BEHOLD,
I COME
QUICKLY

BEHOLD, I COME QUICKLY

THE LAST DAYS AND BEYOND

HOYT W. BREWSTER JR.

DESERET BOOK COMPANY
SALT LAKE CITY, UTAH

Library of Congress Cataloging-in-Publication Data

Brewster, Hoyt W.
    Behold, I come quickly : the last days and beyond / Hoyt W.
Brewster, Jr.
        p.   cm.
    Includes bibliographical references and index.
    ISBN 0-87579-865-9
    1. Eschatology. 2. The Church of Jesus Christ of Latter-day Saints—
Doctrines. 3. Mormon Church—Doctrines. I. Title.
BX8643.E83B74   1994
236'.9'088283—dc20   94-22203
                                                                        CIP

Printed in the United States of America

10   9   8   7   6   5   4   3   2   1

To my beloved companion, Judy,
to Brent and Janice Carroll,
to Dan and Carol Parris,
and to our children, grandchildren,
and future posterity.

May all stand true and faithful
in the trials of the last days!

We *need to overcome fatalism. We know the prophecies of the future. We know the final outcome. We know the world collectively will not repent and consequently the last days will be filled with much pain and suffering. Therefore, we could throw up our hands and do nothing but pray for the end to come so the millennial reign could begin. To do so would forfeit our right to participate in the grand event we are all awaiting. We must all become players in the winding-up scene, not spectators. We must do all we can to prevent calamities, and then do everything possible to assist and comfort the victims of tragedies that do occur.* (Glenn L. Pace, *Ensign,* November 1990, p. 8.)

Be *patient in tribulation until I come; and, behold, I come quickly.* (D&C 54:10.)

CONTENTS

SECTION 1

WHAT HAS BEEN REVEALED ABOUT
THE SECOND COMING

CONTENTS

SECTION 3

THE GATHERINGS

CONTENTS

SECTION 4

THE SECOND COMING

CONTENTS

ABBREVIATIONS

Works frequently cited in this book are abbreviated according to the following list.

CHMR   Smith, Joseph Fielding. *Church History and Modern Revelation.* 2 vols. Salt Lake City: The Council of the Twelve Apostles, 1953.

CR   Conference Reports of The Church of Jesus Christ of Latter-day Saints. Salt Lake City: The Church of Jesus Christ of Latter-day Saints, 1880, 1898 to present.

DCE   Brewster, Hoyt W., Jr. *Doctrine & Covenants Encyclopedia.* Salt Lake City: Bookcraft, 1988.

DNTC   McConkie, Bruce R. *Doctrinal New Testament Commentary.* 3 vols. Salt Lake City: Bookcraft, 1965–73.

DS   Smith, Joseph Fielding. *Doctrines of Salvation.* 3 vols. Compiled by Bruce R. McConkie. Salt Lake City: Bookcraft, 1954–56.

EM   *Encyclopedia of Mormonism.* 4 vols. Edited by Daniel H. Ludlow. New York: Macmillan Publishing Co., 1992.

HC   Smith, Joseph. *History of The Church of Jesus Christ of Latter-day Saints.* 7 vols. 2d ed. rev. Edited by B. H. Roberts. Salt Lake City: The Church of Jesus Christ of Latter-day Saints, 1932–51.

JD   *Journal of Discourses.* 26 vols. London: Latter-day Saints' Book Depot, 1854–86.

JH   Journal History of the Church. LDS Church Archives. Salt Lake City: The Church of Jesus Christ of Latter-day Saints.

JS–H	Joseph Smith–History.
JS–M	Joseph Smith–Matthew.
JSP	Smith, Joseph. Joseph Smith Papers. LDS Church Archives. Salt Lake City: The Church of Jesus Christ of Latter-day Saints.
JST	Joseph Smith Translation (Inspired Version) of the Bible.
MM	McConkie, Bruce R. *The Millennial Messiah: The Second Coming of the Son of Man.* Salt Lake City: Deseret Book Co., 1982.
NWAF	McConkie, Bruce R. *A New Witness for the Articles of Faith.* Salt Lake City: Deseret Book Co., 1985.
OSS	Draper, Richard D. *Opening the Seven Seals: The Visions of John the Revelator.* Salt Lake City: Deseret Book Co., 1991.
ST	Smith, Joseph Fielding. *Signs of the Times.* Salt Lake City: Deseret Book Co., 1974.
THY	Smith, Joseph Fielding. *Take Heed to Yourselves.* Salt Lake City: Deseret Book Co., 1966.
TPJS	Smith, Joseph. *Teachings of the Prophet Joseph Smith.* Selected by Joseph Fielding Smith. Salt Lake City: Deseret Book Co., 1976.
WP	Smith, Joseph Fielding. *The Way to Perfection.* Salt Lake City: The Genealogical Society of The Church of Jesus Christ of Latter-day Saints, 1953.
WW	Cowley, Matthias F. *Wilford Woodruff.* Salt Lake City: Bookcraft, 1964.

WATCH AND BE READY

Perhaps no topic is as fascinating and at the same time so subject to speculation as that of the end of the world. Christianity associates this event with the second coming of Jesus Christ and the commencement of the thousand-year period of peace known as the Millennium. Other religions also look towards a time when the world as we now know it will no longer exist.

The time leading up to the Millennium is known as the last days, a time filled with cataclysmic events and marvelous heavenly manifestations. That we are already living in such a time seems validated by the daily diet of increasing calamities and catastrophes fed to us by the news media.

Ancient prophets and apostles recorded their prophecies not only of the disasters and distresses of the last days, but also of the marvelous blessings and wondrous events that would surely come. Sometimes there is such concern for and emphasis on the negative aspects of the last days that the positive prophecies regarding these times are ignored.

A modern-day apostle of the Lord Jesus Christ, Elder Neal A. Maxwell, has reminded us to maintain a proper perspective: "Yes, there will be wrenching polarization on this planet, but also the remarkable reunion with our colleagues in Christ from the City of Enoch. Yes, nation after nation will become a house divided, but more and more unifying Houses of the Lord will grace this planet. Yes, Armageddon lies ahead. But so does Adam-ondi-Ahman!" (*Ensign*, November 1981, p. 10.)

Thus, while the righteous and the wicked may both suffer the natural consequences coming from calamities associated with the last days, to the righteous the coming of the Lord will be a "great day," while to the wicked it shall be a "dreadful day." (See Malachi 4:5.) The righteous watch for the events foreshadowing the end of the world and the second coming of the Savior, taking whatever precautions they feel are necessary, but they are not in constant disabling distress. Speaking of His return to the earth and the times that would precede it, the Savior said: "Watch therefore. . . . be ye also ready: for in such an hour as ye think not the Son of man cometh." (Matthew 24:42, 44.)

The purpose of this book is to assist in one's efforts to watch and be ready by identifying the signs and events of the last days. In addition to focusing on the last days and the Second Coming, this book will discuss the revealed events of the Millennium and final destiny of this earth and its inhabitants. In this age there is much speculation regarding the last days. This work avoids the popular yet useless speculative tendency in favor of focusing on the revealed word of God through the scriptures and the teachings of those sustained as prophets, seers, and revelators. Two statements by men sustained in these sacred offices will suffice to set the spiritual tone for the rationale and contents of this book.

First, consider this declaration from the tenth prophet and President of The Church of Jesus Christ of Latter-day Saints, President Joseph Fielding Smith:

> Trouble in the earth will continue; there will be distress, calamity, and perplexity among the nations.
>
> We need not look for peace in the immediate future because peace will not come. Nevertheless, we may look forward with rejoicing; we need not be downcast, but in the spirit of faith and hope, and in the fear of the Lord, we should look to the future with feelings of joy, of humility, and of worship, with the desire in our hearts, stronger if possible than ever, of serving the Lord and keeping his commandments, for the day of his coming draws near. (*DS,* 3:51–52.)

Now reflect on this recent testimony from Elder M. Russell Ballard of the Quorum of the Twelve Apostles:

Living in these difficult times . . . requires each one of us to maintain a positive, hopeful perspective about the future. . . .

My message to you today, my brothers and sisters, is simply this: the Lord is in control. He knows the end from the beginning. He has given us adequate instruction that, if followed, will see us safely through any crisis. His purposes will be fulfilled, and someday we will understand the eternal reasons for all of these events. Therefore, today we must be careful to not overreact, nor should we be caught up in extreme preparations, but what we must do is keep the commandments of God and never lose hope!

But where do we find hope in the midst of such turmoil and catastrophe? Quite simply, our one hope for spiritual safety during these turbulent times is to turn our minds and our hearts to Jesus Christ. (*Ensign,* November 1992, pp. 31, 32.)

As you, the reader, study and ponder the teachings and warnings regarding the last days, do not lose hope. Focus on those things that matter most and recognize the overriding hand of the Lord in preparing the world for His second coming.

SECTION 1

WHAT HAS BEEN REVEALED ABOUT THE SECOND COMING

Chapter 1

ALARMISTS AND FALSE PROPHETS

"For there shall arise false Christs, and false prophets, and shall shew great signs and wonders; insomuch that, if it were possible, they shall deceive the very elect."
—MATTHEW 24:24

Tragedy in Texas

In the spring of 1993, the world was stunned to read the following shocking headline in newspapers: "Koresh Leads 85 Cultists, Including 24 Children, to Fiery Deaths in Waco Fortress." This tragic event was another episode in the ongoing fulfillment of prophecies warning of the many false prophets and false Christs that will arise before the end of the world.

In this particular tragedy, a Bible-quoting, gun-wielding fanatic named David Koresh, born Vernon Howell, proclaimed himself to be the latter-day Messiah. "If the Bible is true," he declared, "then I'm Christ." In Waco, Texas, Koresh established a cult known as the Branch Davidians and gathered them inside a compound that he named the Ranch Apocalypse. From this location, Koresh preached his brand of doomsday doctrine.

Because of his cache of firearms, Koresh and his one hundred or so followers were involved in a seven-week standoff with United States federal authorities. During the siege, Koresh said he had the power to open the seven seals described in the Bible's Book of Revelation. By opening them, he declared, he would trigger the end of the world. The

3

siege—and not the world, needless to say—came to a tragic ending when this false prophet and his fanatical followers set fire to their compound and committed themselves, including children, to a fiery death.

False Expectations

While this tragedy was of a large scale in terms of the number of people who died, there have been many smaller tragedies associated with expectations of the Second Coming or the last days. In 1988, for example, in the small community of Marion, Utah, a fanatical self-proclaimed prophet by the name of Adam Swapp took the life of a Utah correctional officer.

Swapp's father-in-law, polygamist John Singer, had been killed in a confrontation with law enforcement officers in 1979. Almost a decade later, Swapp bombed a meetinghouse of the LDS church, setting in motion a confrontation that he believed would bring about the resurrection of Singer, whom Swapp revered as his prophet-leader.

From the day of the Ascension some two thousand years ago, when heavenly messengers proclaimed "this same Jesus, which is taken up from you into heaven, shall so come in like manner as ye have seen him go into heaven" (Acts 1:11), mankind has been anxiously awaiting the return of the resurrected Savior. The Second Coming, the end of the world, the onset of millennial peace on earth—all of these events have long been expected by the faithful, as well as by those whose wicked ways would give them cause to fear such events. Many other expectant people have sold their homes or forsaken their jobs, and even their families, to follow false prophets and teachers into the mountains, wilderness, or faraway places in anticipation of these long-awaited events. Religious organizations—cults, sects, and churches—have evolved around beliefs associated with the last days. For example, the Seventh-Day Adventist movement began as an end-of-the-world revivalist campaign that ended when Christ did not appear as expected.

The movement then changed its focus and the church was established.

In our day the Second Coming and ushering in of the Millennium is generally associated with cataclysmic events. Most of these events are based on scriptural prophecy, but some are the result of fervid imaginations or of misinterpretation of the scriptures. Elder Neal A. Maxwell has observed: "Over the sweep of Christian history, some believers have, by focusing on a few prophecies while neglecting others, prematurely expected the Second Coming. Today, while we are obviously closer to that great moment, we are in the same danger." (*Ensign,* May 1988, p. 7.)

False Prophets

Because of unbelief, many false prophets, and crescending calamities that have become commonplace, many people no longer prepare or watch for the coming of the Lord. "He delayeth his coming," they charge, and like the foolish virgins, they fail to keep their lamps trimmed and ready for the coming of the Bridegroom. (See Matthew 24:48; 25:1–13.)

Without their spiritual lamps trimmed, people are apt to foolishly follow the flame of false prophets. Some of these false prophets are alarmists whose doomsday preachments prey upon the fears of the uninformed and the gullible. Whether deliberately or unwittingly, these false leaders become pawns in the adversary's efforts to discredit true servants of God and to lead astray even the elect of God. A former member of the Quorum of the Twelve Apostles, Elder Delbert L. Stapley, warned: "Satan is stirring up the hearts of men to do iniquity continually; and to thwart, if possible, faith in the great event of Christ's second coming to earth, which I testify is sure to come to pass. Satan is alert and active. We must be more alert and perceptive of the false and insincere schemes of his agents among us." (CR, October 1961, p. 22.)

Admittedly, it may be considered harsh to refer to individuals as agents of Satan, particularly if they believe their efforts

5

are accomplishing some good purpose. Ultimately, however, anyone or anything that puts us at variance with the Lord, His prophets and other anointed servants, or the doctrines and teachings of His gospel and Church, places us in spiritual jeopardy. No matter how well-intentioned or sincere another person may appear to be, we should always be careful about placing our temporal or spiritual welfare in his or her hands.

Beware of Priestcrafts

False prophets and teachers are usually motivated by the desire for either some tangible gain (usually monetary) or praise and popularity. The Book of Mormon describes this as priestcrafts: "Priestcrafts are that men preach and set themselves up for a light unto the world, that they may get gain and praise of the world; but they seek not the welfare of Zion." (2 Nephi 26:29.) The practice of priestcrafts is not confined to false prophets outside The Church of Jesus Christ of Latter-day Saints, for there are persons even within the Church who may be guilty of this sin. Elder Dallin H. Oaks of the Quorum of the Twelve Apostles observed that "a man or woman might serve in Church positions or in private acts of mercy in an effort to achieve prominence or cultivate contacts that would increase income or aid in acquiring wealth. Others might serve in order to obtain worldly honors." (CR, October 1984, p. 14.)

Among those who practice priestcrafts are those who preach for profit by appealing to people's fears. They pronounce doom and chaos. Many of them promote the panic buying of their "essential" products. This is not an indictment against all who seek to understand the signs of the times or who wish to be prepared for possible calamities. Leaders of the Church have always taught the principle of personal and family preparedness, and there are legitimate business ventures that help meet this need by marketing food storage and survival equipment. However, we must be wary of extremism and of those who teach without authority. When one without authority purports to speak for the Lord or His church in promoting products or philosophies for personal gain, we simply say, "Let the buyer beware!" Follow the Lord's true prophet rather than the profit seeker.

Among those who practice priestcrafts are those who preach for popularity. Oftentimes this approach will include the following implied lines of allurement: "I know something that even the Brethren don't know—I have some special insights!" or "The leaders of the Church know what I am doing, and they agree with me. They just haven't spoken out publicly." To any who make such claims, we refer to the warning issued by one of the Lord's recognized servants, Elder Boyd K. Packer of the Quorum of the Twelve Apostles: "Claims of special revelation or secret authority from the Lord or from the Brethren are false on the face of them and really utter nonsense!" (*Ensign,* May 1985, p. 34.) On another occasion, Elder Packer said: "There is safety in learning doctrine in gatherings which are sponsored by proper authority. Some members, even some who have made covenants in the temple, are associating with groups of one kind or another which have an element of secrecy about them and which pretend to have some higher source of inspiration concerning the fulfillment of prophecies than do ward or stake leaders or the General Authorities of the Church. Know this: There are counterfeit revelations which, we are warned, 'if possible . . . shall deceive the very elect, who are the elect according to the covenant.' (JS–M 1:22.)" (*Ensign,* November 1991, p. 21.)

We have been counseled and encouraged to be aware of the signs of the times. As we study and learn to recognize these signs, we must be ever wary of those who give information that is not official Church doctrine. For example, one who designates a specific time for the Second Coming or a time and place of gathering that have not been announced through proper priesthood channels is leading you astray.

Follow the Duly Designated Leaders

Revelation for the Church and, for that matter, the world will come through designated channels. Our fifth article of faith states: "We believe that a man must be called of God, by prophecy, and by the laying on of hands by those who are in authority, to preach the Gospel and administer in the ordinances thereof." Just because one has received the priesthood or even holds a highly visible position in the Church does not mean that he or she is authorized to speak in behalf of the Church. The Church is a kingdom of order. Stewardships have definite parameters. Elders quorum presidents or Relief Society presidents do not receive revelation for bishops. Bishops do not receive revelation for stake presidents. Stake presidents do not receive revelation for General Authorities.

Some years ago while serving as a bishop, I received a telephone call from the personal secretary to the President of the Church. He inquired about a member of my ward and asked what I knew about the individual. He then said, "Bishop, did you know this person has been trying to schedule a personal meeting with the prophet?" When I responded that I knew of no such efforts, I was asked to invite the individual to meet with me and discuss the matter. When the meeting took place, the individual told me of a personal experience with the Three Nephites, who had left a message to be taken to the President of the Church. (The Three Nephites are ancient disciples of Christ who lived in the Americas and were granted the same gift given to the Apostle John by the Savior: they would not taste of death until the Second Coming. [See 3 Nephi 28:1–10.]) I explained that if the Three Nephites had a message for the prophet, they would give it to him directly and not send it through another person. There is order in the Lord's kingdom; revelation and instruction come through proper channels.

I quoted the Prophet Joseph Smith, who declared: "It is contrary to the economy of God for any member of the Church, or any one, to receive instruction for those in authority, higher than themselves; therefore you will see the impropriety of giving heed to them; but if any person have a vision or a visitation from a heavenly messenger, it must be for his own benefit and instruction." (*TPJS,* p. 21.) I also cited the words of President Joseph F. Smith: "It would be absolutely inconsistent, unreasonable and absurd to suppose that after God had called one man and appointed him to this work, that He should pass him by and go to somebody else to accomplish the same purpose." (*JD,* 24:189.) I was not immediately successful in changing the individual's thinking, but with patience and prayer that understanding eventually did come.

There is a great spiritual danger in listening to the ideas of false teachers and leaders, even if we think we are only doing it out of curiosity. President Joseph F. Smith warned:

> We can accept nothing as authoritative but that which comes directly through the appointed channel, the constituted organizations of the Priesthood, which is the channel that God has appointed through which to make known His mind and will to the world. . . .
>
> And the moment that individuals look to any other source, that moment they throw themselves open to the seductive influences of Satan, and render themselves liable to become servants of the devil; they lose sight of the true order through which the blessings of the Priesthood are to be enjoyed; they step outside of the pale of the kingdom of God, and are on dangerous ground. Whenever you see a man rise up claiming to have received direct revelation from the Lord to the Church, independent of the order and channel of the Priesthood, you may set him down as an impostor. (*JD,* 24:188–90.)

Much trouble could be avoided if members of the Church would remember a very basic scripture. The Lord declared that "it shall not be given to any one to go forth to preach my gospel, or to build up my church, except he be ordained by some one who has authority, and it is known to the church that he has authority and has been regularly ordained by the heads of the church." (D&C 42:11.) Elder Boyd K. Packer provided the following commentary on this scripture, a fitting summary to this chapter on alarmists and false prophets:

> There are some among us now who have *not* been regularly ordained by the heads of the Church who tell of

impending political and economic chaos, the end of the world—something of the 'sky is falling, chicken licken' of the fables. They are misleading members to gather to colonies or cults.

Those deceivers say that the Brethren do not know what is going on in the world or that the Brethren approve of their teaching but do not wish to speak of it over the pulpit. Neither is true. The Brethren, by virtue of traveling constantly everywhere on earth, certainly know what is going on, and by virtue of prophetic insight are able to read the signs of the times.

Do not be deceived by them—those deceivers. If there is to be any gathering, it will be announced by those who have been regularly ordained and who are known to the Church to have authority.

Come away from any others. Follow your leaders who have been duly ordained and have been publicly sustained, and you will not be led astray. (*Ensign,* November 1992, p. 73.)

Chapter 2

THE TIMING OF THE SECOND COMING

"I, the Lord God, have spoken it; but the hour and the day no man knoweth, neither the angels in heaven, nor shall they know until he comes."

—D&C 49:7

The Restitution of All Things

In his role as the earthly leader of the ancient Christian church after the ascension of the Savior, the Apostle Peter preached these words to those who had just witnessed the power of his priesthood at work: "Repent ye therefore, and be converted, that your sins may be blotted out, when the times of refreshing shall come from the presence of the Lord; and he shall send Jesus Christ [the second time], which before was preached unto you: Whom the heaven must receive *until the times of restitution of all things,* which God hath spoken by the mouth of all his holy prophets since the world began." (Acts 3:19–21; italics added.)

Although the gospel originally taught to Adam and Eve and others of Old Testament times was reestablished during the earthly ministry of Jesus Christ, the Savior's chief apostle spoke of a yet future "restitution of all things." Implied in this prophetic pronouncement was the fact that Christ's gospel would be taken from the earth, thus necessitating a *restitution,* or *restoration.*

The Apostle Paul similarly taught that "the day of Christ" (His second coming) would not come until a "falling away," or an *apostasy,* had first occurred. (2 Thessalonians 2:1–3.)

11

The message of The Church of Jesus Christ of Latter-day Saints to the world is that a universal apostasy did occur and the restitution spoken of by the Apostle Peter has taken place. In response to prayerful pleading, a young prophet named Joseph Smith was visited by Deity and divinely commissioned to set this restoration in place.

Following the receipt of priesthood authority under the hands of heavenly messengers sent from the presence of God, the Prophet Joseph Smith reestablished the Church of Jesus Christ upon the earth. (See D&C 13:1; 20:1; 27:8, 12; 115:4.)

Another Testament of Jesus Christ Is Revealed

Among the heavenly messengers sent to instruct the Prophet was an angel named Moroni. He first appeared to Joseph Smith on the night of September 21, 1823. At that time the angel revealed the existence of a sacred record of the ancient inhabitants of the Americas. The record contained an account of their history and, more important, the teachings of their prophets and their dealings with God. By the gift and power of God, the Prophet Joseph Smith later translated this record into what today is titled *The Book of Mormon: Another Testament of Jesus Christ.* This inspired book is a companion volume of scripture to the Bible and includes a record of the visit of the resurrected Christ to these ancient people following his ascension.

The coming forth of this scripture with its revealed truths and especially its witness of Jesus Christ as the Son of God and Savior, or Messiah, was an important part of the "restitution of all things." The publication of the Book of Mormon was a prelude to the coming forth of other scripture, for the heavens were once more opened, and revelation was poured out to God's authorized servants on earth.

The Messenger to Precede the Messiah's Coming

A major part of the message that the Angel Moroni gave to Joseph Smith that September night in 1823 was a recitation of biblical prophecies. The angel first quoted from the third and fourth chapters of Malachi. (See JS–H 1:36–39.) This Old Testament prophet foretold of a messenger who would be sent to prepare the way before the Lord, who Himself "shall suddenly come to his temple." (Malachi 3:1.)

During his earthly ministry, Jesus identified John the Baptist as the messenger promised by Malachi. (See Matthew 11:7–10.) While it is true that John's *mortal* ministry prepared the way for the *mortal* ministry of the Messiah, even Jesus Christ, the Baptist also had a second mission to perform in preparing the way for the *second* coming of the Savior. On May 15, 1829, the resurrected John the Baptist bestowed the Aaronic Priesthood on Joseph Smith and his colleague in the work of the Restoration, Oliver Cowdery. (See JS–H 1:68–73; D&C 13:1; 27:8.) John's recorded words were: "Upon you my fellow servants, in the name of Messiah, I confer the Priesthood of Aaron, which holds the keys of the ministering of angels, and of the gospel of repentance, and of baptism by immersion for the remission of sins; and this shall never be taken again from the earth until the sons of Levi do offer again an offering unto the Lord in righteousness." (D&C 13:1; see JS–H 1:69.)

Elijah the Prophet's Return

In reference to another event that would precede the Second Coming, Malachi also prophesied that "the day cometh that shall burn as an oven, and all the proud, yea, and all that do wickedly shall burn as stubble." (Malachi 4:1.) In addition, this ancient seer spoke of the coming of "Elijah the prophet before the coming of the great and dreadful day of the Lord." (Malachi 4:5.)

In anticipation of the return of Elijah, the descendants of Judah annually set a place at the table for this great prophet. Unknown to most of the world is the fact that Elijah has already returned in fulfillment of Malachi's prophecy. On April 3, 1836, this great prophet appeared as a resurrected being to

Joseph Smith and Oliver Cowdery in the newly completed temple in Kirtland, Ohio. Of this great occasion, the Prophet Joseph Smith wrote: "Elijah the prophet, who was taken to heaven without tasting death, stood before us, and said: Behold, the time has fully come, which was spoken of by the mouth of Malachi—testifying that he [Elijah] should be sent, before the great and dreadful day of the Lord come—To turn the hearts of the fathers to the children, and the children to the fathers, lest the whole earth be smitten with a curse— Therefore, the keys of this dispensation are committed into your hands; and by this ye may know that *the great and dreadful day of the Lord is near, even at the doors.*" (D&C 110:13–16; italics added.)

Joseph Smith identified the keys delivered by Elijah as the priesthood authority that would validate or allow "all the ordinances [to] be attended to in righteousness." (*TPJS*, p. 172.)

An Ensign to the Nations

Following his quotations from Malachi, Moroni next "quoted the eleventh chapter of Isaiah, saying that it was about to be fulfilled." (JS–H 1:40.) This chapter of Isaiah is filled with prophecies about the Millennium and events leading up to it. For example, the eleventh verse speaks of the Lord setting "his hand again the second time to recover the remnant of his people." Verse twelve tells of an "ensign for the nations" that shall be set up and to which the outcasts of Israel shall be gathered. This ensign is The Church of Jesus Christ of Latter-day Saints, which is vigorously engaged in the work of gathering the dispersed of Israel to the fold of the True Shepherd in anticipation of his return to earth.

Those Who Will Be Cut Off

During his visit to the young man Joseph Smith, Moroni quoted from the New Testament as follows: "For Moses truly said unto the fathers, A prophet shall the Lord your God raise up unto you of your brethren, like unto me; him shall ye hear in all things whatsoever he shall say unto you. And it shall come to pass, that every soul, which will not hear that prophet, shall be destroyed from among the people." (Acts 3:22–23.)

Moroni declared "that prophet was Christ; but the day had not yet come when 'they who would not hear his voice should be cut off from among the people,' but soon would come." (JS–H 1:40).

In a later revelation given through the Prophet Joseph Smith in 1831, the Lord declared that "the arm of the Lord shall be revealed; and the day cometh that they who will not hear the voice of the Lord, neither the voice of his servants, neither give heed to the words of the prophets and apostles, shall be cut off from among the people." (D&C 1:14.)

Joel's Prophecy of the Last Days

The Angel Moroni quoted "many other passages of scripture" that the Prophet Joseph Smith did not identify, with the exception of the following:

> And it shall come to pass afterward, that I will pour out my spirit upon all flesh; and your sons and your daughters shall prophesy, your old men shall dream dreams, your young men shall see visions: And also upon the servants and upon the handmaids in those days will I pour out my spirit. And I will shew wonders in the heavens and in the earth, blood, and fire, and pillars of smoke. The sun shall be turned into darkness, and the moon into blood, before the great and the terrible day of the Lord come. And it shall come to pass that whosoever shall call on the name of the Lord shall be delivered: for in mount Zion and in Jerusalem shall be deliverance, as the Lord hath said, and in the remnant whom the Lord shall call. (Joel 2:28–32.)

Moroni declared that Joel's prophecy "was not yet fulfilled, but was soon to be" and "that the fulness of the Gentiles was soon to come in." (JS–H 1:41.) Commenting on the part of Joel's prophecy dealing with the promised "wonders in heaven," President Joseph Fielding Smith said:

One wonders if we are not now seeing some of the signs in heaven? Not all, for undoubtedly some of them will be among the heavenly bodies, such as the moon and the sun, the meteors and comets, but in speaking of the heavens, reference is made to that part which surrounds the earth and which belongs to it. It is in the atmosphere where many of the signs are to be given. Do we not see airships of various kinds traveling through the heavens daily? Have we not had signs in the earth and through the earth with the radio, railroad trains, automobiles, submarines and satellites, and many other ways? There are yet to be great signs; the heavens are to be shaken, the sign of the Son of Man is to be given; and then shall the tribes of the earth mourn. (*THY,* pp. 428–29.)

Further reference will be made to this and other aspects of Joel's prophecy later in the book.

Nearness of the Second Coming

The point of referencing these prophecies cited by the Angel Moroni is to suggest that the theme of the last days and Second Coming has been very much a part of the restoration of the gospel of Jesus Christ. Although many prophesied latter-day events are yet to occur, many others have already taken place since the beginning of the Restoration. That the doctrine of the Second Coming is integral to the restored gospel is underscored by the fact that twelve times between October 1830 (see D&C 33:18) and July 1837 (see D&C 112:34), the Lord declared, "I come quickly!" On other occasions he spoke of his coming as being "soon at hand." (D&C 29:9.)

Latter-day apostles have spoken of the time being short and of our days being the "Saturday night of time." Elder Orson F. Whitney, an apostle who served in the early 1900s, wrote:

According to received chronology—admittedly imperfect, yet approximately correct—four thousand years, or four of the seven great days given to this planet as the period of its "temporal existence," had passed before Christ was crucified; while nearly two thousand years have gone by since. Consequently, Earth's long week is now drawing to a close, and we stand at the present moment in the Saturday Evening of Time, at or near the end of the sixth day of human history. Is it not a time for thought, a season for solemn meditation? Morning will break upon the Millennium, the thousand years of peace, the Sabbath of the World! (*Saturday Night Thoughts,* Salt Lake City: Deseret News Press, 1921, p. 12.)

An apostle who lived closer to the present day, Elder Bruce R. McConkie, wrote: "We are now living during the final years of the sixth seal, that thousand year period which began in 1000 A.D. and will continue through the Saturday night of time and until just before the Sabbatical era when Christ shall reign personally on earth, when all of the blessings of the Great Millennium shall be poured out upon this planet. This, accordingly, is the era when the signs of the times shall be shown forth, and they are in fact everywhere to be seen." (*DNTC,* 3:485–86.)

In His great sermon regarding the calamities preceding his second coming, the Savior spoke of the timing of this anticipated event: "But of that day and hour knoweth no man, no, not the angels of heaven, but my Father only." (Matthew 24:36; see also Matthew 25:13; JS–M 1:48.) The Gospel of Mark records the words of the Savior as follows: "But of that day and that hour knoweth no man, no, not the angels which are in heaven, *neither the Son,* but the Father." (Mark 13:32; italics added.)

It should be noted that this statement was made during the Savior's mortality. Perhaps at this time He did not have a perfect knowledge of all things, including the timing of the Second Coming. This knowledge would come to Him following His resurrection and when He had reclaimed His place at the right hand of His Father. In this respect it is of interest to see the difference in wording between a declaration delivered during His mortal ministry and one delivered following His resurrection. In Matthew 5:48, the Savior admonished, "Be ye therefore perfect, even as your Father which is in heaven is perfect." In 3 Nephi 12:48, the *resurrected* Lord admonished, "Therefore I would that ye should be perfect *even as I,* or your Father who is in heaven is perfect." (Italics added.)

It is possible that Mark or other early transcribers added the words "neither the Son" to the Savior's statement. The Joseph Smith Translation omits this exclusive statement. (See JST, Mark 13:47.) It is also possible that Joseph Smith omitted the statement based on his understanding that the resurrected Christ knew all things, including the timing of His second coming.

Latter-day revelation affirms that neither men nor angels know the timing of the Second Coming: "I, the Lord God, have spoken it; but the hour and the day no man knoweth, neither the angels in heaven, nor shall they know until he comes." (D&C 49:7; see also 39:21; 133:11.) In 1844 Joseph Smith declared: "Jesus Christ never did reveal to any man the precise time that He would come. Go and read the Scriptures, and you cannot find anything that specifies the exact hour He would come; and all that say so are false teachers." (*HC,* 6:254.)

More recently, President Joseph Fielding Smith said: "The Lord has never revealed to us when the day will come, but he has given us knowledge enough by which we may know that that day is not far away. When I say 'not far away,' I am not setting any definite number of years. . . . People say all kinds of things but no man knows the day of his coming and no man is going to know and I don't think the Twelve will know it. I have my doubts that the Presidency of the Church will know, because the Lord says he will come when no one is expecting it, but he has given us signs and the world is full of them today, signs of his coming as he draws nigh." (*THY,* pp. 19–20.)

Prepared, We Need Not Fear

If the time of the Second Coming is not known and not to be revealed, why should we concern ourselves with this event? Elder Bruce R. McConkie has provided an answer: "Deliberately and advisedly the actual time of his coming has been left uncertain and unspecified, so that men of each succeeding age shall be led to prepare for it as though it would be in their mortal lives." (*DNTC*, 1:675.)

In a speech given to students at Brigham Young University while he was a member of the Quorum of the Twelve Apostles, Elder Gordon B. Hinckley gave this admonition:

> Certainly there is no point in speculating concerning the day and the hour. Let us rather live each day so that if the Lord does come while we are yet upon the earth we shall be worthy of that change which will occur as in the twinkling of an eye and under which we shall be changed from mortal to immortal beings. And if we should die before he comes, then—if our lives have conformed to his teachings—we shall arise in that resurrection morning and be partakers of the marvelous experiences designed for those who shall live and work with the Savior in that promised Millennium. We need not fear the day of his coming; the very purpose of the Church is to provide the incentive and the opportunity for us to conduct our lives in such a way that those who are members of the kingdom of God will become members of the kingdom of heaven when he establishes that kingdom on the earth. ("We Need Not Fear His Coming," *1979 Devotional Speeches of the Year*, Provo: Brigham Young University Press, p. 83.)

There is a need for each of us as individuals and as members of other units—the family, Church, community—to be prepared for the Second Coming. To this end we familiarize ourselves with the signs and events of the last days.

In the parable of the ten virgins, the Savior taught the importance of preparedness, especially in anticipation of meeting Him (the Bridegroom) when He returns to earth. (See Matthew 25:1–13.) His admonition was that we should "watch!" President Spencer W. Kimball suggested that this parable had specific application to members of the Church:

> I believe the Ten Virgins represent the people of the Church of Jesus Christ and not the rank and file of the world. All of the virgins, wise and foolish, had accepted the invitation to the wedding supper; they had knowledge of the program and had been warned of the important day to come. They were not the gentiles or the heathens or the

pagans, nor were they necessarily corrupt and reprobate, but they were knowing people who were foolishly unprepared for the vital happenings that were to affect their eternal lives.

They had the saving, exalting gospel, but it had not been made the center of their lives. They knew the way but gave only a small measure of loyalty and devotion. . . .

Rushing for their lamps to light their way through the blackness, half of them found them empty. They had cheated themselves. They were fools, these five unprepared virgins. . . . They had heard of his coming for so long, so many times, that the statement seemingly became meaningless to them. (*Faith Precedes the Miracle*, Salt Lake City: Deseret Book Co., 1972, pp. 253–54.)

Although we must be prepared and watch for the signs of the times as if the Savior were coming today, there are extremes to avoid. Elder Neal A. Maxwell cautioned:

[We] need to keep our eyes on more than a few leaves of the fig tree in order to know when summer is nigh (see Matthew 24:32). By analogy, it is one thing to notice strong ocean breakers crashing against the shore, heralding another oncoming storm, and quite another to discern the powerful movements on the ocean's quake-jarred floor foretelling a terrible tidal wave.

In the context of such cautions, I have no hesitancy in saying that there are some signs—but certainly not all— suggesting that "summer is nigh" (Matthew 24:32). We would do well to notice and to ponder, but without either becoming preoccupied or ignoring any sprouting leaves because of being "overcharged" with the "cares of this life" (Luke 21:34). (*Ensign*, May 1988, p. 7.)

Speaking specifically to teenagers, who sometimes seem overwhelmed by the events of the world and feel the end of the world is so close at hand that there will not be an opportunity for them to make or fulfill any long-range plans and dreams, Elder Boyd K. Packer observed:

Teenagers also sometimes think, "What's the use? The world will soon be blown all apart and come to an end." That feeling comes from fear, not from faith. No one knows the hour or the day (see D&C 49:7), but the end cannot come until all of the purposes of the Lord are ful-filled. Everything that I have learned from the revelations and from life convinces me that there is time and to spare for you to carefully prepare for a long life.

One day you will cope with teenage children of your own. That will serve you right. Later, you will spoil your grandchildren, and they in turn spoil theirs. (*Ensign,* May 1989, p. 59.)

The timing of the end of the world and the Second Coming have long been set by the God of heaven and earth. Elder Bruce R. McConkie declared:

As to the Second Coming, the time is fixed, the hour is set, and, speaking after the manner of the Lord, the day is soon to be. The appointed day can be neither advanced nor delayed. It will come at the decreed moment, chosen before the foundations of the earth were laid, and it can be neither hastened by righteousness nor put off by wicked-ness. It will be with our Lord's return as it was with his birth to Mary: the time of each coming was fixed by the Father.

True, no man knows or shall know the day or the hour of our Lord's return; that knowledge is retained in the bosom of heaven, for good and sufficient reasons. But all men may read the signs of the times, and those whose souls are attuned to the things of the Spirit know that the great and dreadful day of the Lord is near, even at the door. But they also know there are many things yet to be done before earth's rightful King comes to change the kingdoms of this world into the kingdom of our God and of his Christ. (*NWAF,* p. 591.)

As noted by Elder McConkie, many things remain to be done before the end of the world. Among these are the fol-lowing events that will be discussed later in the book:

- The return to Jackson County, Missouri
- The building of a temple in Jackson County
- The building of a temple in Old Jerusalem
- The full return of Judah to Israel
- The gospel preached in all the world
- The return of the lost tribes

- The gathering of prophets at Adam-ondi-Ahman in Missouri
- The raising up of two great prophets to minister in Israel
- The Battle of Armageddon
- The sun darkened, moon turned to blood, stars fall from the heavens, and many other wonders and signs

And so we strive to fill our spiritual lamps with the oil of preparedness, of faith and hope, as we watch for the signs of the times and wait for the day that will be great for the righteous and dreadful for the wicked.

SECTION 2

COMMOTION, CONSPIRACIES, AND CONTENTION

Chapter 3

THE ELEMENTS IN COMMOTION

*"For after your testimony cometh the testimony of earthquakes.
. . . And also cometh the testimony of the voice of thunderings,
and the voice of lightnings, and the voice of tempests, and the
voice of the waves of the sea heaving themselves beyond their
bounds. And all things shall be in commotion."*
—D&C 88:89–91

Disasters of Nature

A clever advertising campaign some years ago featured a
woman portraying Mother Nature. All was calm and peaceful
around her until she discovered she had been deceived by the
manufacturers of a product that appeared natural but which
was really artificial. At this point she declared, "It's not nice to
fool Mother Nature" and turned the peaceful setting into one
of natural disaster.

Deity has often displayed displeasure through the forces of
nature. These forces have been used to call the disobedient to
repentance. Certainly the wicked in the days of Noah learned
this lesson in a hard way. (See Genesis 6 and 7.) The forces of
nature also destroyed the wicked in the ancient Nephite civilization at the time of the crucifixion of Christ. A "great storm"
arose, accompanied by "a great and terrible tempest." There
was "terrible thunder" and "sharp lightnings, such as never
had been known in all the land." Some cities were destroyed
by fire, and others sunk into the depths of the sea or covered
by mountains of dirt and debris. "The whole face of the land
was changed." (3 Nephi 8.)

Following this terrible destruction, the cry of the survivors was "O that we had repented before this great and terrible day." (3 Nephi 8:24.) Two thousand years later we face this same challenge: to repent before the "great and terrible day." Certainly the voices of nature are now being heard throughout the earth in calling the people to repentance.

Earthquakes in Divers Places

Among the predicted commotions of nature to take place in the last days is the upheaval and shaking of the earth. As Jesus taught his disciples on the Mount of Olives about the pending doom of Jerusalem and the future calamities preceding His second coming, he declared: "There shall be famines, and pestilences, and earthquakes, in divers places." (Matthew 24:7; see also Mark 13:8; Luke 21:11; JS–M 1:29.) This declaration is repeated in a revelation given in 1831 (see D&C 45:33) and was mentioned by the ancient prophet Moroni as one of the signs of the last days (see Mormon 8:30).

The writings of Isaiah as revealed in the Book of Mormon warn that the Lord would visit the wicked with earthquakes. (See 2 Nephi 27:1–2; compare Isaiah 29:6.) Latter-day revelation indicates that God chastises and calls people to repentance by the voice and testimony of earthquakes. (See D&C 43:25; 87:6; 88:89.) Elder Melvin J. Ballard, who served as an apostle from 1919 to 1939, said: "God is speaking through the elements. The earthquakes, the sea heaving itself beyond its bounds, bringing such dire destruction as we have seen are the voice of God crying repentance to this generation, a generation that only in part has heeded the warning voice of the servants of the Lord." (CR, October 1923, p. 31.)

It is well to add a caution here. The impact of natural disasters such as earthquakes generally affects an entire population of an area, and one must be careful about judging the victims of such disasters. While it is true that the wicked are often pinpointed for such destruction, as in the case of Sodom and Gomorrah (see Genesis 18 and 19), it is also true that the righteous must often suffer along with the wicked. Adversity is often the refining fire that strengthens faith.

Speaking at a general conference in Salt Lake City, President Ezra Taft Benson said the following to the Latter-day Saints: "Too often we bask in our comfortable complacency and rationalize that the ravages of war, economic disaster, famine, and earthquake cannot happen here. Those who believe this are either not acquainted with the revelations of the Lord, or they do not believe them. Those who smugly think these calamities will not happen, that they somehow will be set aside because of the righteousness of the Saints, are deceived and will rue the day they harbored such a delusion." (*Ensign*, November 1980, p. 34.)

The state of Utah, headquarters for The Church of Jesus Christ of Latter-day Saints, is shaken by about seven hundred earthquakes each year. Seismologists have estimated there is a 20 percent chance of an earthquake measuring at least 7.0 on the Richter Scale occurring along Utah's highly populated Wasatch Front before the year 2050. Such a quake would cause shaking of the ground ranging from 70 percent to 100 percent the force of gravity.

Earthquakes are increasingly affecting the people of this planet. President Joseph Fielding Smith researched the numbers of earthquakes and discovered that "'if all earthquakes down to zero magnitude could be detected, the number would be between one and ten million each year.'" Furthermore, he found that "there are about 2,000 earthquakes each year with the magnitude between 5 and 6 [on the Richter Scale] and about 20,000 between 4.0 and 5.0." President Smith thus concluded, "There are around 20,000 earthquakes a year that could be damaging if they occurred in populated areas." (*THY,* p. 430.)

More recently Elder M. Russell Ballard noted the following regarding the frequency of high-intensity earthquakes: "Statistics from the U.S. Geological Survey indicat[e] that earthquakes around the world are increasing in frequency and intensity. According to the article, only two major earthquakes, earthquakes measuring at least six on the Richter scale, occurred during the 1920s. In the 1930s the number increased to five, and then decreased to four during the 1940s. But in the 1950s, nine major earthquakes occurred, followed by fifteen during the 1960s, forty-six during the 1970s, and fifty-two during the 1980s. Already almost as many major earthquakes have occurred during the 1990s as during the entire decade of the 1980s." (*Ensign*, November 1992, p. 31.)

Earth Movements during the Millennium

The Doctrine and Covenants refers to a time when the "earth shall . . . reel to and fro" like a drunkard. (45:48; 49:23; 88:87.) These citations have reference to the Millennium, in that at least two great shakings of the earth will occur in this time period: one at the beginning of the thousand years and one at the conclusion.

The great earthquake ushering in the Millennium will be part of the events surrounding Christ's second coming. When the Savior stands on the Mount of Olives, it will be at a time when the Jewish people are about to be destroyed. At this moment, a great earthquake will cleave the mount in twain. (See Zechariah 14:4; Revelation 11:13; 16:17–20; D&C 45:48.) President Joseph Fielding Smith commented on this momentous occasion: "You can see what a terrible condition it is going to be; and the Jews besieged, not only in Jerusalem but, of course, throughout Palestine are in the siege; and when they are about to go under, then the Lord comes. There will be the great earthquake. The earthquake will not be only in Palestine. There will not be merely the separation of the Mount of Olives, to form a valley that the Jews may escape, but the whole earth is going to be shaken. There will be some dreadful things take place, and some great changes are going to take place." (*ST*, p. 170.)

At the conclusion of the Millennium, the "earth shall remove out of her place" (Isaiah 13:13) as a prelude to becoming a celestial sphere. While this may not include earthquakes, at least as we define them today, it certainly will involve a reeling to and fro of the earth as it hurtles through space to its new destination. More will be said of this later in the book.

Thunderings, Lightnings, and Tempests

Not long ago a terrible thunderstorm rolled through the Salt Lake Valley one night. The sound of thunder shook me from my sleep, and the lightning illuminated the bedroom. One particular clap of thunder put my heartbeat into a quick acceleration, and I anticipated being immediately struck by lightning. Fortunately my fears were not realized, although the strike was so close to the house and so charged with electricity that it turned the lights on in several rooms. This experience gave me a greater appreciation of this prophecy regarding the signs of the last days: "And also cometh the testimony of the voice of thunderings, and the voice of lightnings, and the voice of tempests, and the voice of the waves of the sea heaving themselves beyond their bounds. And all things shall be in commotion; and surely, men's hearts shall fail them; for fear shall come upon all people." (D&C 88:90–91.)

One of the fearful things about storms and tempests is the sense of hopelessness and vulnerability that comes with them. While meteorologists have been helpful in predicting the coming of hurricanes and tidal waves, thereby alerting people to secure their property and take precautions for their personal safety, the predicted path and the exact timing of these tempests have not always been accurate. Any who have experienced these storms or watched the destruction secondhand as reported on television have some idea of how fear can come upon all people.

In 1860 President Brigham Young spoke of the intensity of such forthcoming calamities:

"Do you think there is calamity abroad now among the people?" Not much. All we have yet heard and all we have experienced is scarcely a preface to the sermon that is going to be preached. When the testimony of the Elders ceases to be given, and the Lord says to them, "Come home; I will now preach my own sermons to the nations of the earth," all you now know can scarcely be called a preface to the sermon that will be preached with fire and sword, tempests, earthquakes, hail, rain, thunders and lightnings, and fearful destruction. . . . You will hear of magnificent cities, now idolized by the people, sinking in the earth, entombing the inhabitants. The sea will heave itself beyond its bounds, engulphing [*sic*] mighty cities. . . . Yet the faithful of God's people will see days that will cause them to close their eyes because of the sorrow that will come upon the wicked nations. The hearts of the faithful will be filled with pain and anguish for them. (*JD*, 8:123.)

Destruction by Waters

The summer of 1993 will long be remembered by the citizens of the midwestern United States as the year when the flood of the century took place. The mighty Missouri and Mississippi Rivers heaved themselves beyond their banks, destroying lives and hundreds of millions of dollars in property. Many of the efforts to stay the floodwaters were futile. Man simply did not have the power or the wherewithal to withstand these destructive forces of nature.

Perhaps the force of the flood gave new understanding to Joseph Smith's metaphoric pronouncement in comparing the power of heaven to the power of the Missouri River: "What power shall stay the heavens? As well might man stretch forth his puny arm to stop the Missouri river in its decreed course, or to turn it up stream, as to hinder the Almighty from pouring down knowledge from heaven upon the heads of the Latter-day Saints." (D&C 121:33.)

In 1831 the Lord gave warning that destruction by waters would occur in the last days. The Prophet Joseph and a small group of elders had spent several days traveling by canoe on the Missouri River. During the journey one of the travelers, W. W. Phelps, "in open vision by daylight, saw the destroyer in his most horrible power, ride upon the face of the waters; others heard the noise, but saw not the vision." (*HC,* 1:203.) The following morning, after Joseph Smith had prayed, he received this revelation: "For I, the Lord, have decreed in mine anger many destructions upon the waters. . . . Behold, I, the Lord, in the beginning blessed the waters; but in the last days, by the mouth of my servant John, I cursed the waters. Wherefore, the days will come that no flesh shall be safe upon the waters." (D&C 61:5, 14–15.)

There are several possibilities as to how the waters would be cursed in the last days. Certainly the effect of floods, hurricanes, and typhoons are a possibility as the prophesied storms and tempests increase. Those who have traveled by ship during times of war know of man-made dangers: mines, missiles, and submarines. Yet another possibility is contaminated water. John the Revelator prophesied that "the third part of the sea became blood; and the third part of the creatures which were in the sea, and had life, died; and the third part of the ships were destroyed. . . . And there fell a great star from heaven, burning as it were a lamp, and it fell upon the third part of the rivers, and upon the fountains of waters; and the name of the star is called Wormwood: and the third part of the waters became wormwood; and many men died of the waters, because they were made bitter." (Revelation 8:8–11.)

Wormwood is a plant symbolic of bitterness, calamity, and sorrow. The introduction of wormwood into the waters would make them undrinkable, or at the very least bitter and distasteful. Elder Bruce R. McConkie suggested the possibility of the waters being contaminated by atomic fallout: "Could this be atomic fallout which shall poison a third of the drinking water of the earth?" (*DNTC,* 3:499.)

Volcanic Eruptions

Another force of nature that can wreak terrible destruction in a short period of time is the volcanic eruption. While it may be true that volcanoes have been erupting throughout the earth's

31

history, such eruptions are associated with the signs of the last days. It is of interest to hear the meteorologists and climatologists explain the changing conditions of the earth's weather patterns in connection with recent volcanic eruptions. Ash and heat spewed in the atmosphere have altered the jet streams and have had significant impact on where and when moisture has fallen. Certainly these are signs in the heavens.

There is yet another interesting aspect of the potential impact of volcanic eruptions. Scientists have recently discovered a volcano under nearly a mile of solid ice near the South Pole. It is theorized that heat from this volcano may be the source of voluminous ice streams in western Antarctica and that this abundance of water is lubricating the slide of glaciers across the region's ice sheet. This condition could lead to the catastrophic collapse of an ice sheet that could release enough water into the Pacific Ocean to raise global sea levels by eighteen to twenty feet. Such a disaster would bury in the depths of the seas many of the low-lying areas of the planet where a good portion of the earth's population lives. (See "Chilling Thought: Antarctic Volcano Gives New Meaning to 'Meltdown,'" *Salt Lake Tribune,* 11 February 1993, p. A1.)

The Apostle John saw "a great mountain burning with fire [being] cast into the sea" in the last days. (Revelation 8:8.) The Savior spoke of one of the signs of His coming being "fire, and vapors of smoke." (D&C 45:41.) Such signs could be the result of bombs and missiles, but the language is also descriptive of volcanic eruptions. Furthermore, it seems highly probable that much of the destruction brought upon the ancient Nephite civilization at the time of Christ's crucifixion was volcanic in origin. For example, the "thick darkness" that came upon the land following the violent storms and upheavals of the earth might well have been volcanic cloud and ash. No light could penetrate those "mists of darkness." (3 Nephi 8:20–23.)

It is not inconceivable that a repeat of this destructive force of nature could precede Christ's second coming. Latter-day revelation reminds us that "before the day of the Lord shall come, the sun shall be darkened" (D&C 45:42), and that "the sun shall hide his face, and shall refuse to give light" (D&C 88:87). It is, of course, conceivable that such an occurrence could be brought about by the brightness emanating from the very presence of the Savior: "And so great shall be the glory of his presence that the sun shall hide his face in shame." (D&C 133:49.)

Great Hailstorms, Fire, and Brimstone

Modern revelation speaks of "a great hailstorm sent forth to destroy the crops of the earth." (D&C 29:16.) John the Revelator saw "a great hail out of heaven, every stone about the weight of a talent." (Revelation 16:21.) The immensity of this destruction is evident in the fact that a talent is 75.6 pounds. There are yet other references in the Old and New Testaments that add another dimension to the plague of hail. This could yet be another disaster, for it is spoken of in the context of the final battle of Armageddon. Speaking of Gog, the enemy of God, the prophet Ezekiel proclaims: "And I will plead against him with pestilence and with blood; and I will rain upon him, and upon his bands, and upon the many people that are with him, an overflowing rain, and great hailstones, fire, and brimstone." (Ezekiel 38:22.)

Elder Bruce R. McConkie provided the following commentary on this scene of destruction: "It shall be, in the literal and full sense of the word, as it was with Sodom and Gomorrah. Fire and brimstone will fall upon the armies of the wicked in all nations. That which is going forward in Palestine is but a type and a shadow of that which shall be in all nations and among all peoples. . . . This is a worldwide conflict and . . . all nations are involved." (*MM*, p. 485.)

John the Revelator saw "hail and fire mingled with blood" being cast upon the wicked. (Revelation 8:7.) This calamity could be similar to what Pharaoh and the ancient Egyptians experienced when the Lord God Jehovah "sent thunder and hail, and the fire ran along upon the ground," smiting both man and beast. (See Exodus 9:22–26.)

Famine and Drought

From the days in ancient Egypt when Joseph, son of Jacob, was raised up to save the people from starvation, famine has been a challenge to human survival. (See Genesis 41.)

In the days of the prophet Elijah, the Lord tested the faith of a widow during a severe famine. She was asked to give first of her meager meal to God's prophet before she and her son partook of what was supposed to be their final morsels of food. Because of her faith and obedience, she and her son never wanted for sustenance while the drought and famine continued in the land. (See 1 Kings 17.)

Famine has been prophesied as one of the disasters of the last days. The Savior said "there shall be famines, and pestilences." (Matthew 24:7.) The Lord uses famine as one of the means whereby "the inhabitants of the earth [are] made to feel the wrath, and indignation, and chastening hand of an Almighty God." (D&C 87:6.) The "voice of famines and pestilences of every kind" calls to the nations of the earth to hear the words of God and his servants. (See D&C 43:23–25.)

The Book of Mormon provides a classic example of the Lord's prophet decreeing a drought and famine to bring the disobedient people of his day to repentance: "O Lord do not suffer that this people shall be destroyed by the sword; but O Lord, rather let there be a famine in the land, to stir them up in remembrance of the Lord their God, and perhaps they will repent and turn unto thee. And so it was done, according to the words of Nephi. And there was a great famine upon the land, among all the people of Nephi. And thus . . . the famine did continue, and the work of destruction did cease by the sword but became sore by famine. . . . And it came to pass that the people saw that they were about to perish by famine, and they began to remember the Lord their God." (Helaman 11:4–5, 7.) Fortunately, the people repented, and the prophet pleaded with the Lord to bring an end to the famine. During such troubled times, the righteous often suffer along with the unrighteous.

Elder Bruce R. McConkie made the following observation regarding the famine of Elijah's day and the desolation that will come in the last days:

> When there was a famine in the land, at Elijah's word, a certain barrel of meal did not waste, and a certain cruse of oil did not fail, until the Lord sent again rain on the earth. And it is worthy of note, as Jesus said, that though there were many widows in Israel, unto one only was Elijah sent. (See 1 Kings 17:10–16.)
>
> We do not say that all of the Saints [of the last days] will be spared and saved from the coming day of desolation. But we do say there is no promise of safety and no promise of security except for those who love the Lord and who are seeking to do all that he commands. (*Ensign*, May 1979, p. 93.)

During a drought in the '70s, President Spencer W. Kimball declared:

> Early this year when drouth conditions seemed to be developing in the West, the cold and hardships in the East, with varying weather situations all over the world, we felt to ask the members of the Church to join in fasting and prayer, asking the Lord for moisture where it was so vital and for a cessation of the difficult conditions elsewhere.
>
> Perhaps we may have been unworthy in asking for these greatest blessings, but *we do not wish to frantically approach the matter but merely call it to the attention of our Lord and then spend our energy to put our lives in harmony.*
>
> One prophet said: "When heaven is shut up, and there is no rain, because they have sinned against thee; if they pray toward this place, and confess thy name, and turn from their sin, when thou afflictest them: then hear thou in heaven, and forgive the sin of thy servants, and of thy people Israel, that thou teach them the good way wherein they should walk, and give rain upon thy land, which thou hast given to thy people for an inheritance." (1 Kings 8:35–36.)
>
> The Lord uses the weather sometimes to discipline his

people for the violation of his laws. He said to the children of Israel: "If ye walk in my statutes, and keep my commandments, and do them; then I will give you rain in due season, and the land shall yield her increase, and the trees of the field shall yield their fruit. And your threshing shall reach unto the vintage, and the vintage shall reach unto the sowing time: and ye shall eat your bread to the full, and dwell in your land safely. And I will give peace in the land, and ye shall lie down, and none shall make you afraid: . . . neither shall the sword go through your land." (Lev. 26:3–6.)

With the great worry and suffering in the East and threats of drouth here in the West and elsewhere, we asked the people to join in a solemn prayer circle for moisture where needed. Quite immediately our prayers were answered, and we were grateful beyond expression. We are still in need and hope that the Lord may see fit to answer our continued prayers in this matter. . . .

Perhaps the day has come when we should take stock of ourselves and see if we are worthy to ask or if we have been breaking the commandments, making ourselves unworthy of receiving the blessings. (*Ensign*, May 1977, p. 4; italics added.)

The power of prayer in relieving famine and drought was quite evident in a visit Elder M. Russell Ballard and Bishop Glenn L. Pace made to Ethiopia in 1985. The country was in desperate need of rain. Elder Ballard reported the following:

The Spirit of the Lord was present. Because we had a deep yearning to help our Father's children who were suffering, we offered a special prayer that rain might come to that drought-stricken area. We felt a deep sense of the importance of our mission. I knew that if we called upon the Lord to bless the land, the elements would be tempered. We prayed, brethren, for rain. During the balance of the time we were in Ethiopia it rained every day wherever we traveled. We were grateful to our Heavenly Father because the rain was a special witness to us that he was aware that his sons, bearing his holy priesthood, were about his business in that part of the world. (*Ensign*, May 1985, p. 41.)

36

The Hurricane of Disobedience

Of all the disasters taking place during the last days, the hurricane of disobedience is ultimately the most deadly. Bishop Glenn L. Pace offered these insights: "The whole world seems to be in commotion. Today's news is filled with accounts of large-scale famine, civil unrest, and natural disasters. Even more devastating in the long run is the spiritually destructive hurricane of disobedience to God's commandments that is engulfing the world. This horrible storm is blowing the moral fiber out of the nations of the earth and leaving the land in moral desolation. Many people seem to be oblivious to this hurricane and have become so desensitized they don't even feel a breeze." (*Ensign,* November 1992, p. 12.)

Mankind can survive all forms of natural disaster: houses can be rebuilt, bones can be mended, supplies can be replenished. And even where death has occurred, there is the hope—even the absolute reality—of resurrection and of life beyond the grave. But to lose one's faith and turn from the ways of the Prince of Peace to the wickedness of the master of misery is a disaster of eternal consequences.

At the present time the forces of nature cannot be controlled, except through prayer and priesthood power. However, the plagues and moral pollutions that imperil the spirituality of people can be controlled. The next few chapters will deal specifically with the plagues of the last days that could be avoided if people simply followed a moral life and sought to do the will of God rather than to pursue their own carnal and selfish ways.

Chapter 4

PLAGUES AND POLLUTIONS

"For I, the Almighty, have laid my hands upon the nations, to scourge them for their wickedness. And plagues shall go forth, and they shall not be taken from the earth until I have completed my work, which shall be cut short in righteousness."
—D&C 84:96–97

People in Peril

The nightly news regularly reminds us of the perilous times in which we live. The spreading cancer of moral decay is not only reported in the news but also often celebrated as a preferred lifestyle. The immorality of the rich and famous of the world is frequently portrayed as normal, while those who practice virtue are mocked. Well did the prophet Isaiah warn: "Wo unto them that call evil good, and good evil; that put darkness for light, and light for darkness; that put bitter for sweet, and sweet for bitter!" (Isaiah 5:20.)

Those who seek pleasure in wickedness will one day discover the eternal truth that "wickedness never was happiness." (Alma 41:10.) The adversary promises a life of pleasure, but the reality is that his ways lead to misery, "for he seeketh that all men might be miserable like unto himself." (2 Nephi 2:27.)

The Savior warned that the days preceding his coming would be even "as the days of Noe [Noah] were" (Matthew 24:37; see also Luke 17:26). The days of Noah were filled with corruption and violence throughout the earth. (Genesis 6:11.) In comparing the wicked days of Noah to our day, Elder Neal A. Maxwell said:

We are told . . . that some of the conditions preceding the second coming of the Savior will be as in the days of Noah (see Matthew 24:37–39) and "also as it was in the days of Lot" (Luke 17:28). Noah's time was one of disobedience and wickedness. People were uncomprehending and "knew not until the flood came" (Matthew 24:39; see also Genesis 6:5; 1 Peter 3:20.) The choking cares and pleasures of this life led to the general rejection of Noah's prophetic message. Two especially interesting words are used in the Bible to describe Noah's time: *violence* and *corruption*. (Genesis 6:11). Violence and corruption, seldom strangers to the human scene, appear to be increasing today.

Some of the coarseness and cruelty present at the time of Noah will be replicated, for "the love of many shall wax cold" (Matthew 24:12). Also, peace will have been "taken from the earth" (D&C 1:35). (*Ensign*, May 1988, p. 7.)

That our days are similar to the days of Noah was also affirmed by President Joseph Fielding Smith, who declared:

Our Savior promised that the days preceding his second coming will be typical of the days of the flood. A glance at the sixth chapter of Genesis will reveal the conditions of the world in the days of Noah and the flood and the reason for the cleansing by water. This comparison is not to be taken figuratively, but literally as it is given. The world today is corrupt and filled with violence as it was at that earlier day, for now as then, 'All flesh has corrupted his way upon the earth.' [Gen. 6:12.] The Lord promised that he would never again destroy the entire world with a flood of water, but he did promise to cleanse it the second time with sword and with fire. [See Moses 7:50–51, 58–62.] (*THY*, p. 173.)

Without Natural Affection

When the Savior likened the days before His second coming to those of Noah, he also made reference to the wickedness "in the days of Lot." (See Luke 17:26–30.) Lot was warned to flee the gross perversion of Sodom and Gomorrah, where immorality, including homosexuality, was the accepted way of life. (See Genesis 19; see also JST, Genesis 19.) The Apostle

Paul foresaw these same conditions in the last days: "In the last days perilous times shall come. For men shall be lovers of their own selves, . . . *without natural affection,* . . . lovers of pleasures more than lovers of God." (See 2 Timothy 3:1–4; italics added.)

Commenting on Paul's description of our day, Elder Russell M. Nelson said: "Paul's warnings describe apostasy and other dangers of our day. Some of those perils are contrary to God's purposes and are championed by persuasive people possessing more ability than morality, more knowledge than wisdom." (*Ensign,* November 1992, p. 8.)

A peril "championed by persuasive people possessing more ability than morality" is that of homosexuality. In order to give homosexuality a semblance of legitimacy, this violation of God's laws is depicted as an "alternative lifestyle" with no moral or legal consequences. Great effort has gone into portraying one's so-called sexual preference as a civil right, and those who oppose this lifestyle are branded as "homophobic" or "prejudiced."

In April 1993 an estimated crowd of three hundred thousand people marched on Washington, D.C., in a display of support for so-called gay and lesbian rights. Holding hands, men with men and women with women, the group demanded that the country recognize their civil rights. The march was seen by some as signaling "the coming of age of a political movement."

Many federal, state, and local government agencies, including educational institutions, have made it illegal for anyone receiving their services to discriminate against another because of his or her sexual preferences and practices. On some college campuses, student organizations founded on principles of morality have been threatened with being denied access to school facilities unless they sign a pledge requiring them not to deny membership in their organization to one whose sexual preference and lifestyle may be contrary to the standards and beliefs of the organization. In essence, the rights of moral people are trampled upon to accommodate the lifestyles of the immoral minority. Even the Boy Scouts of America, who have long required members to pledge that they will be "morally straight," have been denied funding, harassed, and sued because the organization has refused to alter its membership and oath requirements.

Political pressure, demonstrations, threats, and man-made legislation will not change what God and His prophets have unalterably declared to be immoral. One of those prophets, President Spencer W. Kimball, declared: "The fact that some governments and some churches and numerous corrupted individuals have tried to reduce such behavior from criminal offense to personal privilege does not change the nature nor the seriousness of the practice." (*Ensign*, November 1980, p. 97.)

Another of God's anointed servants, Elder Boyd K. Packer, sounded the following warning to those who have made covenants with God through the waters of baptism and through other sacred ordinances:

> My message is to you who are tempted either to promote, to enter, or to remain in a life-style which violates your covenants and will one day bring sorrow to you and to those who love you.
>
> Growing numbers of people now campaign to make spiritually dangerous life-styles legal and socially acceptable. Among them are abortion, the gay-lesbian movement, and drug addiction. They are debated in forums and seminars, in classes, in conversations, in conventions, and in courts all over the world. The social and political aspects of them are in the press every day.
>
> The point I make is simply this: there is a *MORAL* and *SPIRITUAL* side to these issues which is universally ignored. For Latter-day Saints, morality is one component which must not be missing when these issues are considered— otherwise sacred covenants are at risk! Keep your covenants and you will be safe. Break them and you will not. . . .
>
> Some challenge us to show where the scriptures specifically forbid abortion or a gay-lesbian or drug-centered life-style. "If they are so wrong," they ask, "why don't the scriptures tell us so in 'letter of the law' plainness?" These issues are not ignored in the revelations. [See, for example,

Leviticus 18:22,29; 20:13; Romans 1:24–27; 1 Corinthians 6:9.] The scriptures are generally positive rather than negative in their themes, and it is a mistake to assume that anything not specifically prohibited in the "*letter* of the law" is somehow approved of the Lord. All the Lord approves is not detailed in the scriptures, neither is all that is forbidden." (*Ensign,* November 1990, p. 84.)

The Plague of AIDS

One of the direct results of the practice of homosexuality in these last days is the plague of AIDS (Acquired Immune Deficiency Syndrome). It is preceded by the HIV infection (Human Immunosuppressive Virus). "AIDS is so deadly," said Dr. John L. Clowe, former president of the American Medical Association, "that by its very diagnosis the patient faces what literally is a death sentence." Dr. Clowe noted further that the "progression from HIV infection to AIDS takes an average of 10 years." During this time, the sexually promiscuous can unknowingly transmit the disease to many others, "keeping the epidemic invisibly alive." ("The Changing World of Aids," *Vital Speeches of the Day,* 15 December 1992, pp. 135, 136.)

Unfortunately, there also are innocent victims of this dread disease: those who are infected by contaminated blood, innocent spouses of promiscuous husbands and wives, or babies infected by their mothers. Elder Russell M. Nelson, who speaks the spiritual language of one called to the holy apostleship and who is an internationally recognized medical doctor, said this about the spread of AIDS: "An epidemic has been forecast—a plague fueled by a vocal few who exhibit greater concern for civil rights than for public health—a plague abetted by the immoral. Some live in lust as though God's commandment to be chaste was written with an asterisk, exempting them from obeying. And regrettably, as in previous plagues, many innocent victims are doomed to suffer." (*Ensign,* November 1992, p. 8.)

It seems reasonable to conclude that the spread of this terrible disease could be at least in partial fulfillment of the plagues that would be part of the last days. A revelation from the Lord in 1832 warned: "For I, the Almighty, have laid my hands upon the nations, to scourge them for their wickedness. And plagues shall go forth, and they shall not be taken from the earth until I have completed my work, which shall be cut short in righteousness." (D&C 84:96–97.)

In 1859 Charles W. Penrose, who became an apostle in 1904, published a sermon identifying many of the disasters and disturbances that would accompany the last days. He said "the passions of human nature will be put to the vilest uses [and] new diseases will silently eat their ghastly way through the ranks of the wicked." (*Millennial Star,* 21:582.) Perhaps this is part of what John the Revelator saw when he prophesied of the plagues to be poured out upon the wicked in the last days: "And there fell a noisome and grievous sore upon the men which had the mark of the beast, and upon them which worshipped his image." (Revelation 16:2.)

President Gordon B. Hinckley, First Counselor in the First Presidency, provided the following commentary on the plague of AIDS:

> There is a plague of fearsome dimensions moving across the world. Public health officials are greatly concerned, and everyone else should be. . . .
>
> AIDS is a commonly fatal malady caused primarily from sexually transmitted disease and secondarily from drug abuse. Unfortunately, as in any epidemic, innocent people also become victims.
>
> We, with others, hope that discoveries will make possible both prevention and healing from this dread affliction. But regardless of such discoveries, the observance of one clearly understandable and divinely given rule would do more than all else to check this epidemic. That is chastity before marriage and total fidelity after marriage.
>
> Prophets of God have repeatedly taught through the ages that practices of homosexual relations, fornication, and adultery are grievous sins. Sexual relations outside the bonds of marriage are forbidden by the Lord. We reaffirm

those teachings. Mankind has been given agency to choose between right and wrong. . . .

Each of us has a choice between right and wrong. But with that choice there inevitably will follow consequences. Those who choose to violate the commandments of God put themselves at great spiritual and physical jeopardy. (*Ensign*, May 1987, pp. 46–47.)

General Decline in Morality

The general decline in morality in the last days is very evident. Nudity, illicit sexual liaisons, pornography, perversion, and filthy language can all be found not only in movie theaters, but also on public television. Ears and eyes are constantly assaulted in public places by vulgarity in conversation, music, advertising, and the printed word.

Immorality is publicly promoted through the distribution of condoms in schools and the advocacy of immoral behavior. For example, a recommended book list for first graders in New York City public schools has included "Heather Has Two Mommies" and "Daddy's Roommate," both of which focus on accepting the gay-lesbian lifestyle. Such moral decay is further illustrated in a recent cartoon showing a man sitting in front of a television from which comes this announcement: "The following program may not be suitable for those of you who still have standards."

In writing about several world conditions that would prevail during the last days, the ancient prophet Moroni foresaw "a day when there shall be great pollutions upon the face of the earth; there shall be murders, and robbing, and lying, and deceivings, and whoredoms, and all manner of abominations; when there shall be many who will say, Do this, or do that, and it mattereth not." (Mormon 8:31.) Commenting on the application of this scripture to these last days, Elder Dallin H. Oaks said: "For many in our day, the profane has become commonplace and the vulgar has become acceptable. Surely this is one fulfillment of the Book of Mormon prophecy that in the last days 'there shall be *great pollutions* upon the face of the earth.'" (*Ensign,* May 1986, p. 49; italics added.)

Elder Boyd K. Packer spoke of the moral pollution spreading its filthy cloud throughout the world today, causing the "pollution index" to spiral upward:

> The Book of Mormon depicts humanity struggling through a "mist of darkness" and defines the darkness as the "temptations of the devil." (1 Ne. 8:23; 12:17.) So dense was that *moral pollution* that many followed "strange roads" and "fell away into forbidden paths and were lost." (See 1 Ne. 8:23–32.)
>
> The deliberate pollution of the fountain of life now clouds our moral environment. The gift of mortal life and the capacity to kindle other lives is a supernal blessing. Its worth is *incalculable!*
>
> The rapid, sweeping deterioration of values is characterized by a preoccupation—even an obsession—with the procreative act. Abstinence before marriage and fidelity within it are openly scoffed at—marriage and parenthood ridiculed as burdensome, unnecessary. Modesty, a virtue of a refined individual or society, is all but gone.
>
> The adversary is jealous toward all who have the power to beget life. He cannot beget life; he is impotent. He and those who followed him were cast out and forfeited the right to a mortal body. His angels even begged to inhabit the bodies of swine. (See Matt. 8:31.) And the revelations tell us that "he seeketh that all men might be miserable like unto himself." (2 Ne. 2:27.)
>
> With ever fewer exceptions, what we see and read and hear have the mating act as a central theme. Censorship is forced offstage as a violation of individual freedom.
>
> That which should be absolutely private is disrobed and acted out center stage. In the shadows backstage are addiction, pornography, perversion, infidelity, abortion, and—the saddest of them all—incest and molestation. In company with them now is a plague of biblical proportion. And all of them are on the increase. (*Ensign,* May 1992, p. 66.)

The Loss and Lessening of Standards and Values

A national chain of retail stores emphasizes its products as having "true value!" Unfortunately, the people of the world in general have let their "true values" slip and slide as they pursue the path of sin. There is an ever-widening gap between the ways of the world and those true values and standards to which all people should adhere.

Recently an athlete with superstar status admitted to having contracted the HIV infection as a result of years of promiscuous living. Because of this athlete's public confession, one reporter suggested he should be "held up as a modern-day hero." The athlete promised to become a spokesman for AIDS awareness, stating, "I want young people to realize they can practice safe sex." There was no mention of moral abstinence or right and wrong by this "modern-day hero," simply the *practice* of so-called safe sex.

It is interesting to note the type of individuals held up as heroes by youth. In a recent survey, the top three categories of most admired people for youth were (1) TV/movie stars, (2) rock musicians, and (3) professional athletes. In another survey of most-admired people, the top ten chosen by young men included three movie stars, three professional athletes, a film director, and a rock star, while five of the top ten chosen by young women were movie stars.

As a whole the values of these admired people are not consistent with the standards taught in the scriptures by the prophets or embraced by other men and women of virtue and integrity. A survey of Hollywood's influential television writers and executives revealed that they are "far less religious than the general public and diverge sharply from traditional values on such issues as abortion, homosexual rights and extramarital sex:

> While nearly all of the 104 Hollywood professionals interviewed had a religious background, 45 percent now say they have no religion, and of the other 55 percent only 7

percent say they attend a religious service as much as once a month.

This group has had a major role in shaping the shows whose themes and stars have become staples in our popular culture. . . .

Eighty percent of the respondents said they did not regard homosexual relations as wrong, and 51 percent did not deem adultery as wrong. Of the 49 percent who called extramarital affairs wrong, only 17 percent felt that way strongly, the study said. Nearly all—97 percent—favored the right of a woman to choose an abortion, 91 percent holding that view strongly. (John Dart, in *Los Angeles Times,* 19 February 1983, part 2, p. 5; as quoted in Gordon B. Hinckley, *Ensign,* November 1983, p. 45.)

President Gordon B. Hinckley offered the following observations regarding the difference between the ways of the world and the values upheld by The Church of Jesus Christ of Latter-day Saints:

Some time ago I read a letter to a newspaper editor which was highly critical of the Church. I have forgotten the exact language, but it included a question something like this: "When are the Mormons going to stop being different and become a part of the mainstream of America?"

About this same time there came to my desk a copy of an address given by Senator Dan Coats of Indiana. He spoke of a study made by "a commission of educational, political, medical and business leaders" dealing with the problems of American youth. The committee issued a report called *Code Blue.* That report, according to the Senator, concluded: "Never before has one generation of American teenagers been less healthy, less cared for, or less prepared for life than their parents were at the same age." He went on to say, "I have seen the parade of pathologies—they are unending and increasing:

"Suicide is now the second leading cause of death among adolescents, increasing 300 percent since 1950.

"Teen pregnancy has risen 621 percent since 1940. More than a million teenage girls get pregnant each year. Eighty-five percent of teenage boys who impregnate teenage girls eventually abandon them.

"The teen homicide rate has increased 232 percent since

47

1950. Homicide is now the leading cause of death among fifteen- to nineteen-year-old minority youth. . . .

"Every year substance abuse claims younger victims with harder drugs. A third of high school seniors get drunk once a week. The average age for first-time drug use is now thirteen years old."

The report reached a shocking conclusion. It said: "The challenges to the health and well-being of America's youth are not primarily rooted in illness or economics. Unlike the past, the problem is not childhood disease or unsanitary slums. The most basic cause of suffering . . . is profoundly self-destructive *behavior*. Drinking. Drugs. Violence. Promiscuity. A crisis of behavior and belief. A crisis of character." (*Imprimis,* Sept. 1991, p. 1.)

When I read those statements, I said to myself, if that is the mainstream of American youth, then I want to do all in my power to persuade and encourage our young people to stay away from it. (*Ensign,* May 1992, pp. 69–70.)

In prophesying about the last days, the Book of Mormon prophet Nephi, son of Lehi, proclaimed: "For the time speedily cometh that the Lord God shall cause a great division among the people, and the wicked will he destroy; and he will spare his people, yea, even if it so be that he must destroy the wicked by fire." (2 Nephi 30:10; see also D&C 63:53–54.)

Elder Neal A. Maxwell contrasted the ways of the world with the values embraced by The Church of Jesus Christ of Latter-day Saints: "The Church is pulling away from the world at a rate that would be noticeable even if the world were standing still in its standards. But the world is pulling away even from standards it once held. Thus the Church and the world are parting company like two speeding cars going in opposite directions." (*Deposition of a Disciple,* Salt Lake City: Deseret Book Co., 1976, p. 63.) As people contemplate their own values and the impact that personal decisions will have on the rest of their mortal lives as well as the long hereafter, the words of Elder Dean L. Larsen of the Seventy are worth pondering:

The challenging conditions we find in the world today should be no surprise to us. As we approach the time of the Savior's return, wickedness will increase. There will be more temptations in our daily lives, and they will become more intense. It will become more acceptable in the world to break the laws of God or to disregard them altogether. The stigma attached to immoral, dishonest behavior will disappear.

In this difficult environment we will be expected to steer our own course in an upward direction. . . . It will neither be acceptable nor safe to remain on the plateaus where our present conduct has kept us. Abrupt downward forces, represented by increasing wickedness in the world, can only be offset by forces that move correspondingly upward. Our lives must be better than they have ever been before. This simply means that we will become increasingly different from those around us whose lives follow the world's way. It is not easy to be different. There are intense pressures that work against us. But we must clearly understand that it is not safe to move in the same direction the world is moving, even though we remain slightly behind the pace they set. Such a course will eventually lead us to the same problems and heartaches. It will not permit us to perform the work the Lord has chosen us to do. It would disqualify us from his blessing and his protecting care. . . .

But there are too many whose lives are being contaminated by the worldly trends. This is not a light matter. The judgments of God will not be withheld from those who willfully, knowing who they are and what is expected of them, allow themselves to be drawn along the precarious paths of worldly conduct. (*Ensign,* May 1983, pp. 34–35.)

Blasphemy and Mockery of Sacred Things

A major cause of the downfall of the ancient Nephite civilization was that they made "a mock of that which was sacred." (Helaman 4:12.) In our day the Lord has warned, "Trifle not with sacred things." (D&C 6:12.) Those persons who promote the values and wickedness of the world today often mock that which is held sacred by the righteous. Sacred covenants, ceremonies, clothing, words, books, buildings—none have escaped the finger of scorn nor the tongue of blasphemy of the wicked.

From the beginning the adversary and his followers have sought to discredit Deity and to mock God's ways.

In the Book of Revelation, John describes a beast who, representing earthly kingdoms, is controlled by the devil: "And [the beast] opened his mouth in blasphemy against God, to blaspheme his name, and his tabernacle, and them that dwell in heaven." (Revelation 13:6.) The beast is busy blaspheming all that is held sacred throughout the earth today. Of particular interest to the adversary is anything or anyone connected with God's kingdom on earth. Prophets are scorned, ordinances are ridiculed, and the righteous are belittled. The holy name of Deity is blasphemed when used in concert with gutter language and misused in everyday expressions. The sacred functions of procreation are spoken of in filth, and even a name that God holds most dear—that of "mother"—is defiled. Is it any wonder that our Father in Heaven has been so protective of the identity of our Mother in Heaven?

The Apostle Paul described the "perilous times" of the last days in warning us against "blasphemers." He then counseled, "from such turn away." (See 2 Timothy 3:1–5.) In addition to refusing to embrace or to use the words of blasphemers, there might be other implications for us in Paul's admonition. Perhaps the "turning away" also means that we should turn our eyes and ears away from movies, television, and music that mock and blaspheme God and anything that should be held sacred.

The prayer of us all should be like that of the ancient psalmist: "Set a watch, O Lord, before my mouth; keep the door of my lips. Incline not my heart to any evil thing, to practise wicked works with men that work iniquity." (Psalm 141:3–4.) And one of the first of the Ten Commandments given anciently on Mount Sinai should still be among the first to be observed in our day: "Thou shalt not take the name of the Lord thy God in vain; for the Lord will not hold him guiltless that taketh his name in vain." (Exodus 20:7.)

An appropriate conclusion to this section on profanity and

to this chapter on plagues and moral pollutions is found in the words of President Spencer W. Kimball: "It is not enough to refrain from profanity or blasphemy. We need to make important in our lives the name of the Lord. While we do not use the Lord's name lightly, we should not leave our friends or our neighbors or our children in any doubt as to where we stand. Let there be no doubt about our being followers of Jesus Christ." (*Ensign*, November 1978, p. 6.)

Chapter 5

SATAN'S ASSAULT ON THE FAMILY

"And he became Satan, yea, even the devil, the father of all lies, to deceive and to blind men, and to lead them captive at his will, even as many as would not hearken unto my voice."

—MOSES 4:4

The Father of Lies

One of the most significant signs of the last days, and probably the most dangerous, is the all-out assault that Satan is making on the family. He has an intense hatred of anything associated with the family—marriage, mother, father, children—for he himself will never be a true father.

When *the* Father laid out His plans for the progression of His children, Satan opposed those plans and offered his own amendment to God's perfect plan, a counterproposal that included the denial of agency and his desire to displace our Father in Heaven. (See Moses 4:1–4; Abraham 3:27–28.) Satan's promise "that one soul shall not be lost" was a lie, for he could not have forced all of Father's children to follow him. And if under his plan an atonement were to be required, this selfish spirit son of God could not have accomplished it. He had neither the love nor the willpower to have borne up under the suffering that was later required of the Only Begotten in Gethsemane and on Calvary. Thus it is appropriate that he "who was a liar from the beginning" (D&C 93:25) should be dubbed "the father of all lies" (2 Nephi 2:18; Moses 4:4). His compulsion to lie and to deceive preceded his encounter with

Adam and Eve in the Garden of Eden, and it continues in these days.

The scornful but accurate title of "father of all lies" is the only way Satan will ever have the title of father. Because he is eternally damned—denied the right to a body, to a wife, to fatherhood and children, and to extended posterity—he is intensely hateful of all that he cannot possess and is in constant rebellion against that holy Being who has asked us to address Him simply as "Father."

To the degree that he can experience satisfaction, the adversary takes pleasure (not genuine happiness, for he is incapable of that experience) in the destruction of the family. Marital discord, divorce, neglected and abused children, abortion, the misuse of procreative powers—all of these are consistent with the desires of that evil being who "seeketh that all men might be miserable like unto himself." (2 Nephi 2:27; see also verse 18.)

As the timing of the Second Coming draws closer, the adversary has intensified his campaign of hatred against the family. The potential destructiveness of this assault on the family is evidenced in these words of Bishop Victor L. Brown:

> At the present time, there are wars and rumors of wars. Yet, may I suggest that there is another war currently going on in the world—a war more destructive than any armed conflict—yes, a war between good and evil, between freedom and slavery, between the Savior and Satan. Satan's legions are many. In their battle to enslave mankind, they use weapons such as selfishness; dishonesty; corruption; sexual impurity, be it adultery, fornication, or homosexuality; pornography; permissiveness; drugs; and many others. I believe Satan's ultimate goal is to destroy the family, because if he would destroy the family, he will not just have won the battle; he will have won the war. (*Ensign,* January 1974, p. 108.)

The Breakdown of the Family

The success of Satan's assault on the family is found in these words of Elder James E. Faust of the Quorum of the Twelve

Apostles: "In recent times, society has been plagued with a cancer from which few families have escaped. I speak of the disintegration of our homes." (*Ensign*, May 1993, p. 35.) The spiraling numbers of divorces, spouse and child abuse, broken homes, absentee parents, and abortions all bear witness to the assault being made on the family. Even the titles and callings of "father" and "mother" have come under attack.

In a speech given to the Catholic League for Religious and Civil Rights in Washington, D.C., in 1992, then United States Attorney General William P. Barr made these observations regarding the breakdown of the family:

> The most significant feature of contemporary society has been the battering of the family, and its disintegration.
> Today, in America, we have soaring illegitimacy rates. Today, almost 30 percent of children are born out of wedlock—about a quadrupling in 25 years.
> In many inner-city areas, the illegitimacy rate is as high as 80 percent.
> And America also now has among the highest divorce rates in the world—divorce is as common as marriage.
> As a consequence of this, we now have the highest percentage of children living in single-parent households.
> This breakdown of the family is particularly distressing because it is the family that is the principal institution by which we conduct moral education—by which we transmit moral values from generation to generation.
> As the family is weakened, so is our ability to transmit values to the next generation.
> And, it is the breakdown of the family that is at the root of most of our social problems today. ("The Judeo-Christian Tradition vs. Secularism," 6 October 1992.)

While divorce has always been a challenge to a stable society, it has become increasingly so in recent years. In 1960, 74 percent of all United States households were headed by a married couple; by 1990 this figure had declined to 56 percent.

The breakdown of the family has not been confined to the United States, but it is happening worldwide. In a speech delivered in the summer of 1993, Mr. John Banks, Minister of Police for New Zealand, stated:

> It is within the family that children learn such values as love, responsibility, communication, respect for authority and faith in God. They learn about living up to one's potential, leaving the world a better place, doing the right thing and doing things right. . . .
>
> When the traditional family unit is undermined, as it has been, self-reliance is lost and responsibility disappears. These have been replaced by a dependence, often long-term, on the Government and manipulation by social engineers. The destruction of the family unit provides the setting which leads young people to the treadmill of drug abuse and crime. Children need mothers and fathers. A welfare cheque is not a husband. The State is not a father. Where there are not mature, responsible parents around to teach boys how to be good citizens, gangs often serve in their place. ("Make Our Country Good and Great," *Vital Speeches of the Day,* 1 September 1993, p. 682.)

Absentee Parents

Among the most difficult social problems of our day is the rise in juvenile crime and violence. It is of interest to note that recent statistics show that "the most accurate predictor of violent crime and burglary in neighborhoods is not race or income but rather the percent of households without fathers." Furthermore, research has shown that "seventy percent of all juveniles in long-term correctional facilities did not live with their father while growing up." (Richard Witmire, "Life without Father Breaking Hearts, Homes across U.S.," *Salt Lake Tribune,* 19 June 1993, p. A1.)

The importance of fathers in the home was emphasized by Elder James E. Faust, who said: "Fathers are not optional family baggage. We need to honor the position of the father as the primary provider for physical and spiritual support." Elder Faust further noted the importance of both fathers and mothers: "It is useless to debate which parent is most important. No one would doubt that a mother's influence is paramount with newborns and in the first years of a child's life. The father's influence increases as the child grows older. However, each parent is necessary at various times in a child's development." (*Ensign*, May 1993, p. 35.)

The absence of mothers in the home has also had a destructive impact on the family. While serving as a counselor in the First Presidency, President Nathan Eldon Tanner said: "Satan and his cohorts are using scientific arguments and nefarious propaganda to lure women away from their primary responsibilities as wives, mothers, and homemakers. We hear so much about emancipation, independence, sexual liberation, birth control, abortion, and other insidious propaganda belittling the role of motherhood, all of which is Satan's way of destroying woman, *the home and the family—the basic unit of society*." (*Ensign*, January 1974, p. 7.)

It is recognized that out of economic necessity (not simply material desires), some mothers must work outside the home. However, the prophets and other servants of God have admonished mothers to carefully count the cost to the children and the family before making such a move. Bishop H. Burke Peterson, while serving as a counselor in the Presiding Bishopric of the Church, observed:

> One of the great tragedies of our day is the confusion in the minds of some which would cause mothers to go to work in the marketplace. Satan, that master of deceit, would have us believe that when we have problems with our children, the answer may be a nicer home in a finer neighborhood, that they might have their own bedroom, or better quality clothes, and maybe their own car. Satan would have us believe that money or the things money can buy are more important in the home than mother.
>
> Now there are some mothers with school-age children who are the breadwinners of their family and they must work; they are the exception. Fathers and mothers, before you decide you need a second income and that mother must go to work out of the home, may I plead with you: first go to the Lord in prayer and receive his divine approbation. Be sure he says yes. Mothers with children and teenagers at home, before you go out of your homes to

56

work, please *count the cost* as carefully as you count the profit. Earning a few dollars more for luxuries cloaked in the masquerade of necessity—or a so-called opportunity for self-development of talents in the business world, a chance to get away from the mundane responsibilities of the home—these are all satanic substitutes for clear thinking. They are counterfeit thoughts that subvert the responsibilities of motherhood." (*Ensign*, May 1974, p. 32.)

Genocide of the Unborn

The most vile assault on the family is genocide of the unborn. Abortion is one of the devil's most widespread techniques in his ongoing war against the plan of salvation. The killing of innocent children through abortion is epidemic. Elder Russell M. Nelson has noted that this war on the unborn "*annually* claims more casualties than the total number of fatalities from all the wars of this nation." (*Ensign*, May 1985, p. 11.)

Could abortion be one of the things Paul had in mind when he spoke of there being those "without natural affection" as one of the signs of the last days? (2 Timothy 3:3.) What is more unnatural than for a mother to willingly submit to procedures that kill the child she has conceived and is carrying? Is the killing of the unborn a modern manifestation of what the Lord anciently referred to when he described people who, "without affection, . . . hate their own blood"? (Moses 7:33.) Could abortion be one of the things the Prophet Joseph Smith had in mind when he saw in vision "women killing their own daughters?" (*HC*, 3:391.)

In Old Testament times there was an abominable form of worship in which children were offered as fiery sacrifices to the fire god Molech. Elder Theodore M. Burton of the Seventy drew a comparison between this ancient abomination and modern-day abortion: "We shudder as we read in [the Old Testament] of the sacrifices of idol worshipers of that time who fed their children into the fiery maw of the iron god Molech. Is personal selfishness which results in abortion any less repulsive to God, as modern people through abortion offer the sacrifice of their children to their idol of selfish materialism?" (*Ensign*, May 1979, p. 73.)

Unfortunately, this very moral issue has been turned into a political issue, and efforts continue to establish abortion as a civil right rather than a damnable sin. Politicians have made the support of abortion a condition for one to be selected to serve in the judicial system. Anciently the prophet Isaiah cried out against such leaders: "O my people, they who lead thee cause thee to err and destroy the way of thy paths." (Isaiah 3:12; 2 Nephi 13:12.)

In commenting on Isaiah's scriptural pronouncement, Elder Ezra Taft Benson observed: "Consider these words [of Isaiah] seriously when you think of those political leaders who are promoting birth control and abortion." (*Improvement Era*, December 1970, p. 46.) Later he also observed: "Innocent-sounding phrases are now used to give approval to sinful practices. Thus, the term 'alternate life-style' is used to justify adultery and homosexuality, *'freedom of choice' to justify abortion,* 'meaningful relationship' and 'self-fulfillment' to justify sex outside of marriage." (*Ensign*, November 1982, p. 59; italics added.)

In spite of the efforts of politicians to popularize and legalize sin, the position of the Church and its prophets is clear. President Spencer W. Kimball declared: "Abortion must be considered one of the most revolting and sinful practices in this day." (*Ensign*, May 1975, p. 7.) And Elder Ezra Taft Benson has likewise denounced abortion: "We oppose and abhor the damnable practice of wholesale abortion and every other unholy and impure act which strikes at the very foundation of the home and family, our most basic institutions." (*Ensign*, July 1973, p. 41.)

In an official declaration, the First Presidency of The Church of Jesus Christ of Latter-day Saints published this statement on the issue of abortion:

> In view of the widespread public interest in the issue of abortion, we reaffirm that The Church of Jesus Christ of

Latter-day Saints has consistently opposed elective abortion. More than a century ago, the First Presidency of the church warned against this evil. We have repeatedly counseled people everywhere to turn from the devastating practice of abortion for personal or social convenience.

The church recognizes that there may be rare cases in which abortion may be justified—cases involving pregnancy by incest or rape; when the life or health of the woman is adjudged by competent medical authority to be in serious jeopardy; or when the fetus is known by competent medical authority to have severe defects that will not allow the baby to survive beyond birth. But these are not automatic reasons for abortion. Even in these cases, the couple should consider an abortion only after consulting with each other, and their bishop, and receiving divine confirmation through prayer." ("LDS Position on Abortion," *Deseret News*, 12 January 1991, p. B6.)

The Lord declared to the ancient Israelites that one who "hurt a woman with child, so that her fruit depart from her, ... he shall be surely punished." (Exodus 21:22.)

John Calvin, the sixteenth-century religious reformer, provided some thoughts worth pondering: "If it seems more horrible to kill a man in his own house than in a field, because a man's house is his place of most secure refuge, it ought surely to be deemed more atrocious to destroy a *fetus* in the womb before it has come to light." (As quoted by Russell M. Nelson in *Ensign*, May 1985, p. 12.) A twentieth-century apostle, Elder Neal A. Maxwell, expressed his feelings on abortion in connection with his gratitude for the Atonement: "I thank the Father that His Only Begotten Son did not say in defiant protest at Calvary, 'My body is my own!' I stand in admiration of women today who resist the fashion of abortion, by refusing to make the sacred womb a tomb!" (*Ensign*, May 1978, p. 10.)

An Eternal Perspective on Family

While it is recognized that some people, through no fault of their own, will be deprived of a partner or children in this life, the eternal perspective of the family must not be lost. God is fair! God is just! No blessing will be withheld from the righteous in the eternities, though there may be temporary deprivation in mortality. Lucifer, that master of deceit—that most miserable of all creatures, he who is without hope of ever having a family himself—would fain discourage and dishearten those whose righteous desires for a family have not yet been granted.

In response to the hopelessness that the adversary promotes, consider what has been said by several special witnesses of Jesus Christ whom we sustain as prophets, seers, and revelators:

Elder Boyd K. Packer declared: "Any soul who by nature or circumstance is not afforded the blessing of marriage and parenthood or who innocently must act alone in rearing children, working to support them, will not be denied in the eternities any blessing—provided they keep the commandments. [See D&C 137:7–9.] As President Lorenzo Snow promised: 'That is sure and positive.'" (*Ensign,* November 1993, p. 23.) A fellow apostle, Elder Dallin H. Oaks, stated:

> We know that many worthy and wonderful Latter-day Saints currently lack the ideal opportunities and essential requirements for their progress. Singleness, childlessness, death, and divorce frustrate ideals and postpone the fulfillment of promised blessings. . . . But these frustrations are only temporary. The Lord has promised that in the eternities no blessing will be denied his sons and daughters who keep the commandments, are true to their covenants, and desire what is right.
>
> Many of the most important deprivations of mortality will be set right in the Millennium, which is the time for fulfilling all that is incomplete in the great plan of happiness for all of our Father's worthy children. We know that will be true of temple ordinances. I believe it will also be true of family relationships and experiences.
>
> I pray that we will not let the challenges and temporary diversions of mortality cause us to forget our covenants and lose sight of our eternal destiny. (*Ensign,* November 1993, p. 75.)

Chapter 6

CONSPIRACIES OF THE LAST DAYS

"Behold, verily, thus saith the Lord unto you: In consequence of evils and designs which do and will exist in the hearts of conspiring men in the last days, I have warned you, and forewarn you."

—D&C 89:4

Conspiring Men

Tobacco and alcohol consumption are so much a part of everyday life that a question might be raised as to why they are referred to in a book on the last days. Is the common use of these products really a sign preceding the Second Coming? The answer lies in a revelation received by the Prophet Joseph Smith in 1833. In this revelation, known as the Word of Wisdom, the Lord warned against the "evils and designs which do and will exist in the hearts of *conspiring men in the last days.*" (D&C 89:4; italics added.)

Who are these "conspiring men?" One need only peruse a periodical or view television, particularly a sporting event, to note the advertising designed to entice one to consume products harmful to the body and the spirit. While the "Marlboro man" has ridden off into the sunset of television advertising (because of the government ban on tobacco advertising via radio and television), another tobacco company has conspired to create a cartoon character named "Joe Camel," who is designed to sell cigarettes from the slick pages of periodicals. A younger clientele is targeted, with the hope that a lifelong habit can be formed.

And what about the advertising for alcoholic beverages? A wide variety of alcoholic products is portrayed as fun and popular, the way to success, the "in" thing to do. Yet the promises are shallow and short-lived. The reality of alcohol's destructive power was described in a speech given by Neal A. Maxwell when he was vice president of the University of Utah. To a group of college students, he spoke of the "awful arithmetic" of alcohol: "If as many of your generation maintain, the ultimate obscenity is violence and needless death, then alcohol is obscene in terms of the people it kills and maims on our highways and the numerous child beatings it causes in homes and all the other tragedies that grow out of the misuse of alcohol." ("This Matter of Relevancy," 16 May 1969, pp. 2–3.)

Elder Joseph B. Wirthlin of the Quorum of the Twelve Apostles gives some indication of how different society might be if the resources now used in rectifying abuse of alcohol, tobacco, and other drugs were free to be used in other areas: "Imagine the results we would see if the total populace were to live this law of health and never abuse their bodies with alcoholic beverages, tobacco, and other harmful substances. What magnitude of decline would we see in automobile accidents, illness and premature death, fetal defects, crime, squandered dollars, broken homes, and wasted lives resulting from alcohol and other addictive drugs? How much would lung cancer, heart disease, and other ailments caused by cigarette smoking decrease?" (*Ensign*, November 1991, p. 16.) The cost to society in suffering, loss of lives, loss of income, destruction of families, and disruption of employment from the abuse of alcohol, tobacco, and other drugs is almost incalculable, the terrible cost rising each year. However, some idea of the annual cost is gleaned from the following figures of the late 1980s:

- 10.6 million adults are alcoholics
- Alcohol is a factor in one-half of traffic deaths.
- More Americans have now been killed in alcohol-related auto accidents than in all the wars ever fought by Americans.

- 320,000 annual deaths can be attributed to tobacco.
- 125,000 annual deaths can be attributed to alcohol.
- An estimated one-half of Americans have tried drugs.
- An estimated one-half of crimes are drug related.
- The federal government has launched an $8 billion battle against illicit drugs (prisons, police, etc.). (See *Ensign,* November 1988, p. 7; November 1989, p. 49.)

The Terrible Toll of Drugs

One of the most insidious signs of the last days is the increase in the use of illicit drugs. Some of the criminal by-products of drug usage include prostitution, AIDS, robbery, assault, and murder. President Ezra Taft Benson commented on the conspiracy in the last days to spread the use of addictive substances, especially drugs:

> The Lord foresaw the situation of today when motives for money would cause men to conspire to entice others to take noxious substances into their bodies. [See D&C 89:4.] Advertisements which promote beer, wine, liquors, coffee, tobacco, and other harmful substances are examples of what the Lord foresaw. But the most pernicious example of an evil conspiracy in our time is those who induce young people into the use of drugs. My young brothers and sisters, in all love, we give you warning that Satan and his emissaries will strive to entice you to use harmful substances, because they well know if you partake, your spiritual powers will be inhibited and you will be in their evil power. Stay away from those places or people which would influence you to break the commandments of God. Keep the commandments of God and you will have the wisdom to know and discern that which is evil." (*Ensign,* May 1983, pp. 54–55.)

As part of the scenario preceding the Second Coming, the Apostle John described the wicked who did not repent "of their murders, nor of their sorceries, nor of their fornication, nor of their thefts." (Revelation 9:21.) The word *sorceries* has its origin in the Greek *pharmakeia,* which means "pharmacy" or

63

"drugs." Clearly the Revelator saw the rampant use of drugs in the last days.

One official of the United States government commented on the drain that drugs are having on worldwide resources: "I know from firsthand knowledge what a scourge illicit narcotics are to this country and others. The drain on the human and monetary resources of the world being caused by this dilemma is inestimable and threatens the very foundations of freedom." (As quoted by Gordon B. Hinckley in *Ensign*, November 1989, p. 49.)

Satan's Slavery

Satan uses the weakness of the flesh, the desire for unnatural stimulants and experiences, and the curiosity to taste forbidden fruits to enslave men, women, youth, and even children in his ongoing, relentless battle to destroy agency. The success of the adversary in this respect was noted by Elder Russell M. Nelson: "Through chemical means, one can literally become disconnected from his or her own will!" (*Ensign*, November 1988, p. 7.)

Satan was unsuccessful in his bid to convert us to his enslaving plan in the premortal world of spirits. However, he is having great success in enslaving physical bodies with substance addiction. There are few, if any, alcoholics or drug addicts who deliberately set out to become a slave to a habit. Many thought they would sample the forbidden fruit for a season or "just this once" before returning to abstinence and freedom's safe ground. In this respect, Elder Neal A. Maxwell offered the following warning: "Why do some of our youth risk engaging in ritual prodigalism, intending to spend a season rebelling and acting out in Babylon? . . . Though planning to return later, many such stragglers find that alcohol, drugs, and pornography will not let go easily. Babylon does not give exit permits gladly. It is an ironic implementation of that ancient boast: 'One soul shall not be lost.' (Moses 4:1.)" (*Ensign*, November 1988, p. 33.)

To enslave the body to an addictive habit is to give away control of the Spirit. Elder Stephen L Richards noted that "injury to the body [from substance abuse] may be comparatively trivial to the damage to the soul in the destruction of faith and the retardation of spiritual growth." (In CR, April 1949, p. 141.) The risk of addiction and the loss of one's spiritual moorings are far too great for anyone to risk trifling with forbidden fruits. Elder Russell M. Nelson observed: "From an initial experiment thought to be trivial, a vicious cycle may follow. From trial comes a habit. From habit comes dependence. From dependence comes addiction. Its grasp is so gradual. Enslaving shackles of habit are too small to be sensed until they are too strong to be broken. Indeed, drugs are the modern 'mess of pottage' for which souls are sold. No families are free from risk." (*Ensign*, November 1988, p. 6.)

Other Conspiring Men

There is another dimension of obedience to the Word of Wisdom that should not be overlooked. Elder Russell M. Nelson noted: "As you develop courage to say no to alcohol, tobacco, and other stimulants, you gain additional strength. You can then refuse conspiring men—those seditious solicitors of harmful substances or smut. You can reject their evil enticements to your body." (*Ensign*, November 1985, p. 31.)

Is there any doubt that the intention of the smut peddlers—those *other conspiring men*—is to seduce and enslave the weak willed and wayward, to addict them to pornography and perversion? Resistance to sin is built through obedience. Strength to stand spiritually strong in one area provides power to resist temptation in another. Those who resist the allurement of addictive substances reap the promise that the "destroying angel shall pass by them." (D&C 89:21.) They shall not be subject to the plagues, diseases, and misery caused by violations of the Lord's Word of Wisdom.

Secret Combinations

The Book of Mormon warns of secret combinations that will threaten civilization in the last days. There is no question that the worldwide drug cartels and crime syndicates that produce and peddle pornography are filled with evil and conspiring men. However, there are also wicked people who conspire to take away constitutional freedoms and to make serfs of free men, women, and children.

Secret combinations are formed to gain unrighteous power over others and have existed on this earth from the day that Cain entered into an evil alliance with Satan against his brother Abel. (See Moses 5:29–31.) These societies prospered during the days of the Gadianton robbers among the ancient Nephites and Lamanites and were a direct cause of the downfall of that civilization, as well as its predecessor, the Jaredite nation. "Had among all people" (Ether 8:20), secret combinations surely exist today as well. The prophet Moroni foresaw their rise in the last days and warned against allowing them to gain control:

> And whatsoever nation shall uphold such secret combinations, to get power and gain, until they shall spread over the nation, behold, they shall be destroyed. . . .
>
> Wherefore, O ye Gentiles, it is wisdom in God that these things should be shown unto you, that thereby ye may repent of your sins, and suffer not that these murderous combinations shall get above you, which are built up to get power and gain. . . .
>
> Wherefore, the Lord commandeth you, when ye shall see these things come among you that ye shall awake to a sense of your awful situation, because of this secret combination which shall be among you; or wo be unto it, because of the blood of them who have been slain; for they cry from the dust for vengeance upon it, and also upon those who built it up.
>
> For it cometh to pass that whoso buildeth it up seeketh to overthrow the freedom of all lands, nations, and countries; and it bringeth to pass the destruction of all people, for it is built up by the devil, who is the father of all lies. (Ether 8:22–25.)

President Ezra Taft Benson added his own insights regarding the secret combinations of the last days: "I testify that wickedness is rapidly expanding in every segment of our society. (See D&C 1:14–16; 84:49–53.) It is more highly organized, more cleverly disguised, and more powerfully promoted than ever before. Secret combinations lusting for power, gain, and glory are flourishing. A secret combination that seeks to overthrow the freedom of all lands, nations, and countries is increasing its evil influence and control over America and the entire world. (See Ether 8:18–25.)" (*Ensign*, November 1988, p. 87.) Almost three decades earlier, while a member of the Quorum of the Twelve Apostles, Elder Benson had referred to these secret combinations as both conspiratorial communism and as a "gigantic criminal conspiracy which would seek to rule the world." (CR, October 1961, p. 71.)

The secret combinations of the last days are not confined to one group nor to worldwide organizations, but include any combination of people whose purpose is to get unrighteous gain and power over others. The far-reaching tentacles of secret combinations were described by President Benson in a talk given in 1978: "Yes, there is a conspiracy of evil. The source of it all is Satan and his hosts. He has a great power over men to 'lead them captive at his will, even as many as would not hearken' to the voice of the Lord. (Moses 4:4.) His evil influence may be manifest through governments; through false educational, political, economic, religious, and social philosophies; through secret societies and organizations; and through myriads of other forms. His power and influence are so great that, if possible, he would deceive the very elect. As the second coming of the Lord approaches, Satan's work will intensify through numerous insidious deceptions." (*Ensign*, May 1978, p. 33.)

Enemies in Secret Chambers

In January 1831 the Lord revealed to the members of His fledgling church that "the enemy in the secret chambers seeketh your lives." (D&C 38:28.) Secret plottings against the Prophet Joseph Smith and his followers have led to many martyrdoms and much persecution since the time of the restoration of the fulness of the gospel of Jesus Christ. (See Hoyt W. Brewster, Jr., *Martyrs of the Kingdom,* Salt Lake City: Bookcraft, 1990.)

Dallin H. Oaks and Marvin S. Hill have written: "The murder of Joseph and Hyrum Smith at Carthage, Illinois, was not a spontaneous, impulsive act by a few personal enemies of the Mormon leaders, but a deliberate political assassination, committed or condoned by some of the leading citizens in Hancock County." (*Carthage Conspiracy: The Trial of the Accused Assassins of Joseph Smith,* Urbana, Illinois: University of Illinois Press, 1975, p. 6.)

Recent assassinations of missionaries serving in South America have been precipitated by secret conspiracies, mostly radical political groups seeking publicity. While these events are very visible, receiving wide publicity, there is perhaps an even more sinister type of enemy meeting in secret chambers, plotting the destruction of The Church of Jesus Christ of Latter-day Saints and its leaders. (See D&C 38:13.) This type of enemy seeks to portray himself or herself as a friend of the Church, or even a loyal supporter thereof, but in reality is a wolf in sheep's clothing. (See Matthew 7:15.) The Apostle Paul warned of such individuals: "For I know this, that after my departing shall grievous wolves enter in among you, not sparing the flock. Also of your own selves shall men arise, speaking perverse things, to draw away disciples after them." (Acts 20:29–30.)

Paul spoke further of those "in the latter times [that] shall depart from the faith, . . . speaking lies in hypocrisy." (1 Timothy 4:1–2.) While Paul was making direct reference to the apostasy that took place in the early Christian church, the application of his warning to the last days is very meaningful. For there are those of our day who have entered the flock in an effort "to draw away disciples after them."

The eleventh prophet of this last dispensation of times, President Harold B. Lee, commented on the wolves among us: "There are some as wolves among us. By that, I mean some who profess membership in this church who are not sparing the flock. And among our own membership, men are arising speaking perverse things. Now *perverse* means diverting from the right or correct, and *being obstinate in the wrong,* willfully, in order to draw the weak and unwary members of the Church away after them." (*Ensign,* January 1973, p. 105; second italics added.) One of the earmarks of the wolves is their obstinacy in the face of counsel, correction, or reproof: "I have my agency," they cry. "I have the right to freedom of thought and expression! I will not be silenced!"

According to the policy of The Church of Jesus Christ of Latter-day Saints, apostasy includes "members who repeatedly act in clear, open and deliberate public opposition to the church or its leaders; (or) persist in teaching as Church doctrine information that is not church doctrine after being corrected by their bishops or higher authority." ("Church Isn't Conducting a 'Purge,' LDS Apostle Says," *Deseret News,* 2 October 1993, p. A5.)

Bishop Richard C. Edgley, counselor in the Presiding Bishopric, spoke of those who seek to displace or discredit the leaders whom God has chosen to lead His church: "There are the so-called 'learned' that have let their intellect undermine their spiritual moorings and who would also attempt to lead the faithful away from those who are appointed by the Lord to lead. There are those who feel that our leaders are out of touch with the realities of the day. They would attempt to lead members by substituting their own knowledge for the revelations from God to His prophets. And, unfortunately, there are those who would so follow. Christ warned, 'Beware of false prophets, which come to you in sheep's clothing, but inwardly they are ravening wolves. (Matt. 7:15.)'" (*Ensign,* May 1993, p. 12.)

From the day that Joseph Smith was first called of God to be His earthly prophet, there have been individuals who have sought to counsel the Lord and His servants on matters that are clearly not within their stewardship. Counsel from these self-appointed critics usually turns to faultfinding, with a resultant loss of the Spirit. Unrepentant and unwilling to receive and follow proper counsel, these critics will be severed from the Church, either by formal action or their own withdrawal. (See D&C 1:14.)

While serving as a member of the Council of the Twelve Apostles, Elder Harold B. Lee warned about the loss of the Spirit by critics: "There are those among us who would set themselves up as critics of the Church, saying that the Church has gone out of the way. Some splintered apostate clans even from the beginning of this dispensation have made fictitious claims to authority. We should warn these, as well as those who are in danger of being led astray, of what the Prophet [Joseph Smith] predicted. He said, 'That man who rises up to condemn others, finding fault with the Church, saying they are out of the way, while he himself is righteous, then know assuredly that that man is [on the way] to apostasy; and if he does not repent, [he] will apostatize, as God lives.' [*TPJS*, pp. 156–57.]" (CR, October 1965, pp. 129–30.)

God's Work Will Not Fail

The critics and enemies of the Lord's work may find temporary success in causing the weak and the proud to stumble and fall, but they will not stop or greatly hinder the work. In a reprimanding revelation, Joseph Smith was reminded by the Lord "that it is not the work of God that is frustrated, but the work of men." (D&C 3:3.) Then follows this interesting warning: "For although a man may have many revelations, and have power to do many mighty works, yet if he boasts in his own strength, and sets at naught the counsels of God, and follows after the dictates of his own will and carnal desires, he must fall and incur the vengeance of a just God upon him." (Verse 4.)

The Old Testament prophet Daniel saw the establishment of God's kingdom upon the earth in the last days and proclaimed that it "shall never be destroyed . . . [but] shall stand for ever." (Daniel 2:44; see also D&C 65:2.) The Church of Jesus Christ of Latter-day Saints is that kingdom! Regarding the Church's ability to withstand attacks and persecution, the Prophet Joseph Smith boldly proclaimed: "No unhallowed hand can stop the work from progressing; persecutions may rage, mobs may combine, armies may assemble, calumny may defame, but the truth of God will go forth boldly, nobly, and independent, till it has penetrated every continent, visited every clime, swept every country, and sounded in every ear, till the purposes of God shall be accomplished, and the Great Jehovah shall say the work is done." (*HC,* 4:540.)

He who is *the* Head of the Church, even Jesus Christ, declared: "Verily, thus saith the Lord unto you—there is no weapon that is formed against you shall prosper." (D&C 71:9.)

More recently, Elder Neal A. Maxwell testified of the ultimate success of God's work:

> Growing out of our faith in the Lord is our sustaining of His anointed leaders. . . . Faithful Church members have what Peter called an "unfeigned love of the brethren." (1 Pet. 1:22.) Collectively but not perfectly, those sustained do the work to which God has called them. *As with Joseph Smith, so it is for his succeeding Brethren. The operative promise persists: namely, the people of the Church will never be turned away "by the testimony of traitors."* (D&C 122:3.) But the faithful know something about divine determination. They know that *the Lord's purposes will finally triumph,* for "there is nothing that the Lord thy God shall take in his heart to do but what he will do it." (Abr. 3:17.) Of that divine determination and divine love I gladly and publicly testify in the holy name of Jesus Christ. (*Ensign,* May 1991, p. 91; italics added.)

Numerous other testimonies could be cited regarding the unfailing nature of the restored gospel of Jesus Christ as proclaimed by The Church of Jesus Christ of Latter-day Saints. Perhaps three will suffice to conclude this chapter on conspiracies in the last days:

While serving as a counselor in the First Presidency of the

Church, President Hugh B. Brown testified: "I leave you my testimony of the restoration of the gospel, and I want you to know that the President and all of us have confidence in you, that you will not let us down nor be untrue to yourselves nor become traitors to the cause. Furthermore, you may be sure that ultimately righteousness will triumph. Truth will prevail. The Church has been organized and set up. It is the kingdom of God, and it will never be thrown down." (CR, October 1961, p. 87.)

President Joseph Fielding Smith, tenth prophet of this last dispensation, declared: "The time will never come when we will not be able to put confidence and exercise faith in the teachings and in the instruction of those who lead us." (*DS*, 1:243.)

Finally, consider this declaration from President Heber J. Grant: "Any Latter-day Saint who thinks for one minute that this Church is going to fail is not really a converted Latter-day Saint. There will be no failure in this Church. It has been established for the last time, never to be given to another people and never to be thrown down." ("Message of Inspiration," *Church News,* 27 October 1962, p. 2.)

Chapter 7

THE CONSTITUTION BY A THREAD

*"Even this nation will be on the verge of crumbling to pieces
and tumbling to the ground and when the Constitution is on
the brink of ruin this people will be the staff upon which the
nation shall lean and they shall bear the Constitution away
from the very verge of destruction."*

—JSP, 10 MARCH 1844

An Inspired Document

Latter-day Saints have long loved and cherished the United
States Constitution. This basic document of law received a
divine stamp of approval in an 1833 revelation to the Prophet
Joseph Smith in which the Lord declared, "I established the
Constitution of this land, by the hands of wise men whom I
raised up unto this very purpose." (D&C 101:80.) In a revelation given several months earlier, the Lord had counseled his
people to befriend "the constitutional law of the land" (D&C
98:6).

The Prophet Joseph Smith expressed his feelings for this
inspired instrument of freedom in these words: "The Constitution of the United States is a glorious standard; it is founded
in the wisdom of God. It is a heavenly banner; it is to all those
who are privileged with the sweets of its liberty, like the cool-
ing shades and refreshing waters of a great rock in a thirsty and
weary land. It is like a great tree under whose branches men
from every clime can be shielded from the burning rays of the
sun. . . . The Constitution of the United States is true." (*HC*,
3:304.)

Other latter-day prophets have testified of the inspired nature of the Constitution. President George Albert Smith, eighth prophet of this dispensation, declared: "I am saying to you that to me the Constitution of the United States of America is just as much from my Heavenly Father as the Ten Commandments." (CR, April 1948, p. 182.)

President David O. McKay, who followed President George Albert Smith as the Lord's latter-day prophet, proclaimed: "Next to being one in worshiping God there is nothing in this world upon which this Church should be more united than in upholding and defending the Constitution of the United States." (In CR, October 1939, p. 105.) Finally, President Ezra Taft Benson, thirteenth prophet of the dispensation of the fullness of times, said: "I reverence the Constitution of the United States as a sacred document. To me its words are akin to the revelations of God." (*Ensign,* November 1987, p. 7.)

Although the Constitution is an inspired document, it should be noted that it is not perfect. Appropriate amendments have been added to it as times and circumstances have changed. President Brigham Young explained: "The signers of the Declaration of Independence and the framers of the Constitution were inspired from on high to do that work. But was that which was given to them perfect, not admitting of any addition whatever? No; for if men know anything, they must know that the Almighty has never yet found a man in mortality that was capable, at the first intimation, at the first impulse, to receive anything in a state of entire perfection. They laid the foundation, and it was for after generations to rear the superstructure upon it. It is a progressive—a gradual work." (*JD,* 7:14.)

President John Taylor added that "even this [Constitution], good as it was, was not a perfect instrument; it was one of those stepping stones to a future development in the progress of a man to the intelligence and light, the power and union that God alone can impart to the human family." (*JD,* 21:31.)

A Future Threat to the Constitution

It is said that on July 19, 1840, the Prophet Joseph declared that the United States "will be on the verge of crumbling to pieces and tumbling to the ground." At this critical point, *"when the Constitution is on the brink of ruin,"* the Latter-day Saints apparently will reach out and "bear the Constitution away from the very verge of destruction." (JSP, 10 March 1844; italics added.)

While we are unable to specifically document Joseph Smith's having uttered these or similar words, several of his contemporaries claimed to have heard him make such statements. For example, in 1871 Eliza R. Snow said: "I heard the prophet say, 'The time will come when the government of these United States will be so nearly overthrown through its corruption, that *the Constitution will hang as it were by a single hair,* and the Latter-day Saints—the Elders of Israel—will step forward to its rescue and save it.'" (JH, 24 July 1871; italics added.)

Similar wording can be found in an utterance of Elder Parley P. Pratt, who is quoted as saying the following in 1841 regarding the United States government: "The government is fallen and needs redeeming. It is guilty of *Blood* and cannot stand as it now is but will come so near desolation as to *hang as it were by a single hair!!!!!*" (George A. Smith Papers, LDS Church Archives, 21 January 1841; second italics added.)

On Independence Day in 1854, President Brigham Young declared: "Will the Constitution be destroyed? No: it will be held inviolate by this people; and, as Joseph Smith said, 'The time will come when the *destiny of the nation will hang upon a single thread.* At that critical juncture, this people will step forth and save it from the threatened destruction.' It will be so." (JD, 7:15; italics added.)

Less than one year later, President Young spoke again of a future threat to the constitutional government of the United States: "Brethren and sisters, our friends wish to know our feelings towards the Government. I answer, they are first-rate, and we will prove it too, as you will see if you only live long enough, for that we shall live to prove it is certain; and *when the Constitution of the United States hangs, as it were, upon a single thread,* they will have to call for the 'Mormon' Elders to save it from utter destruction; and they will step forth and do it." (*JD*, 2:182; italics added.)

Elder Orson Hyde recalled a slightly different wording of Joseph Smith's alleged statement regarding the Constitution than did some of his contemporaries:

> It is said that brother Joseph in his lifetime declared that the Elders of this Church should step forth at a particular time when the Constitution should be in danger, and rescue it, and save it. This may be so; but I do not recollect that he said exactly so. I believe he said something like this—that *the time would come when the Constitution and the country would be in danger of an overthrow,* and said he, *If the Constitution be saved at all, it will be by the Elders of this Church.* I believe this is about the language, as nearly as I can recollect it.
>
> The question is whether it will be saved at all, or not. I do not know that it matters to us whether it is or not: the Lord will provide for and take care of his people, if we do every duty, and fear and honour him, and keep his commandments; and he will not leave us without a Constitution. (*JD*, 6:152; italics added.)

It appears that President Brigham Young thought the predicted governmental and constitutional crisis would occur in his days. He spoke the following words in April 1868: "And I tell you further, Elders of Israel, that you do not know the day of your visitation, neither do you understand the signs of the times, for if you did you would be awake to these things. *Every organization of our government, the best government in the world, is crumbling to pieces.* Those who have it in their hands are the ones who are destroying it. How long will it be before the words of the prophet Joseph will be fulfilled? He said if the Constitution of the United States were saved at all it must be done by this people." (*JD*, 12:204; italics added.)

More than one hundred years later, President Ezra Taft Benson expressed his feelings regarding the fulfillment of the prediction attributed to Joseph Smith: "I have faith that the Constitution will be saved as prophesied by Joseph Smith. It will be saved by the righteous citizens of this nation who love and cherish freedom. It will be saved by enlightened members of this Church—among others—men and women who understand and abide the principles of the Constitution." (*Ensign*, November 1987, p. 7.) "We are fast approaching that moment prophesied by Joseph Smith." (Ibid, p. 6.)

People to Look to the Latter-day Saints for Protection

Perhaps the predicted governmental crisis will occur amid civil strife and widespread warfare. On August 31, 1879, President John Taylor uttered these words of warning:

> We have got to establish a government upon the principle of righteousness, justice, truth and equality and not according to the many false notions that exist among men. And then the day is not far distant when this nation will be shaken from centre to circumference. And now, you may write it down, any of you, and I will prophesy it in the name of God. And then will be fulfilled that prediction to be found in one of the revelations given through the Prophet Joseph Smith. [See D&C 45:65–71.] Those who will not take up their sword to fight against their neighbor must needs flee to Zion for safety. And they will come, saying, we do not know anything of the principles of your religion, but we perceive that you are an honest community; you administer justice and righteousness, and we want to live with you and receive the protection of your laws, but as for your religion we will talk about that some other time. Will we protect such people? Yes, all honorable men. *When the people shall have torn to shreds the Constitution of the United States the Elders of Israel will be found holding it up* to the nations of the earth and proclaiming liberty and equal rights to all men, and extending the hand of fellowship to the oppressed of all nations. This is part of the programme, and as long as we do what is right and fear God, he will help us and stand by us under all circumstances." (*JD*, 21:8; italics added.)

More will be said in chapter 9 about the forthcoming strife and warfare that will engulf all nations, including the United States of America. It appears that just as "wise men [were] raised up" by the Lord to establish the Constitution (D&C 101:80), he will similarly raise up wise men in the last days to save it from destruction.

Chapter 8

"THE LOVE OF MANY SHALL WAX COLD"

"And because iniquity shall abound, the love of many shall wax cold."

—MATTHEW 24:12

The Loss of Love

The prophecy that in the last days "the love of many shall wax cold" is found in three different scriptures. (See Matthew 24:12; D&C 45:27; JS–M 1:10.) To "wax cold" is to lose the warmth of love and to become increasingly self-centered, inconsiderate, and uncaring of others.

When asked to identify "the great commandment in the law," the Savior responded by citing two commandments: "Thou shalt love the Lord thy God with all thy heart, and with all thy soul, and with all thy mind. This is the first and great commandment. And the second is like unto it, Thou shalt love thy neighbour as thyself. On these two commandments hang all the law and the prophets." (Matthew 22:36–40.) In the last days many have lost their love of their neighbor and of God. They have turned from worshipping Deity to worshipping the things of this world: material possessions, power, prestige, and pleasures. The self-centered approach to life is epitomized in the selfish slogan "Look out for number one!"

Society is presently plagued with increasing evidences of love waxing cold: rudeness, divorce, lawsuits, abuse, rape, beatings, gang violence, murder, theft, vandalism, and freeway and drive-by shootings. In general, there has been a turning away from love, courtesy, and consideration for others. On all sides we see the fulfillment of the Apostle Paul's prophecy "that in the last days . . . men shall be lovers of their own selves, . . . lovers of pleasures more than lovers of God." (2 Timothy 3:1–2, 4.)

Grim Facts

In 1992 the Attorney General of the United States reported that violence had increased 500 percent in thirty years. The number of violent crime attempts increased 11 percent from 1990 to 1991. A 1993 survey indicated that 3.5 million people are killed by violent action each year in the United States.

Violence among young people is particularly distressing. The editors of *Fortune* magazine provided the following information: "Of the 65 million Americans under 18, [fully 20%] live in poverty, 22% live in single-parent homes, and almost 3% live with no parent at all. Violence among the young is . . . rampant. . . . Playground fights that used to end in bloody noses now end in [some fatalities]. Schools that once considered talking in class a capital offense are routinely [checking children] for weapons, questioning them about drugs. . . . A good public education, safe streets, and family dinners—with both father and mother present—seem like quaint memories of a far distant past." (Louis S. Richman, "Struggling to Save Our Kids," *Fortune,* 10 August 1992, p. 34.)

The evidence of increasing violence in the public schools is vividly seen in comparing two surveys: "Not long ago, in a California school system, the top seven problems were listed as: talking out of turn; chewing gum; making noise; running in the halls; cutting in line; dress code violations; and littering.

"By the 1980's, in the same school system, the top seven problems were drug abuse; alcohol abuse; pregnancy; suicide; rape; robbery; and assault." (William P. Barr, "The Judeo-Christian Tradition vs. Secularism," speech delivered to the Catholic League for Religious and Civil Rights, Washington, D.C., 6 October 1992.)

Consider these recent examples of increasing violence and

evidence of the loss of love among the young people in our society:

 • An eight-year-old boy walked into a school cafeteria and pointed a BB gun at the stomach of a pregnant teacher. Smiling, he pulled the trigger.

 • Following a concert in the downtown area of a metropolitan city, a seventeen-year-old boy was pulled from his car, senselessly beaten, and shot to death while hundreds of onlookers stood by.

 • Six children, ranging in age from eight to thirteen, terrorized an 87-year-old woman as she returned from the grocery store. She was physically and verbally abused, and her apartment was ransacked during the attack.

 • A seventeen-year-old spectator at a Little League baseball game was killed when he was hit with a bat that one player swung at another player. The umpire's home was later firebombed, and a threatening note left behind warned, "Testify and you're dead!"

 • A 1991 survey showed that 20 percent of high school students admitted to carrying weapons to school.

 • Children are now participating in ride-by shootings on bicycles.

 • Two girls, ages fourteen and fifteen, armed with 9mm semiautomatic pistols, hijacked a car from a man and went on a joyride.

 • A group of teenagers raped and stabbed a woman 132 times. The reason? "There was nothing to do, and so I guess we had the impression of going out to the field and kill somebody."

 • Two ten-year-old boys kidnapped a two-year-old child and viciously beat him to death with bricks and stones. They then disposed of the body on a train track.

The increasing violence by children and teenagers was summed up by professor Jack Levin, who teaches sociology and criminology at Northeastern University in Boston: "Hatred is hip. Killing is cool. . . . We're seeing a callous disregard for human life that we've never seen before." (As quoted in *Deseret News*, 29 September 1992, p. A1.)

Reaping the Winds of Violence

The loss of love and the resultant increase of violence in the world can be attributed in part to the increase of violence in television, videos, and movies. The Apostle Paul warned that "whatsoever a man soweth, that shall he also reap." (Galatians 6:7.) Society has "sown the wind," and it is "reap[ing] the whirlwind." (Hosea 8:7.)

In the middle 1960s, when the entertainment media was relatively mild compared with the media today, Elder Richard L. Evans of the Quorum of the Twelve Apostles observed that "the evil that seems to fascinate men most today is violence." (Tom Wolfe, as quoted in CR, October 1965, p. 43.) President N. Eldon Tanner spoke of the consequences of this fascination with violence: "We are drowning our youngsters in violence, cynicism, and sadism piped into the living room and even the nursery. The grandchildren of the kids who used to weep because The Little Match Girl froze to death now feel cheated if she isn't slugged, raped, and thrown into a Bessemer converter." (*Ensign*, July 1973, p. 10.)

More recently, Elder M. Russell Ballard spoke out against the increasing violence that comes into the homes on the television screen and is portrayed on the larger screen in movie theaters:

> Dr. [Victor] Cline said that the mental diet is as important as the nutritional diet. "The amount of violence a child sees at 7 predicts how violent he will be at 17, 27, and 37. Children's minds are like banks—whatever you put in, you get back 10 years later with interest." He said that violent television teaches children, step-by-step, "how to commit violent acts, and it desensitizes them to the horror of such behavior and to the feelings of victims." Dr. Cline said that *America is suffering from "an explosion of interpersonal violence like we have never seen before.* . . . The violence is because of violence in our entertainment." (See "Therapist says

82

children who view TV violence tend to become violent," *Deseret News,* 24 Mar. 1989, p. B-2.) (*Ensign,* May 1989, p. 78; italics added.)

Another of the Lord's apostles, Elder Marvin J. Ashton, warned of the addictive behavior that comes from violence—a terrible form of obscenity as one assaults a fellow human being, a son or daughter of God—or from being involved in other types of obscenities, such as pornography: "A person who becomes involved in obscenity soon acquires distorted views of personal conduct. He becomes unable to relate to others in a normal, healthy way. Like most other habits, an addictive effect begins to take hold of him. A diet of violence or pornography dulls the senses, and future exposures need to be rougher and more extreme. Soon the person is desensitized and is unable to react in a sensitive, caring, responsible manner, especially to those in his own home and family. Good people can become infested with this material and it can have terrifying, destructive consequences." (*Ensign,* November 1977, p. 71.)

This increase in violence, often associated with filth, is not limited to the land of America. It is a worldwide cancer of the last days. Elder Gordon B. Hinckley reported: "The flood of pornographic filth, the inordinate emphasis on sex and violence are not peculiar to this land. The situation is as bad in Europe and in many other areas. News stories tell of the production in Denmark of a filthy, erotic, and blasphemous movie to be produced on the life of the Son of God. The whole dismal picture indicates a weakening rot seeping into the very fiber of society." (CR, October 1975, p. 56.)

The world has stooped to a vile level when he who represents the epitome of love, even the sinless Son of God, who selflessly sacrificed Himself to bring about the Atonement in our lives, is vilified in blasphemous ways.

The war against the Lord, His church, His ways, and His servants has intensified in these last days. Satan is as active as he has ever been since he lost his self-serving bid and the resultant battle for control of men's souls in the pre-earth life. He who is not capable of love has intensified his efforts to destroy love and replace it with contention, violence, hatred, and war.

The Downfall of Ancient Civilizations

Classic examples of Satan's tactics in destroying two civilizations can be found in the Book of Mormon. The first of these, the Jaredite civilization, flourished in the ancient Americas from shortly after the Tower of Babel (circa 2000 B.C.) until its destruction around 590 B.C.

The Jaredite society became characterized by secret combinations, violence, murder, and war: "Now there began to be a war upon all the face of the land, every man with his band fighting for that which he desired. And there were robbers, and in fine, all manner of wickedness upon all the face of the land. . . . And they did meet in great anger." (Ether 13:25–27.) Perhaps the most telling description of their state of mind is found in these fateful words: "*They were drunken with anger,* even as a man who is drunken with wine." (Ether 15:22; italics added.)

The second civilization whose destruction is recorded in the Book of Mormon was one that lasted from roughly B.C. 600 to about A.D. 421. Like the Jaredites before them, this second civilization succumbed to the sin of contention, allowing their love of God and man to wax cold. Their condition was described by the prophet Mormon: "Satan stirreth them up continually to anger one with another. . . . For so exceedingly do they anger that it seemeth me that they have no fear of death; and they have lost their love, one towards another; and they thirst after blood and revenge continually." (Moroni 9:3, 5.)

A Prophet's Admonition

During the early years of his ministry as the Lord's prophet and spokesman on earth, President Ezra Taft Benson spoke frequently and fervently about the importance of studying the Book of Mormon. He noted that one of the reasons "why we must make the Book of Mormon a center focus of study is that it was written for our day. The Nephites never had the book; neither did the Lamanites of ancient times. It was meant for us." President Benson cited examples of where the prophets of Book of Mormon times had indicated they were writing to a future generation (see 2 Nephi 25:21; Jacob 1:3; Enos 1:15–16; Jarom 1:2; Mormon 7:1; 8:34–35) and then commented:

> If they saw our day, and chose those things which would be of greatest worth to us, is not that how we should study the Book of Mormon? We should constantly ask ourselves, "Why did the Lord inspire Mormon (or Moroni or Alma) to include that in his record? What lesson can I learn from that to help me live in this day and age?"
>
> And there is example after example of how that question will be answered. For example, in the Book of Mormon we find a pattern for preparing for the Second Coming. A major portion of the book centers on the few decades just prior to Christ's coming to America. By careful study of that time period, we can determine why some were destroyed in the terrible judgments that preceded His coming and what brought others to stand at the temple in the land of Bountiful and thrust their hands into the wounds of His hands and feet.
>
> From the Book of Mormon we learn how disciples of Christ live in times of war. From the Book of Mormon we see the evils of secret combinations portrayed in graphic and chilling reality. In the Book of Mormon we find lessons for dealing with persecution and apostasy. We learn much about how to do missionary work. And more than anywhere else, we see in the Book of Mormon the dangers of materialism and setting our hearts on the things of the world. Can anyone doubt that this book was meant for us and that in it we find great power, great comfort, and great protection? (*Ensign,* November 1986, pp. 6–7.)

Thus, a study of the Book of Mormon will help humble people of the last days to avoid making the same mistakes that destroyed those of former days. However, prophecy will be fulfilled, and the love of many will continue to wax cold during these last days before the Second Coming.

Chapter 9

WARS AND RUMORS OF WARS

"And ye shall hear of wars and rumours of wars: see that ye be not troubled: for all these things must come to pass, but the end is not yet. For nation shall rise against nation, and kingdom against kingdom."

—MATTHEW 24:6–7

Satan Rages in the Hearts of Men

John the Revelator, who saw both the past and the future, proclaimed: "And there was war in heaven; Michael and his angels fought against the dragon; and the dragon and his angels fought against Michael; And the dragon prevailed not. . . . Neither was there place found in heaven for the great dragon, who was cast out; that old serpent called the devil, and also called Satan, which deceiveth the whole world; he was cast out into the earth; and his angels were cast out with him." (JST, Revelation 12:6–8.) Although he was unsuccessful in his first war, Satan has continued to promote warfare here on earth. He rages in the hearts of men, fomenting anger and hatred, which lead to wars and bloodshed. (See Moses 6:15.)

The ancient Nephite prophet-general Mormon provided insights regarding how depraved warfare can become. He described the bloodthirsty depravity of the Nephite soldiers as the curtain was fast falling on their civilization: "They are without order and without mercy. . . . And they have become strong in their perversion; and they are alike brutal, sparing none, neither old nor young; and they delight in everything save that which is good. . . . They are without principle, and past feeling." (Moroni 9:18–20.)

Prophecies of Wars in the Last Days

Although warfare and bloodshed have essentially been a curse on this planet from the day that Cain slew Abel, the widespread presence of wars and rumors of wars throughout the earth is one of the prophesied signs of the last days. The Savior spoke of this coming bane on mankind during His final days on earth. (See Matthew 24:6–7; see also JS–M 1:28–29.) He repeated this prophetic utterance in a revelation given to the Prophet Joseph Smith in 1831. (See D&C 45:26.)

One need only glance through the daily newspaper or listen to news reports to get a glimpse of how this prophecy is being fulfilled. Almost daily the media feeds us a diet of disputes throughout the world that turn into skirmishes and finally into full-fledged fighting with declared and undeclared wars. Nearly as soon as a precarious truce is worked out in one area, another fight breaks out somewhere else. Each time a worldwide conflict ends, there is a surge of hope that war is at an end. And yet anger, fighting, bloodshed, and wars continue. And so it will be until the Second Coming.

Joseph Smith's Prophecy on War

In March 1831 the Lord revealed to the Prophet the imminency of wars, including in the United States: "Ye hear of wars in foreign lands; but, behold, I say unto you, they are nigh, even at your doors, and not many years hence ye shall hear of wars in your own lands." (D&C 45:63.)

Almost two years later, on Christmas Day in 1832, the Prophet Joseph Smith uttered this remarkable prophecy regarding war:

> Verily, thus saith the Lord concerning the wars that will shortly come to pass, beginning at the rebellion of South Carolina, which will eventually terminate in the death and

misery of many souls; and the time will come that war will be poured out upon all nations, beginning at this place. For behold, the Southern States shall be divided against the Northern States, and the Southern States will call on other nations, even the nation of Great Britain, as it is called, and they shall also call upon other nations, in order to defend themselves against other nations; and then war shall be poured out upon all nations. . . . And thus, with the sword and by bloodshed the inhabitants of the earth shall mourn. (D&C 87:1–3, 6.)

This prophecy was given twenty-nine years before the first gun was fired on Fort Sumter by rebel forces from South Carolina. Handwritten copies of the revelation had been carried by some of the leading elders between the time of the prophecy in 1831 and the commencement of hostilities in 1861.

Elder Orson Pratt, one of those called to the original Quorum of Twelve Apostles in 1835, related his experience in teaching Joseph's prophecy:

When I was a [young man], I traveled extensively in the United States and the Canadas, preaching this restored Gospel. I had a manuscript copy of this revelation [D&C 87], which I carried in my pocket, and I was in the habit of reading it to the people among whom I traveled and preached. As a general thing the people regarded it as the height of nonsense, saying the Union was too strong to be broken; and I, they said, was led away, the victim of an impostor. I knew the prophecy was true, for the Lord had spoken to me and had given me revelation. I knew also concerning the divinity of this work. Year after year passed away, while every little while some of the acquaintances I had formerly made would say, "Well, what is going to become of that prediction? It's never going to be fulfilled." Said I, "Wait, the Lord has his set time." By and by it came along, and the first battle was fought at Charleston, South Carolina. This is another testimony that Joseph Smith was a Prophet of the Most High God; he not only foretold the coming of a great civil war at a time when statesmen even never dreamed of such a thing, but he named the very place where it should commence." (*JD*, 18:224–25.)

Elder B. H. Roberts, who served as a General Authority from 1888 until his death in 1933, provided additional insights regarding the 1832 prophecy. Speaking of the proclamation that these forthcoming wars, including the Civil War, would "end in the death and misery of many souls," Elder Roberts said: "This, however, was contrary to the expectations both of the North and the South. The South claimed that in a short time they would be able to compel the North to acknowledge them as an independent nation. While Abraham Lincoln was equally confident in his ability to put his foot upon the neck of the Rebellion and crush out its life." (*JD*, 25:142.)

To date, only World War II has exceeded the Civil War in casualties for the United States. Almost 215,000 servicemen were killed in action during the war between the states.

Elder Roberts provided further insight into another aspect of the Prophet's remarkable prophecy:

> The Southern States were to call on Great Britain to assist them. Did they do it? Yes. The Southern States Confederacy sent two men, Messrs. Mason and Slidell, to negotiate with the English government, with the view of getting assistance; but they were captured and brought back to the United States. This is a familiar matter of history. England, too, was to call upon other nations to protect themselves against other nations. Has this been done? To answer that question we have but to allude to the treaties now existing between Great Britain and other European nations. Thus you see this prophecy, so far as we have read it [D&C 87:1–3], has been minutely fulfilled— fulfilled in every particular, and the rest of it will be, so fast as the wheels of time shall bring the events due. (*JD*, 25:143.)

As prophesied, war will continue to spread to other nations until the coming of the Son of Man.

A Continuation of Warfare and Bloodshed

As the Civil War raged, Elder Wilford Woodruff, then of the Quorum of the Twelve Apostles, uttered the following statement regarding those who reject the gospel and the ongoing nature of warfare and bloodshed: "Will there ever be any more peace among them? No, not until the earth is drenched with the blood of the inhabitants thereof. When the spirit of the Gospel leaves any people it leaves them in a worse condition than it found them, the spirit of ferocity, darkness and war will take hold of that people, and the time will come when every man that does not take his sword against his neighbor will have to go to Zion for safety." (*JD*, 10:15.)

In 1879 President John Taylor, who succeeded Brigham Young as the Lord's prophet on earth, spoke of the bloodshed of the Civil War and then declared: "I tell you today the end is not yet. You will see worse things than that, for God will lay his hand upon this nation, and they will feel it more terribly than ever they have done before; there will be more bloodshed, more ruin, more devastation than ever they have seen before. . . . There is yet to come a sound of war, trouble and distress, in which brother will be arrayed against brother, father against son, son against father, a scene of desolation and destruction that will permeate our land until it will be a vexation to hear the report thereof." (*JD*, 20:318.)

There has been much speculation on the nature of this prophesied bloodshed. The exact fulfillment remains to be seen. However, the rioting that has torn apart cities in the United States in the past few years, destroying property and lives, could well be a partial fulfillment of President Taylor's proclamation. So too could be the gang violence, murder, and crimes of aggression that have made so many of our metropolitan streets unsafe.

In a later speech, President Taylor indicated that bloodshed would not be limited to the United States but would be worldwide: "The world . . . is full of confusion, and there will be worse confusion by and by. We had a great war upon this continent some years ago; but there will yet be wars pass through these United States, and through other nations, until it will be mournful to hear the report of the bloodshed, the sorrow and the trouble that will be caused thereby." (*JD*, 24:200.)

The Lord decreed the universal nature of contention and warfare in a revelation received in 1831: "I, the Lord, am angry with the wicked; I am holding my Spirit from the inhabitants of the earth. I have sworn in my wrath, and decreed wars upon the face of the earth, and the wicked shall slay the wicked, and fear shall come upon every man; and the saints also shall hardly escape." (D&C 63:32–33.)

Thus, not only will the wicked suffer the effects of warfare but also the Saints. In this respect, Elder Bruce R. McConkie made an interesting observation: "We do not say that all of the Saints will be spared and saved from the coming day of desolation. But we do say there is no promise of safety and no promise of security except for those who love the Lord and who are seeking to do all that he commands.

"It may be, for instance, that nothing except the power of faith and the authority of the priesthood can save individuals and congregations from the atomic holocausts that surely shall be." (*Ensign*, May 1979, p. 93.)

And what if some Saints do suffer and die? With an eternal perspective in mind, they will not "charge God foolishly" but declare, as did Job, "blessed be the name of the Lord." (Job 1:21–22.)

Warfare Technology Fulfills Ancient Prophecy

Modern technology has increased the capability of mankind to spread war and destruction far and wide. Many years ago Elder Joseph Fielding Smith, then a member of the Quorum of the Twelve Apostles, observed: "Since the Civil War in the United States, warfare has undergone wonderful changes. The nations have been in a mad race to outdo each other. The steel battleship has made it necessary for the steel gun that will pierce the battleship's armor. Bigger guns mean thicker armor plate. Science has been at its wits end in each of the nations, devising ways and means for further and more terrible destruction. The

World War increased this madness rather than being the means of bringing permanent peace." (*The Progress of Man,* Salt Lake City: The Genealogical Society of Utah, 1952, p. 401.)

The Revelator described weaponry and armament unknown to the ancients: "And the shapes of the locusts were like unto horses prepared unto battle; and on their heads were as it were crowns like gold, and their faces were as the faces of men. And they had hair as the hair of women, and their teeth were as the teeth of lions. And they had breastplates, as it were breastplates of iron; and the sound of their wings was as the sound of chariots of many horses running to battle. And they had tails like unto scorpions, and there were stings in their tails: and their power was to hurt men five months." (Revelation 9:7–10.)

Elder Bruce R. McConkie provided the following commentary on John's description: "In prophetic imagery John here seeks to describe a war fought with weapons and under circumstances entirely foreign to any experience of his own or of the people of that day. . . . [See also Joel 2:1–11.]

"It is not improbable that these ancient prophets were seeing such things as men wearing or protected by strong armor; as troops of cavalry and companies of tanks and flame throwers; as airplanes and airborne missiles which explode, fire shells and drop bombs; and even *other weapons yet to be devised* in an age when warfare is the desire and love of wicked men." (*DNTC,* 3:502–3; italics added.)

The Revelator further described locusts that could kill and torment men as scorpions but would "not hurt the grass . . . neither any green thing." The results of their sting would be that "men [would] seek death, and . . . not find it." (Revelation 9:3–6.) Elder McConkie suggested that "perhaps John is seeing such things as the effects of poisonous gas, or bacteriological warfare, or atomic fallout, which disable but do not kill." (*DNTC,* 3:502). Indeed, a revelation in the Doctrine and Covenants seems descriptive of nuclear and chemical warfare: "Wherefore, I the Lord God will send forth flies upon the face of the earth, which shall take hold of the inhabitants thereof, and shall eat their flesh, and shall cause maggots to come in upon them; and their tongues shall be stayed that they shall not utter against me; and their flesh shall fall from off their bones, and their eyes from their sockets." (D&C 29:18–19; see also Zechariah 14:12.)

Anyone who has read a description of the physical condition of a person who has been exposed to nuclear, chemical, or bacteriological weaponry can surely envision a fulfillment of this prophecy. One commentary suggested that the plague of flies would include a "plague of microbes, or bacilli, new to the scientific world and with which they will not be able to cope." (Hyrum M. Smith, and Janne M. Sjodahl, *Doctrine and Covenants Commentary,* Salt Lake City: Deseret Book Co., 1954, p. 152.)

The Lord's Purposes Will Be Accomplished

In spite of Satan's seeming success in promoting war and contention, it is important to remember that in the end the Lord's purposes will be brought to pass. The adversary's greatest efforts will not prevail in stopping God's work.

In a revelation given in 1838 during the height of mobbings against the Saints in Missouri, the Lord provided a comforting reminder of who is really in charge: "Have I not made the earth? Do I not hold the destinies of all the armies of the nations of the earth?" (D&C 117:6.)

Regarding the ultimate power and purposes of the Lord, President John Taylor said: "Whatever the opinions and ideas of men may be, it will be found at last that the Lord rules, manipulates and manages the affairs of men, of nations and of the world, and therefore, *neither this nation nor any other nation can do anything more than God permits.* He sets up one nation, and puts down another, according to the counsels of his own will. And he has done this from the beginning, whether men believe it or not." (*JD,* 23:333; italics added.)

One of the Lord's latter-day Apostles, Elder George Q. Morris, observed:

> But bear in mind that the Lord is directing this world. We are frequently reminded that conditions have been so developed in the powers of warfare that an accident or a rash move could set in operation those powers which might destroy our civilization. But let us bear in mind that this world is in the hands of God. All these things will happen only so far as they are in accordance with his plans and his purposes. And *let us not waste our time and our energy and get into a nervous condition about what is going to happen to the world.* That is not our sphere of responsibility. The Lord will take care of that. It remains for us to be devoted to the upbuilding of his kingdom and facing whatever conditions may come to us. (CR, April 1959, p. 102; italics added.)

Elder Morris's admonition not to waste time and energy fretting about future world conditions is wise counsel.

More recently, President Spencer W. Kimball offered this advice at the opening session of a general conference of the Church: "Love one another, brothers and sisters! Have love in your homes and in your hearts! Be peacemakers even though we must live in a world filled with wars and rumors of wars! (See D&C 45:26.) Follow the counsel you will receive in this general conference. And I'll do my best to do likewise. Trust the Lord and His unfolding purposes even when His purposes are not always completely clear to us at the moment." (*Ensign,* May 1982, p. 5.)

And so, as we anticipate a continued increase of wars and rumors of wars prior to the Second Coming, culminating in the great battle of Armageddon, we put our trust in the Lord.

Chapter 10

ARMAGEDDON

*"The kings of the earth and of the whole world . . . gather . . .
to the battle of that great day of God Almighty. . . . And he
gathered them together into a place called in the Hebrew tongue
Armageddon."*

—REVELATION 16:14,16

Meaning of Armageddon

The name *Armageddon* is one that both intrigues and evokes
great fear, yet its only mention in all of scripture is found in the
apocalyptic writings of the Apostle John. Much has been written and spoken on the subject, some of it inspired and much
of it mere speculation.

The following definitions from the LDS Bible Dictionary
provide assistance in understanding the meaning of
Armageddon:

• "Armageddon. A Greek transliteration from the Hebrew
Har Megiddon, or Mountain of Megiddo. The valley of
Megiddo is in the western portion of the plain of Esdraelon 50
miles north of Jerusalem. Several times the valley of Megiddo
was the scene of violent and crucial battles during [Old
Testament] times (Judg. 5:19; 2 Kgs. 9:27; 23:29). A great and
final conflict taking place at the second coming of the Lord is
called the battle of *Armageddon* because it too will be fought in
the same locale and will be decisive. See Zech. 11–14, especially 12:11; Rev. 16:14–21."

• "Esdraelon. The Greek form of the Hebrew word Jezreel.
The 'great plain of Esdraelon' is also known in the [Old

Testament] as the 'valley of Megiddo'; it separates the hills of Samaria from those of Galilee, and is the most fertile part of Palestine. It was crossed by several important highways, and for that reason often provided a battleground (Judg. 4; 5; 7; 1 Sam. 31; 2 Chr. 35:20–27; cf. Rev. 16:16)."

At the southern entrance to the valley of Esdraelon is a city presently known as *Tell el-Mutesellim* but anciently known as Megiddo. This city stands as a sentinel to the twenty-by-fourteen-mile valley. The name in Hebrew means "the place of troops," a name most appropriate in terms of its standing in ancient battles and its future role in the final conflict before the Second Coming. Megiddo will serve as the command center for the armies of the evil alliance in this last battle of our telestial earth.

Just prior to the Savior's return to earth to reign during a millennium of peace, the most vicious war in history will be raging. Its major battleground will be from the valley of Megiddo to Jerusalem, where some two hundred million warriors ("two hundred thousand thousand" in Revelation 9:16) will be seeking to destroy Israel, but the war will be a worldwide conflict between good and evil. Elder Bruce R. McConkie said: "That which is going forward in Palestine is but a type and a shadow of that which shall be in all nations and among all peoples. We must remind ourselves that this is a worldwide conflict and that all nations are involved." (*MM*, p. 485.)

Identity of Gog and Magog

The leader of the two-hundred-million-man army is identified in the scriptures as Gog. The prophet Ezekiel identified him as having come from the land of Magog. (See Ezekiel 38:2.) Although the collective name of "Gog and Magog" has frequently been given to this evil warrior, he should correctly be referred to as "Gog *of* Magog."

The LDS Bible Dictionary provides the following description of Gog: "King of Magog, whose invasion of Israel was prophesied by Ezekiel (Ezek. 38; 39). The prophecy points to a time when the heathen nations of the north would set themselves against the people of God and would be defeated, and led to recognize Jehovah as King. All this appears to be at the second coming of the Lord. Another battle, called the battle of Gog and Magog, will occur at the end of the 1,000 years. This is described by John in Rev. 20:7–9; see also D&C 88:111–116."

The name *Gog* may have reference to one leader or to a combination of leaders who will make up the evil alliance. Elder Bruce R. McConkie states: "Gog and Magog are all the nations of the earth who take up the sword against Israel and Jerusalem in the day of Armageddon. Their identities remain to be revealed when the battle alliances are made." (*MM*, p. 481.)

There have been speculative efforts to identify the nations that will be on opposite sides of this final battle before the Millennium. As noted in the above commentary by Elder McConkie, "their identities remain to be revealed." One need only reflect on the quick demise of the once powerful Soviet Union to understand how foolish it is to assign specific identities to the future combatants of Armageddon. However, all nations will be involved in this conflict: "No nation in any land will be neutral. This coming conflict will be universal, and out of it will come the final day of destruction and burning. It will exceed in horror, intensity, and scope all prior wars. It is only in the last days that there are enough people on earth to field armies of the required size, and only now do we have the weapons to slay millions at a single blast." (*MM*, pp. 449–50.)

Events Preceding Armageddon

A commentary on the Old Testament published by The Church of Jesus Christ of Latter-day Saints provides the following information regarding some important events that must occur before the battle of Armageddon commences:

> 1. The house of Israel will be gathered from among the heathen (the Gentiles) and returned to their own land (see Ezekiel 36:24; 37:21).

2. The land of Israel will be rebuilt and reinhabited by the covenant people (see Ezekiel 36:10–12, 33–36).

3. The land will become highly productive and fruitful, even like the Garden of Eden (see Ezekiel 36:8, 29–30, 34–35).

4. There will be one nation in the land of Israel again (see Ezekiel 37:22).

5. Jerusalem will be reestablished as the capital city of the Israelites (see Zechariah 1:16–17; 2:12; 12:6; 3 Nephi 20:46).

6. Judah will become powerful in politics and warfare (see Isaiah 19:16–17; Zechariah 10:3, 5–6).

7. A great combination of organizations serving Satan will arise in the last days. This combination has several names: the "beast . . . out of the sea" (Revelation 13:1), representing the kingdoms of the earth (see JST, Revelation 13:1; 17:8–14; Bruce R. McConkie, *Doctrinal New Testament Commentary* 3:520); the "great and abominable church," "the church of the devil," "the great whore," and "the mother of . . . abominations" (Revelation 17:1,5). (*Old Testament Student Manual: 1 Kings–Malachi,* Salt Lake City: The Church of Jesus Christ of Latter-day Saints, 1981, p. 292.)

To the above list we add two significant additions. First, many of the inhabitants of the land—the seed of Judah, believers in the old covenant—must accept the new and everlasting covenant: the restored gospel of Jesus Christ. In order for Judah to be considered truly gathered, this tribe of Israel must accept the true Messiah and receive the saving covenants and ordinances of his gospel under the hands of their brethren from the tribe of Ephraim. Elder McConkie provides the following insight to this aspect of gathering:

> Judah will gather to old Jerusalem in due course; of this, there is no doubt. But this gathering will consist of accepting Christ, joining the Church, and receiving anew the Abrahamic covenant as it is administered in holy places. The present assembling of people of Jewish ancestry into the Palestinian nation of Israel is not the scriptural gathering of Israel or of Judah. It may be prelude thereto, and some of the people so assembled may in due course be

gathered into the true church and kingdom of God on earth, and they may then assist in building the temple that is destined to grace Jerusalem's soil. But a political gathering is not a spiritual gathering, and the Lord's kingdom is not of this world. (*NWAF*, pp. 519–20.)

The second additional event that must occur before Armageddon is the building of a holy temple in old Jerusalem. This will be built and operated under the direction of the First Presidency of The Church of Jesus Christ of Latter-day Saints. The presence of this temple—the mountain of the Lord's House—will be a major factor in the battle for Jerusalem in the days of Armageddon.

A Religious War

Biblical and ancient language scholar Dr. Richard D. Draper suggested that a major objective of the armies of Gog will be "the Mountain of the Lord's House, for . . . the battle is essentially religious: one ideology and theology against another. Therefore, the beast must eventually destroy the Mountain of the Lord's House, the seat of God's power on earth, if he is to reign supreme." (*OSS*, pp. 180–81.)

Elder McConkie also taught that Armageddon would be "a religious war. The forces of antichrist are seeking to destroy freedom and liberty and right; they seek to deny men the right to worship the Lord; they are the enemies of God. The one-third who remain in the land of Israel [see Zechariah 13:8–9] are the Lord's people. They believe in Christ and accept Joseph Smith as his prophet and revealer for the last days." (*MM*, pp. 465–66.)

"One host is for God and his cause; the other fights against him. Both hosts are comprised of wicked and worldly men, but one is defending freedom, and the other would destroy liberty and enslave men. One defends free institutions, freedom in government, freedom to worship the god of one's choice according to one's own conscience, and the other, Lucifer-like, seeks to overthrow liberty and freedom in all its forms." (Ibid, p. 457.)

Lucifer will resort to the use of every form of black magic and sophistry he can to build his armies of Armageddon. One of the original Apostles of this last dispensation, Elder Orson Pratt, taught:

> [Lucifer] will gather up millions upon millions of people into the valleys around about Jerusalem in order to destroy the Jews after they have gathered. How will the Devil do this? He will perform miracles to do it. The Bible says the kings of the earth and the great ones will be deceived by these false miracles. It says there shall be three unclean spirits that shall go forth working miracles, and they are spirits of devils. Where do they go? To the kings of the earth; and what will they do? Gather them up to battle unto the great day of God Almighty. Where? Into the valley of Armageddon. And where is that? On the east side of Jerusalem.
>
> When he gets them gathered together, they do not understand any of these things; but they are given up to that power that deceived them, by miracles that had been performed, to get them to go into that valley to be destroyed. (*JD*, 7:189.)

The Beast at Bay

Although they will wreak great destruction and destroy many lives, the armies of Gog will be prohibited in their objective of conquering Jerusalem for a period of time. Two latter-day prophets will successfully hold these armies at bay. (See Parley P. Pratt, *A Voice of Warning and Instruction to All People,* New York: W. Sandford, 1837, p. 80.)

John the Revelator described the ministry of these two prophets: "And I will give power unto my two witnesses, and they shall prophesy a thousand two hundred and threescore days, clothed in sackcloth. These are the two olive trees, and the two candlesticks standing before the God of the earth. And if any man will hurt them, fire proceedeth out of their mouth, and devoureth their enemies; and if any man will hurt them, he must in this manner be killed. These have power to shut heaven, that it rain not in the days of their prophecy: and have power over waters to turn them to blood, and to smite the earth with all plagues, as often as they will." (Revelation 11:3–6.)

The specified time of their ministry is "a thousand two hundred and threescore days," or three and one-half years. This is the same time as the Savior's mortal ministry. However, it would be wise not to be too confined in placing parameters on this period. Elder McConkie noted "the detailed application of the 42 months to this period is yet to be revealed." (*DNTC,* 3:509.)

Latter-day revelation gives some understanding to the nature of these two witnesses: "They are two prophets that are to be raised up to the Jewish nation in the last days, at the time of the restoration, and to prophesy to the Jews after they are gathered and have built the city of Jerusalem in the land of their fathers." (D&C 77:15.)

Elder Bruce R. McConkie further identified these two prophets:

> These two shall be followers of that humble man, Joseph Smith, through whom the Lord of Heaven restored the fulness of his everlasting gospel in this final dispensation of grace. No doubt they will be members of the Council of the Twelve or of the First Presidency of the Church. Their prophetic ministry to rebellious Jewry shall be the same in length as was our Lord's personal ministry among their rebellious forebears.
>
> The two olive trees, and the two candlesticks [are] Symbols of the two witnesses; meaning, perhaps, that as olive trees, they shall provide oil for the lamps of those who go forth to meet the Bridegroom . . . and that as lamp stands they shall reflect to men that light which comes from Him who is the Light of the World. (*DNTC* 3:509–10.)

At the end of their designated ministry—"when they shall have finished their testimony," the Revelator tells us—"the beast . . . shall overcome them, and kill them." For three and one-half days, their dead bodies will lie in the streets of Jerusalem while the wicked of the world "shall rejoice over them, and make merry, and shall send gifts one to another; because these two prophets tormented them that dwelt on the earth." (Revelation 11:7–10.) Jerusalem will then be overrun and ravished: "For I will gather all nations against Jerusalem to battle; and the city shall be taken, and the houses rifled, and the women ravished; and half of the city shall go forth into captivity, and the residue of the people shall not be cut off from the city." (Zechariah 14:2.) "Every one that is found shall be thrust through; and every one that is joined unto them shall fall by the sword. Their children also shall be dashed to pieces before their eyes; their houses shall be spoiled, and their wives ravished." (Isaiah 13:15–16.)

Just when it seems that the wicked have won this final battle, their victory celebration will be cut short with the resurrection of the two slain prophets: "And after three days and an half the Spirit of life from God entered into them, and they stood upon their feet; and great fear fell upon them which saw them. And they heard a great voice from heaven saying unto them, Come up hither. And they ascended up to heaven in a cloud; and their enemies beheld them. And the same hour was there a great earthquake, and the tenth part of the city fell, and in the earthquake were slain of men seven thousand; and the remnant were afrighted, and gave glory to the God of heaven." (Revelation 11:11–13.)

The Great Earthquake

The number who are slain in the earthquake may not be limited to the seven thousand mentioned by John. Richard Draper has explained that "the number is probably not to be taken literally. Rather, it signifies, as in other places, fullness and completeness. Thus, the specific number doomed to death all died during this judgment." (*OSS,* p. 124.)

This great earthquake, of a magnitude never before recorded on the Richter Scale, will be "such as was not since men were upon the earth." (Revelation 16:18.) "The mountains shall be thrown down, and the steep places shall fall." (Ezekiel 38:20.) "Every island [shall flee] away" (Revelation 16:20) as the earth's land masses join together (see D&C 133:23; Isaiah 62:4). "All nations shall be shaken." (Haggai 2:6–7.)

The Savior will make His appearance during this earthquake: "And then shall the Lord set his foot upon this mount [of Olives], and it shall cleave in twain, and the earth shall tremble, and reel to and fro, and the heavens also shall shake." (D&C 45:48.) "And his feet shall stand in that day upon the mount of Olives, which is before Jerusalem on the east, and the mount of Olives shall cleave in the midst thereof toward the east and toward the west, and there shall be a very great valley; and half of the mountain shall remove toward the north, and half of it toward the south." (Zechariah 14:4.)

The besieged people of Judah will escape through the valley created by the earthquake and will recognize the resurrected Lord as their long-awaited Messiah, yet they will sorrow at seeing the wounds of the crucifixion in His body. (See Zechariah 14:5; 12:10; 13:6; D&C 45:51–53.)

Supper of the Great God

The Lord will pour out destruction upon the armies of Gog. Fire, brimstone, and great hailstones will rain on these wicked warriors. (See Ezekiel 38:22.) "It shall be, in the literal and full sense of the word, as it was with Sodom and Gomorrah. Fire and brimstone will fall upon the armies of the wicked in all nations," said Elder McConkie. (*MM*, p. 485.)

In their anger, wickedness, and panic, the warriors of Gog will even slay one another: "A great tumult from the Lord shall be among them; and they shall lay hold every one on the hand of his neighbour, and his hand shall rise against the hand of his neighbour." (Zechariah 14:13; see also Ezekiel 38:21). Only one-sixth of this massive army will survive. (See Ezekiel 39:2.) So devastating will be their annihilation that it will take seven months to bury most of their dead. Following this, permanent employment will be had by burial teams that will continue to seek out the corpses left lying throughout the land. (See Ezekiel 39:11–16.)

While the bodies of these once-mighty warriors are lying exposed to nature, the beasts and the birds will feast upon their flesh in what the Apostle John calls "the supper of the great God." (See Revelation 19:17–18.) Thus will the prophetic words of Ezekiel be fulfilled: "Thou shalt fall upon the mountains of Israel, thou, and all thy bands, and the people that is with thee: I will give thee unto the ravenous birds of every sort, and to the beasts of the field to be devoured." (Ezekiel 39:4.)

The armaments, weapons of war, and supplies left by the armies of Gog will be so vast that they will serve as a source of fuel and other resources for the inhabitants of the land of Israel for the next seven years. (See Ezekiel 39:8–10.) The total dead throughout the world will be incalculable. "Who shall count the number of dead bodies?" queried Elder McConkie. "The slain will be a third of the inhabitants of the earth itself, however many billions of people that may turn out to be." (*MM*, p. 453.)

Before this great and dreadful day, however, much prophecy must still be fulfilled. The chapters that follow will continue to outline these prophesied events of the last days.

SECTION 3

THE GATHERINGS

Chapter 11

GATHERING THE COVENANT PEOPLE

"And this gospel of the kingdom shall be preached in all the world for a witness unto all nations; and then shall the end come."

—MATTHEW 24:14

The Abrahamic Covenant

An important dimension of understanding the last days is to grasp the significance of a covenant the Lord made to the ancient prophet Abraham:

> My name is Jehovah, and I know the end from the beginning; therefore my hand shall be over thee.
>
> And I will make of thee a great nation, and I will bless thee above measure, and make thy name great among all nations, and thou shalt be a blessing unto thy seed after thee, that in their hands they shall bear this ministry and Priesthood unto all nations; and I will bless them through thy name; for as many as receive this Gospel shall be called after thy name, and shall be accounted thy seed, and shall rise up and bless thee, as their father; and I will bless them that bless thee, and curse them that curse thee; and in thee (that is, in thy Priesthood) and in thy seed (that is, thy Priesthood), for I give unto thee a promise that this right shall continue in thee, and in thy seed after thee (that is to say, the literal seed, or the seed of the body) shall all the families of the earth be blessed, even with the blessings of the Gospel, which are the blessings of salvation, even of life eternal. (Abraham 2:8–11.)

Consider the promise to Abraham that all who would "receive this gospel" down through the ages would "be accounted as thy seed." This covenant was understood by the Apostle Paul, who taught that all who accepted Christ, and were baptized, became "Abraham's seed, and heirs according to the promise [covenant]." (See Galatians 3:26–29.) The Prophet Joseph Smith taught that those who are not literal descendants of Abraham but who accept the gospel, are baptized, and receive the Gift of the Holy Ghost will have their blood purged and become "actually of the seed of Abraham." (*HC*, 3:380.)

Abraham was further promised the land of Canaan as an everlasting inheritance and a posterity as numerous as the sand upon the seashore or the stars in the heavens. Through his posterity, all nations of the earth would be blessed. (See Genesis 17:6–8; 22:17–18.) The blessings of the gospel of Jesus Christ, including the priesthood and all the saving ordinances and covenants, can only be administered through the rightful heirs of the Abrahamic covenant. In these the last days, it is Abraham's posterity of the tribe of Ephraim who have been given the responsibility to lead out in blessing the nations of the earth through the priesthood.

"It is Ephraim, today, who holds the priesthood," said President Joseph Fielding Smith. "It is with Ephraim that the Lord has made covenant and has revealed the fulness of the everlasting gospel. It is Ephraim who is building temples and performing the ordinances in them for both the living and for the dead." (*DS*, 3:252.)

In October 1852 the First Presidency issued an epistle that stated in part: "The invitation is to all, of every nation, kindred and tongue, who will believe, repent, be baptized, and receive the Gift of the Holy Ghost, by the laying on of hands, Come home: come to the land of Joseph, to the Valleys of Ephraim." (JH, 13 October 1852.)

The Gospel Taken to All the World

The gathering of the seed of Abraham to the covenant in the last days actually began in the spring of 1820 in a secluded grove in upstate New York. (See JS–H 1:5–20.) When the young man Joseph Smith received a visitation from God the Father and His Son Jesus Christ and was called to do God's work, he became the first to be gathered in the last days, although it would still be several years before priesthood authority would be restored and saving ordinances administered. Millions have since been gathered as the covenant people have sought to fulfill the Lord's admonition to "teach all nations, baptizing them in the name of the Father, and of the Son, and of the Holy Ghost." (Matthew 28:19.)

The Savior taught his ancient disciples that "this gospel of the kingdom shall be preached in all the world for a witness unto all nations; and then shall the end come." (Matthew 24:14.) He repeated this promise in a latter-day revelation given through his Prophet: "For, verily, the sound must go forth from this place into all the world, and unto the uttermost parts of the earth—the gospel must be preached unto every creature, with signs following them that believe. And behold the Son of Man cometh." (D&C 58:64–65.)

The Old Testament prophet Daniel foresaw the establishment of God's kingdom in the last days and compared it to a "stone . . . cut out without hands" that "became a great mountain and filled the whole earth." (Daniel 2:34–35; see also verses 44–45.) This prophecy was reemphasized in 1831 when the Lord declared: "The keys of the kingdom of God are committed unto man on the earth, and from thence shall the gospel roll forth unto the ends of the earth, as the stone which is cut out of the mountain without hands shall roll forth, until it has filled the whole earth." (D&C 65:2.)

The fulfillment of that prophecy continues as the physical and political barriers to nations continue to be broken down. The doors of more and more nations have been opened to the preaching of the restored gospel, and units of the covenant people are being established. However, a question remains in the minds of many: Given the circumstances of the world, can the gospel really be taken to *all* nations?

In response to this query of doubt, we quote the words of Elder Boyd K. Packer: "We accept the responsibility to preach the gospel to every person on earth. And if the question is asked, 'You mean you are out to convert the entire world?' the answer is 'Yes. We will try to reach every living soul.'

"Some who measure that challenge quickly say, 'Why, that's impossible! It cannot be done!'

"To that we simply say, 'Perhaps, but we shall do it anyway.'" (*Ensign*, November 1975, p. 97.)

Now consider two prophetic pronouncements of Elder Bruce R. McConkie. The first statement was given at a meeting of religious educators held at Brigham Young University in 1978, and the second, at a general conference of the Church:

> • Some day, in the providence of the Lord, we shall get into Red China and Russia and the Middle East, and so on, until eventually the gospel will have been preached everywhere, to all people; and this will occur before the second coming of the Son of Man. . . .
>
> I have no hesitancy whatever in saying that before the Lord comes, in all those nations we will have congregations that are stable, secure, devoted, and sound. We will . . . have progressed in spiritual things to the point where they have received all of the blessings of the house of the Lord. That is the destiny. . . .
>
> People from all nations will have the blessings of the house of the Lord before the Second Coming. ("All Are Alike unto God," *1978 Religious Educators' Symposium,* Salt Lake City: The LDS Church Educational System, 1979, p. 3.)
>
> • Looking ahead, we see the gospel preached in all nations and to every people with success attending.
>
> We see the Lord break down the barriers so that the world of Islam and the world of Communism can hear the message of the restoration; and we glory in the fact that Ishmael—as well as Isaac—and Esau—as well as Jacob— shall have an inheritance in the eternal kingdom.
>
> We see congregations of the covenant people worshipping the Lord in Moscow and Peking and Saigon. We see Saints of the Most High raising their voices in Egypt and India and Africa.

We see stakes of Zion in all parts of the earth; and Israel, the chosen people, gathering into these cities of holiness, as it were, to await the coming of their King. (*Ensign,* May 1980, p. 72.)

President Ezra Taft Benson has added his testimony to the truthfulness of the above testimonies of his fellow Apostles: "With all my soul I testify that this work will go forward till every land and people have had opportunity to accept our message. Barriers will come down for us to accomplish this mission, and some of us will see this done. Our Heavenly Father will cause conditions in the world to change so that His gospel can penetrate every border." (*The Teachings of Ezra Taft Benson,* Salt Lake City: Bookcraft, 1988, p. 174.)

It must be remembered that the Lord is ultimately in control and can change circumstances quickly to suit His divine purposes. In this respect another of His Apostles, Elder David B. Haight, recounted the fast-changing world events of 1990, which included the collapse of Communism in many nations:

During a brief period of weeks, we have witnessed some phenomenal changes in the world, particularly in the Eastern bloc countries, changes which God-fearing men attribute to the hand of the Almighty in bringing about His glorious purposes to fill the earth with the knowledge of the Lord. Walls have come down, gates have opened, and millions of voices have chorused the song of freedom! We rejoice in the dawning of a brighter day.

The news media have made the events in eastern Europe appear as a purely political revolution even though many of the oppressed have recognized it as a "religious renaissance" and have acknowledged the influence of divine intervention. . . .

The transformation of once-mighty man-made empires with such speed and determination has released new springs of faith and hope in the hearts of hundreds of millions of oppressed souls. Where there was despair, now the bright light of freedom shines forth. This only could have happened in such a miraculous way by the intervening hand of the Almighty! "Is anything too hard for the Lord?" (Gen. 18:14.) (*Ensign,* May 1990, p. 23.)

In spite of opposition, the Lord's timetable will be met. The Prophet Joseph Smith boldly proclaimed: "Persecutions may rage, mobs may combine, armies may assemble, calumny may defame, but the truth of God will go forth boldly, nobly, and independent, till it has penetrated every continent, visited every clime, swept every country, and sounded in every ear, till the purposes of God shall be accomplished, and the Great Jehovah shall say the work is done." (*HC,* 4:540.)

Gathered to Zion

Those who are gathered to the large sheepfold, or Church of the Good Shepherd, are also gathered into subunits of the Church, where undershepherds minister to and watch over them. The ancient prophet and record keeper Moroni evidently understood this principle when he wrote the following of new converts: "And after they had been received unto baptism, and were wrought upon and cleansed by the power of the Holy Ghost, they were numbered among the people of the church of Christ; and their names were taken that they might be remembered and nourished by the good word of God, to keep them in the right way, to keep them continually watchful unto prayer, relying alone upon the merits of Christ, who was the author and the finisher of their faith." (Moroni 6:4.)

The prophet Isaiah taught the concept of gathering to Church units. (See Isaiah 54:2.) His words were later quoted by the resurrected Savior during His visit to the inhabitants of the ancient Americas: "Enlarge the place of thy tent, and let them stretch forth the curtains of thy habitations; spare not, lengthen thy cords and strengthen thy stakes." (3 Nephi 22:2.)

In his dedicatory prayer of the Kirtland Temple in 1836, the Prophet Joseph Smith petitioned the Lord "to appoint unto Zion other stakes beside this one which thou hast appointed [in Kirtland, Ohio], that the gathering of thy people may roll on in great power and majesty." (D&C 109:59.) According to the Lord, the gathering to the stakes of Zion is "for a defense, and for a refuge from the storm, and from wrath when it shall be poured out without mixture upon the whole earth." (D&C 115:6.)

Where there are not sufficient numbers of the covenant people to establish stakes, then smaller units are established to which they gather, for Christ declared, "Where two or three are gathered together in my name, there am I in the midst of them." (Matthew 18:20.)

The Place for Gathering

When The Church of Jesus Christ of Latter-day Saints was first established, its members gathered to central locations. It was expected of new converts to "gather to Zion," or the headquarters of the Church. Early gatherings took place in New York, Ohio, Missouri, Illinois, and finally in the Rocky Mountains as the leadership of the fledgling faith moved to new locations.

While there have been isolated attempts to encourage members to remain in their native areas in order to strengthen the Church in locations outside the central stakes of Zion, immigration to central locations of the Church, particularly in the Rocky Mountains, continued well into the twentieth century. During an area conference in Mexico City in 1972, Elder Bruce R. McConkie boldly proclaimed: "[The] revealed words speak of . . . there being congregations of . . . covenant people of the Lord *in every nation, speaking every tongue,* and *among every people* when the Lord comes again. . . .

"The place of gathering for the Mexican Saints is in Mexico; the place of gathering for the Guatemalan Saints is in Guatemala; the place of gathering for the Brazilian Saints is in Brazil; and so it goes throughout the length and breadth of the whole earth. . . . Every nation is the gathering place for its own people." (Mexico and Central America Area Conference Report, 16 August 1972, p. 45.)

One year later President Harold B. Lee quoted Elder McConkie's words in general conference and, in effect, announced that the pioneering phase of gathering was over.

The gathering was now to be out of the world into the Church in every nation. (See CR, April 1973, p. 7.)

And so the gathering of the covenant people continues in great earnestness. But instead of being gathered to the Rocky Mountains, the Saints of the last days are gathering to units of Zion within their own native areas.

Chapter 12

THE GATHERING OF THE DEAD

"And it shall come to pass in the last days, that the mountain of the Lord's house shall be established in the top of the mountains, and shall be exalted above the hills; and all nations shall flow unto it. And many people shall go and say, Come ye, and let us go up to the mountain of the Lord, to the house of the God of Jacob."

—ISAIAH 2:2–3; SEE ALSO MICAH 4:1–2; 2 NEPHI 12:2–3

The Mountain of the Lord

One of the glorious signs of the last days is the building of temples throughout the earth. Temples are different from ordinary church buildings or houses of worship. Temples are sacred sanctuaries in which the Saints of God, acting for themselves or as proxies for the dead, enter into covenants of salvation, receive inspired instruction, and seek to qualify to enter into the presence of the Lord. A temple is literally a house of the Lord.

In writing of the nature of ancient temple worship, the noted Latter-day Saint scholar Dr. Richard Cowan said that "ancient peoples thought of the temple as being the highest point in the human world, the best place to observe and learn the ways of the heavens. Consequently many ancient temples were built atop mountains." (*Temples to Dot the Earth,* Salt Lake City: Bookcraft, 1989, p. 2.) When an actual building dedicated as a temple was not available, the Lord frequently used mountaintops as sacred sanctuaries in which to instruct His prophets. Three experiences illustrate such occurrences.

Moses was summoned to climb the sacred slopes of Mount Sinai, where in the presence of Deity he was instructed, "Put off thy shoes from off thy feet, for the place whereon thou standest is holy ground." (Exodus 3:5.) The Jaredite prophet Mahonri Moriancumer, who is referred to in scripture simply as "the brother of Jared," ascended the heights of mount Shelem, where he not only conversed with the Lord, but saw Him as well. (See Ether 3.) Nephi "was caught away in the Spirit of the Lord, yea, into an exceedingly high mountain" where he was instructed in sacred things by the Spirit of the Lord. (1 Nephi 11.)

Ancient prophets such as Isaiah, Micah, and Nephi all proclaimed that "in the last days, that the mountain of the Lord's house shall be established in the top of the mountains." (Isaiah 2:2–3; Micah 4:1– 2; 2 Nephi 12:2–3.) While serving as a member of the Quorum of the Twelve Apostles, Elder LeGrand Richards declared that the Salt Lake Temple "is that house of the God of Jacob." (CR, October 1975, p. 77.) A temple can appropriately be referred to as "the mountain of the Lord." (See *DCE,* p. 372.) Elder Bruce R. McConkie extended the application of this ancient prophecy: "This has specific reference to the Salt Lake Temple and to the other temples built in the top of the Rocky Mountains, and it has a general reference to the temple yet to be built in the New Jerusalem in Jackson County, Missouri. Those in all nations, be it noted, shall flow to the houses of the Lord in the tops of the mountains, there to make the covenants out of which eternal life comes." (*NWAF,* p. 539.)

Latter-day Temple Building

One of the prophecies cited by the Angel Moroni during his nocturnal visit with the Prophet Joseph Smith on September 21, 1823, was the promised return of Elijah "before the coming of the great and dreadful day of the Lord." (JS–H 1:36–39; see also D&C 2; Malachi 4:5–6.)

This prophecy was fulfilled on April 3, 1836, when the prophet Elijah appeared in the newly dedicated Kirtland Temple and conferred the priesthood keys of the sealing powers to God's earthly prophet, Joseph Smith, and his associate in the work, Oliver Cowdery. (See D&C 110:13–16.) President Joseph Fielding Smith declared that without the restoration of these sealing powers, the temple work for the dead could not be accomplished. (See *DS*, 2:122).

The far-reaching impact of this restoration of priesthood power and authority was noted by Elder Boyd K. Packer: "This signal event went unheeded by the world, but it would influence the destiny of every soul who has ever lived or will live. Things began quietly to happen. The Church became a temple-building church." (*The Holy Temple,* Salt Lake City: Bookcraft, 1980, p. 141.) Within one year of the organization of the Church, the Lord revealed that a temple was to be built in Independence, Missouri. (See D&C 57:1–5.) While this temple is yet to be built, scores of other temples have since been built and dedicated to accomplish the work of salvation for the living and the dead.

Following a decade in which the First Presidency had announced the building of thirty-one new temples in twenty-two countries, President Gordon B. Hinckley observed: "These are important and vital days in the work of the Lord. . . . We are living in one of the most significant and important epochs in the history of the Church and in the history of God's work among His people. We are living in the greatest era of temple building ever witnessed." (*Ensign*, November 1985, p. 54.)

The significance of temples in the last days, and in the theology of The Church of Jesus Christ of Latter-day Saints, is summed up in a declaration that President Howard W. Hunter made at a regional representatives' seminar on April 5, 1991: "This must be the ultimate vision of every priesthood and auxiliary leader. The whole purpose of the Church operating smoothly at the local level is to qualify individuals to return to the presence of God. That can only be done by their accepting the covenants, receiving the ordinances, and then living in accordance with all they have covenanted to do in the temples of our Lord." (See *Church News,* 13 April 1991, p. 6.)

Temples will continue to cover the earth in the days ahead. Some have been announced, others are in the process of being built, and the sites of some are yet to be revealed to the Lord's servants. Two announced temples yet to be built occupy an important role in fulfilling premillennial prophecy:

"Before the Second Coming, gathered *Judah, as directed by Ephraim, shall build up anew the Old Jerusalem and prepare therein a holy temple; and gathered Ephraim, aided by Manasseh, shall build a New Jerusalem in an American Zion and prepare therein a holy temple.* It is to these two temples in particular that the Lord shall come at his glorious return, and it is from these two cities—Zion in America and Jerusalem in Old Canaan—that the governance and worship of the world will be directed. . . .

"The building of these two world capitals will commence before the Second Coming and continue during the Millennium." (*NWAF,* pp. 586–87; italics added.)

The Temple at New Jerusalem

As earlier noted, an 1831 revelation announced the site of a temple at Independence, Missouri. (See D&C 57:1–5.) In a letter "sent to the brethren in Zion, the 25th of June, 1833," the Prophet Joseph Smith indicated that this temple to be built in Jackson County would actually be a complex of twelve temples, two of which would be for the lesser, or Aaronic, Priesthood. (See *HC,* 1:357–58.) Under this arrangement, President Joseph Fielding Smith suggested that "provision will be made for some ceremonies and ordinances which may be performed by the Aaronic Priesthood and a place provided where the sons of Levi may offer their offering in righteousness. This will have to be the case because *all things are to be restored.*" (*DS,* 3:93.)

Elder Orson Pratt gave a further description of this temple complex:

> There will be 24 different compartments in the Temple that will be built in Jackson County. The names of these compartments were given to us some . . . years ago; the names we still have, and when we build these 24 rooms, in a circular form and arched over the centre, we shall give the names to all these different compartments just as the Lord specified through Joseph Smith. . . . Perhaps you may ask for what purpose these 24 compartments are to be built. I answer not to assemble . . . the Saints all in one place, but these buildings will be built with a special view to the different orders, or in other words the different quorums or councils of the two Priesthoods that God has ordained on the earth. That is the object of having 24 rooms so that each of these different quorums, whether they be High Priests or Seventies, or Elders, or Bishops, or lesser Priesthood, or Teachers, or Deacons, or Patriarchs, or Apostles, or High Councils, or whatever may be the duties that are assigned to them, they will have rooms in the Temple of the Most High God, adapted, set apart, constructed, and dedicated for this special purpose. Now, I have not only told you that we shall have these rooms, but I have told you the object of these rooms in short, not in full. But will there be any other buildings excepting those 24 rooms that are all joined together in a circular form and arched over the center—are there any other rooms that will be built—detached from the Temple? Yes. There will be tabernacles, there will be meeting houses for the assembling of the people on the Sabbath day. There will be various places of meeting so that the people may gather together; but the Temple will be dedicated to the Priesthood of the Most High God, and for most sacred and holy purposes. (*JD*, 24:24–25.)

Elder Pratt noted that the Latter-day Saints would "*build it after the pattern that the Lord gave to his servant Joseph, the Prophet, and also according to the pattern that he shall hereafter show, if the pattern is not already given in full.*" (*JD*, 21:330; italics added).

In a continuing description of this magnificent edifice, Elder Pratt said that "a cloud of glory [would] rest upon that temple by day. . . . [and] a flaming fire will rest upon the temple by night." There will be "no need of any artificial light," continued Elder Pratt, "for the Lord God will be the light thereof." (Ibid., 330–31.)

In 1878 Elder Wilford Woodruff, who was destined to become the fourth President of the Church, described a remarkable dream in which he saw the temple being built: "I saw myriads of angels . . . and above their heads there was a pillar-like cloud. . . . I saw people coming from the river and from distant places to help build the Temple. It seemed as though there were hosts of angels helping to bring material for the construction of that building. Some were in Temple robes, and the pillar-like cloud continued to hover over the spot." (*WW*, p. 505.)

The temple will, of course, be built under the direction of the First Presidency of The Church of Jesus Christ of Latter-day Saints. There have been occasional rumors that the temple might be built independent of that direction. Of one such rumor, Elder McConkie emphatically declared:

> An occasional whiff of nonsense goes around the Church acclaiming that the Lamanites will build the temple in the New Jerusalem and that Ephraim and others will come to their assistance. This illusion is born of an inordinate love for Father Lehi's children and of a desire to see them all become now as Samuel the Lamanite once was. The Book of Mormon passages upon which it is thought to rest have reference not to the Lamanites but to the whole house of Israel. The temple in Jackson County will be built by Ephraim, meaning the Church as it is now constituted; this is where the keys of temple building are vested, and it will be to this Ephraim that all the other tribes will come in due course to receive their temple blessings. (*NWAF*, p. 519.)

Because of persecution, the Saints were prevented from building the temple in Jackson County during the days of Joseph Smith. The Lord acknowledged this temporary hindering in an 1838 revelation. (See D&C 124:49–51.) However, the temple must yet be built, for "there is none other place appointed." (D&C 101:20.) An 1834 revelation proclaimed that "this generation shall not all pass away until an house shall be built unto the Lord, and a cloud of glory shall rest upon it." (D&C 84:4–5.) How can we explain the fact that the temple is still not built?

Many explanations for this seeming paradox have been given, but the fact remains that to this date we do not have a complete understanding of its meaning. Of this we are assured: the Lord's purposes will not fail, and someday we will have a complete understanding of the matter. In the meantime, we wait patiently for its fulfillment, as President Joseph Fielding Smith has noted, "Over one hundred years have passed since the site of Zion was dedicated and the spot for the temple was chosen. . . . We have not been released from this responsibility, nor shall we be. The word of the Lord will not fail. . . . When the Lord is ready for it to be accomplished, he will command his people, and the work will be done." (*WP,* pp. 268–69.)

The Temple in Old Jerusalem

Just as we are certain that a temple will be built in the New Jerusalem before the Second Coming, we have a similar conviction of the reality of a yet-to-be-constructed temple in old Jerusalem:

> Old Jerusalem, the ancient holy city, has been and will again be a temple city. On three occasions of which we know, the Lord's own earthly house, as a priceless gem in a heaven-set crown, has graced the ground that is now claimed by the Jews and trodden down of the Gentiles. *Solomon* built a majestic mansion for the Lord in the day of Israel's glory. *Zerubbabel* built it anew when the remnant returned from bondage in Babylon. And *Herod*—a wretched, evil man whose every act bore Satan's stamp—built it for the final time in the day our Lord made flesh his tabernacle. This is the temple—one of the architectural wonders of the world, whose marble blocks were covered with gold, and whose influence upon the people cannot be measured—this is the temple that was torn apart, stone

by stone, by Titus and his minions. (*MM*, p. 277; italics added.)

The destruction of the temple of Herod was a fulfillment of the Savior's prophecy that "there shall not be left here upon this temple, one stone upon another, that shall not be thrown down." (JST, Mark 13:1–5.) However, the promise of a new temple is sure:

> And thus was it to be in Jerusalem until the promised day when a new temple should arise—perhaps on the very site of the old one—in which the gospel ordinances of the new kingdom shall be performed.
>
> This new temple shall be the one of which Ezekiel spoke. "I will make a covenant of peace" with Jewish Israel when they return to the ancient fold, saith the Lord. "It shall be an everlasting covenant with them"—even the fulness of the everlasting gospel, which is the new and the everlasting covenant—"and I will place them, and multiply them, and will set my sanctuary [my temple] in the midst of them for evermore. My tabernacle also shall be with them; yea, I will be their God, and they shall be my people. And the heathen shall know that I the Lord do sanctify Israel, when my sanctuary shall be in the midst of them for evermore." (Ezek. 37:26–28.) (*MM*, p. 278.)

This temple will have some unique features. Elder Orson Pratt stated:

> The Temple at Jerusalem will undoubtedly be built, by those who believe in the true Messiah. Its construction will be, in some respects different from the Temples now being built. It will contain the *throne of the Lord,* upon which he will, at times, personally sit, and will reign over the house of Israel for ever. It *may also contain twelve other thrones,* on which the twelve ancient Apostles will sit, and judge the twelve tribes of Israel. It will, very likely, have an apartment, with a table, on which *food and drink* will be prepared, such as are *suitable to the taste and happiness of immortal resurrected beings,* thus fulfilling the words of Jesus—"Ye that have followed me in the regeneration [resurrection] shall eat and drink at my table, and sit upon twelve thrones, judging the twelve tribes of Israel." [Matthew 19:28.] (*JD,* 19:20; italics added.)

The Prophet Joseph Smith declared: "Judah must return, Jerusalem must be rebuilt, and the temple, and water come out from under the temple, and the *waters of the Dead Sea be healed* . . . before the Son of Man will make His appearance." (*HC,* 5:337; italics added.) How will "the waters of the Dead Sea be healed?" It is possible that the great quake at the time of the Second Coming "will evidently create a huge spring in Jerusalem which will form a new river, flowing westward to the Mediterranean Sea and eastward to the Dead Sea (see Zechariah 14:8–9; Joel 3:18; Ezekiel 47:1–5). Because of this river, the Dead Sea will have its waters healed, that is, it will become a lake with verdant foliage surrounding its shores and fish teeming in its waters (see Ezekiel 47:6–12; Smith, *Teachings of the Prophet Joseph Smith,* p. 286)." (*Old Testament Student Manual: 1 Kings–Malachi,* Salt Lake City: LDS Church Educational System, 1981, p. 294.)

The Old Testament prophet Zechariah, who saw those who would build this future temple, declared, "And they that are far off shall come and build in the temple of the Lord." (Zechariah 6:15.) The identity of "they that are far off" was suggested by Elder McConkie:

> Who are those "that are far off" who shall come to Jerusalem to build the house of the Lord? Surely they are the Jews who have been scattered afar. By what power and under whose authorization shall the work be done? There is only one place under the whole heavens where the keys of temple building are found. There is only one people who know how to build temples and what to do in them when they are completed. That people is the Latter-day Saints. The temple in Jerusalem will not be built by Jews who have assembled there for political purposes as at present. It will not be built by a people who know nothing whatever about the sealing ordinances and their application to the living and the dead. It will not be built by those who know nothing about Christ and his laws and the mysteries reserved for the saints. But it will be built by Jews who have come unto Christ, who once again are in the true fold of their ancient Shepherd, and who have learned anew about temples because they know that Elijah did come, not to sit

in a vacant chair at some Jewish feast of the Passover, but to the Kirtland Temple on April 3, 1836, to Joseph Smith and Oliver Cowdery. The temple in Jerusalem will be built by The Church of Jesus Christ of Latter-day Saints." (*MM*, pp. 279–80.)

And so the role of The Church of Jesus Christ of Latter-day Saints continues in accomplishing the work of gathering the dead that constitutes part of the signs preceding the Second Coming. As will be shown later, this work will not be completed at that "great day" but will continue with intensity throughout the Millennium.

Chapter 13

THE GATHERING OF JUDAH

"And I will remember the covenant which I have made with my people; and I have covenanted with them that I would gather them together in mine own due time, that I would give unto them again the land of their fathers for their inheritance, which is the land of Jerusalem, which is the promised land unto them forever, saith the Father."

—3 NEPHI 20:29

The Scattering of Judah

The tribe of Judah has been the victim of captivity and dispersion on several occasions. In 701 B.C., more than two hundred thousand Jews were carried into Assyrian captivity. (See 2 Kings 18:13.) The Babylonian king Nebuchadnezzar deported many Jews from the land of Judaea in 597 B.C. and again in 586 B.C. (See 2 Kings 24:14; 25:11; 2 Chronicles 36:6–10; Jeremiah 52.)

In 536 B.C. the Persian king Cyrus overthrew Babylon and decreed that the Jews should return to their homeland and rebuild their temple. (See Ezra 1). Some Jews who had become comfortable in their transplanted surroundings chose to remain away from the land of their forefathers and became known as the "diaspora." The Jewish nation remained essentially intact in Palestine until about 70 A.D., when the Roman legions under Titus destroyed Jerusalem, slaughtering many of the Jewish people and scattering the rest.

The extent of their suffering during the past centuries was described by the prophet Zenos and reported by Nephi: "And as for those who are at Jerusalem, saith the prophet, they shall be scourged by all people, because they crucify the God of Israel, and turn their hearts aside, rejecting signs and wonders, and the power and glory of the God of Israel. And because they turn their hearts aside, saith the prophet, and have despised the Holy One of Israel, they shall wander in the flesh, and perish, and become a hiss and a by-word, and be hated among all nations." (1 Nephi 19:13–14; see also 3 Nephi 16:9.)

The Promise to Gather Judah a Second Time

As one of the signs of the last days, "the Messiah will set himself again the second time to recover [the dispersed]." (2 Nephi 6:14.) "I will bring you out from the people, and will gather you out of the countries wherein ye are scattered," proclaimed the Lord through his prophet. (Ezekiel 20:34.)

When the resurrected Redeemer visited the inhabitants of ancient America, He declared: "And I will remember the covenant which I have made with my people; and I have covenanted with them that I would gather them together in mine own due time, that I would give unto them again the land of their fathers for their inheritance, which is the land of Jerusalem, which is the promised land unto them forever, saith the Father." (3 Nephi 20:29.)

While serving as a member of the Council of the Twelve Apostles, Elder Wilford Woodruff spoke of the destiny of the Jewish people:

> The Lord has decreed that the Jews should be gathered from all the Gentile nations where they have been driven, into their own land, in fulfillment of the words of Moses their law-giver. And this is the will of your great Eloheim, O house of Judah, and whenever you shall be called upon to perform this work, the God of Israel will help you. You have a great future and destiny before you and you cannot avoid fulfilling it; you are the royal chosen seed, and the God of your father's house has kept you distinct as a nation for eighteen hundred years, under all oppression of the whole Gentile world. *You may not wait until you believe on*

*Jesus of Nazareth, but when you meet with Shiloh your king, you
will know him; your destiny is marked out, you cannot avoid it."*
(*WW,* p. 509; italics added.)

The Dedication of the Holy Land
to the Return of the Jews

In order to facilitate the return of Judah to its homeland, the
Prophet Joseph Smith appointed two members of the Council
of the Twelve Apostles to travel to the Holy Land and dedicate
it for that purpose. Elders Orson Hyde and John E. Page
received this divine commission in April 1840. Elder Page was
not faithful to his calling, but Elder Hyde, who was of Jewish
descent, exercised the faith necessary to fulfill his mission.

Nearly ten years prior to his call to the Holy Land, Orson
Hyde had received an inspired blessing that included this
promise: "In due time thou shalt go to Jerusalem, the land of
thy fathers, and be a watchman unto the house of Israel; and
by thy hands shall the Most High do a great work, which shall
prepare the way and greatly facilitate the gathering of that
people." (As quoted in *HC,* 4:375.)

On the morning of October 24, 1841, Orson Hyde
climbed the slopes of Mount Olivet and dedicated the land. In
part, his prayerful petition included these words:

> Grant, therefore, O Lord, in the name of thy well-
> beloved Son, Jesus Christ, to remove the barrenness and
> sterility of this land, and let springs of living water break
> forth to water its thirsty soil. Let the vine and olive produce
> in their strength, and the fig tree bloom and flourish. Let
> the land become abundantly fruitful when possessed by its
> rightful heirs; let it again flow with plenty to feed the
> returning prodigals who come home with a spirit of grace
> and supplication; upon it let the clouds distil virtue and
> richness, and let the fields smile with plenty. Let the flocks
> and the herds greatly increase and multiply upon the
> mountains and the hills; and let Thy great kindness con-
> quer and subdue the unbelief of Thy people. Do Thou
> take from them their stony heart, and give them a heart of
> flesh; and may the sun of Thy favor dispel the cold mists of

darkness which have beclouded their atmosphere. Incline them to . . . come like clouds and like doves to their windows. Let the large ships of the nations bring them from the distant isles; and let kings become their nursing fathers, and queens with motherly fondness wipe the tear of sorrow from their eye. . . .

Thou, O Lord, . . . inspire the hearts of kings and the powers of the earth to look with a friendly eye towards this place, and with a desire to see Thy righteous purposes executed in relation thereto. Let them know that it is Thy good pleasure to restore the kingdom unto Israel—raise up Jerusalem as its capital, and constitute her people a distinct nation and government. . . .

Let not their enemies prevail against them, neither let pestilence or famine overcome them, but let the glory of Israel overshadow them, and the power of the Highest protect them. (As quoted in *HC,* 4:457.)

To further emphasize the importance of the Jews returning to their homeland, President George A. Smith, first counselor to President Brigham Young in the First Presidency, was assigned to rededicate the Holy Land to the return of the Jews. In a letter dated October 15, 1872, President Young and President Daniel H. Wells, second counselor in the First Presidency, said to President Smith, "When you get to the land of Palestine, we wish you to dedicate and consecrate that land to the Lord, that it may be blessed with fruitfulness, preparatory to the return of the Jews, in fulfilment of prophecy and the accomplishment of the purposes of our heavenly Father." (As quoted in Eliza R. Snow, *Biography and Family Record of Lorenzo Snow,* Salt Lake City: Deseret News Co., 1884, p. 496.)

The April 1873 issue of the *Millennial Star,* the official Church publication in England, gave this account of the rededication: "On the 2nd [of April 1873] President George A. Smith, Elders Lorenzo Snow and Albert Carrington of the Twelve Apostles, Elders Feramorz Little, Paul A. Schettler and Thomas W. Jennings, and sister Eliza R. Snow, went to Mount Olivet and engaged in Divine worship; in the course of the service dedicating and consecrating the land to the Lord, invoking Him in his own due time to restore the 'early and latter rains,' to restore fruitfulness to the soil, and to hasten the gathering of the Jews and the rebuilding of Jerusalem. All engaged felt greatly blessed of the Lord." (35:200–201.) Elder B. H. Roberts also identified a Miss Clara A. Little as being part of this small group of pilgrims. (See *A Comprehensive History of The Church of Jesus Christ of Latter-day Saints,* Century One, 6 vols., Salt Lake City: The Church of Jesus Christ of Latter-day Saints, 1930, 5:474.)

Fulfillment of Prophecy

In March 1842 Elder Orson Hyde wrote the offices of the *Millennial Star* and offered these insights regarding the gathering of the Jews: "It was by political power and influence that the Jewish nation was broken down, and her subjects dispersed abroad; and I will here hazard the opinion, that by political power and influence they will be gathered and built up; and further, that England is destined in the wisdom and economy of heaven to stretch forth the arm of political power, and advance in the front ranks of this glorious enterprize." (2:168–69.)

Elder Hyde's statement was an elaboration on scriptural prophecy regarding the gathering of Judah as recorded in both the Bible and the Book of Mormon: "And it shall come to pass that they shall be gathered in from their long dispersion, from the isles of the sea, and from the four parts of the earth; and the nations of the Gentiles shall be great in the eyes of me, saith God, in carrying them forth to the lands of their inheritance. Yea, the kings of the Gentiles shall be nursing fathers unto them, and their queens shall become nursing mothers; wherefore, the promises of the Lord are great unto the Gentiles, for he hath spoken it, and who can dispute?" (2 Nephi 10:8–9; see also 2 Nephi 6:6–7; Isaiah 49:22–23.)

The literal fulfillment of these prophetic pronouncements took place when England took control of the Holy Land, displacing the previous overlords, the Turks. Shortly after the British army marched into Jerusalem on December 11, 1917, the following declaration was issued by Lord Balfour, England's Secretary of State for Foreign Affairs: "His Majesty's Government views with favor the establishment in Palestine of a National Home for the Jewish people, and will use their best endeavors to facilitate the achievement of this object." (As quoted in *ST*, p. 66.)

As a show of good faith, Great Britain appointed a Jew as governor of the land. President Joseph Fielding Smith made the following observation of this appointment:

> When Viscount Herbert Samuel, a Jew, was sent to govern Palestine in 1920, it was a significant event for this was the first time that a Jew had ruled in Palestine since the destruction of Jerusalem. According to the word of our Savior they were not to do so until the time of the Gentiles was fulfilled. We have reached, it appears, that fulfillment. This is a sign that the day of the return is here and Judah is to be redeemed from all his rebellion and will once more occupy the lands of his inheritance. Nations may oppose it; Arabs may fight it; but every opposition in the due time of the Lord will melt away and Israel will again possess the land 'northward and southward, and eastward and westward,' for all this land was given to Abraham and Israel by the Lord, for an everlasting possession. (*ST*, p. 234.)

Opposition to Jewish Immigration

Initially, Great Britain gave great support to the Balfour Declaration. Millions of English pounds were spent in making the land inhabitable for the new immigrants. The United States and wealthy Jews throughout the world also gave financial assistance. However, after some initial enthusiasm there came some backsliding, as noted by President Joseph Fielding Smith:

> Then came a change of heart by the British Government. On the Balfour Declaration was placed modified interpretations, a backing away from the broader interpretations in relation to making Palestine a "Jewish Home." British statesmen (or were they politicians?) declared that

it was never intended that Palestine should become a Jewish nation—a National Home, where they might have self-government. The English ardor for the Jews had cooled. Two reasons seem apparent. One is oil in the Arabic country. The other, they did not wish to offend the Arabs of Palestine and drive the Arabic world into the camp of England's enemies. In 1922, Winston Churchill issued a White Paper which was considered by the Jews as "a serious whittling down of the Balfour Declaration." (*ST*, p. 216.)

The British government began restricting the immigration of Jews. Shiploads of Jewish refugees were turned away by British gunboats. On the other hand, immigration by Arabs to Palestine was encouraged. Arabs were commanded by their leaders not to sell any land to the Jews on penalty of death.

When another White Paper was issued in 1939, it was seen as a complete rejection of the Balfour Declaration. The paper included this statement: "His Majesty's Government believe that the framers of the Mandate in which the Balfour Declaration was embodied could not have intended that Palestine should be converted into a Jewish State against the will of the Arab population of the country." (As quoted in *ST*, pp. 219–20.)

Establishment of the State of Israel

The United States continued to stand behind the concept of a Jewish homeland. On October 22, 1938, President Franklin D. Roosevelt said the United States was "for the maintenance of Palestine as a Jewish national home without limitation." He further stated that "everything within the power of the United States Government would be done to prevent the curtailment of Jewish immigration into Palestine." (*Current History*, December 1938, p. 26; as quoted in W. Cleon Skousen, *Prophecy and Modern Times*, Salt Lake City: Deseret Book Co., 1948, p. 80.)

In May 1947 the United Nations Special Committee on Palestine (UNSCOP) was formed to consider permanent government for Palestine. The report was completed on August 31, 1947. The Majority Report called for a partitioning of Palestine into an Arab state, a Jewish state, and the City of Jerusalem. The General Assembly of the United Nations voted on November 29, 1947, to partition Palestine by October 1, 1948, in accordance with the Majority Report. The plan called for Great Britain to withdraw by August 1, 1948, but British leaders requested that withdrawal take place by May 14, 1948. On May 15, 1948, the British government terminated its supervisory government of Palestine. The Jewish people immediately declared the independence of their newly formed sovereign state. The first country to recognize its existence was the United States.

Although in Old Testament times the Jewish nation had been known as the kingdom of Judah, or the southern kingdom, these modern-day descendants of Abraham, Isaac, and Jacob through the tribe of Judah named their country "Israel." President Joseph Fielding Smith provided the following commentary on this choice of name: "It seems a little strange that in this present time, when again the government of the Jews is established, that they call it *Israel instead of Judah.* In doing so, perhaps they have built better than they knew, for eventually this land is to be inhabited by those of the other tribes of Israel and it will not be a kingdom just of Jews." (*ST*, p. 234; italics added.)

Independence did not come without its pains. Several wars and uncounted skirmishes have been part of the price paid by the citizens of Israel. However, against overwhelming odds they have fiercely maintained their independence.

What Constitutes the Gathering of the Jews?

An important aspect of the gathering of Judah is their return to the land of their forefathers. In this respect, Elder George Q. Morris of the Quorum of the Twelve Apostles made the following declaration in April 1960:

"Strangely enough when the State of Israel was reborn in 1948, it was a nation of 600,000, the same number which the Bible reports that Moses led out of bondage in Egypt. It now numbers some two million, the same number which it is said populated the ancient Kingdom of Solomon, when Israel was in all its glory." ([As quoted from] *Know the Word: Israel,* "Around the World Program" by Peggy Mann.)

That is why we may now say that the Jews have returned to Palestine. . . .

I think perhaps we may well now not continue saying the Jews are going to gather in Jerusalem. I think now we may well say they have gathered. (CR, April 1960, p. 101.)

However, there is another and more important element of the prophesied gathering. Elder Bruce R. McConkie stated:

Portions of Jewish Israel hold forth in various nations or have gathered in a political sense to the land of their fathers. *This gathering, however, is simply one that puts persons of the proper lineage in the same geographic locale where their ancestors dwelt; it is not the true gathering of Israel of which the prophets speak. . . .*

What, then, is involved in the gathering of Israel? The gathering of Israel consists in believing and accepting and living in harmony with all that the Lord once offered his ancient chosen people. It consists of having faith in the Lord Jesus Christ, of repenting, of being baptized and receiving the gift of the Holy Ghost, and of keeping the commandments of God. It consists of believing the gospel, joining the Church, and coming into the kingdom. It consists of receiving the holy priesthood, being endowed in holy places with power from on high, and receiving all the blessings of Abraham, Isaac, and Jacob, through the ordinance of celestial marriage. And it may also consist of assembling to an appointed place or land of worship. . . .

The present assembling of people of Jewish ancestry into the Palestinian nation of Israel is not the scriptural gathering of Israel or of Judah. It may be prelude thereto, and some of the people so assembled may in due course be gathered into the true church and kingdom of God on earth, and they may then assist in building the temple that is destined to grace Jerusalem's soil." (*NWAF,* pp. 511, 515, 519; italics added.)

As noted in chapter 12, the converted Jews are destined to build a temple under the direction of the First Presidency of

The Church of Jesus Christ of Latter-day Saints. This seems consistent with the Lord's admonition to "let them who be of Judah flee unto Jerusalem, unto the mountains of the Lord's house." (D&C 133:13.)

Thus, while we watch with great interest the continuing strengthening of a Jewish homeland, we look forward with great eagerness to the day when Judah shall be converted to Christ and truly be gathered.

Chapter 14

THE RESTORATION OF THE TEN TRIBES

"Moses appeared before us, and committed unto us the keys of the gathering of Israel from the four parts of the earth, and the leading of the ten tribes from the land of the north"

—D&C 110:11

A Basic Belief of Latter-day Saints

When Joseph Smith outlined the basic beliefs of the Latter-day Saints in a letter to the editor of the *Chicago Tribune* in 1841, he included among these Articles of Faith this statement: "We believe in the literal gathering of Israel and in the restoration of the Ten Tribes." (Articles of Faith 1:10.)

Previous to penning these beliefs, the Prophet Joseph and his associate in the work of the Restoration, Oliver Cowdery, had been visited by Moses in the Kirtland Temple in 1836 and received from him the keys "leading . . . the ten tribes from the land of the north." (D&C 110:11.) Additionally, in 1831 Joseph had received a revelation in which the Lord proclaimed the following as one of the prophesied events of the last days:

> And they who are in the north countries shall come in remembrance before the Lord; and their prophets shall hear his voice, and shall no longer stay themselves; and they shall smite the rocks, and the ice shall flow down at their presence.
> And an highway shall be cast up in the midst of the great deep.
> Their enemies shall become a prey unto them.
> And in the barren deserts there shall come forth pools

of living water; and the parched ground shall no longer be a thirsty land.

And they shall bring forth their rich treasures unto the children of Ephraim, my servants.

And the boundaries of the everlasting hills shall tremble at their presence.

And there shall they fall down and be crowned with glory, even in Zion, by the hands of the servants of the Lord, even the children of Ephraim.

And they shall be filled with songs of everlasting joy.

Behold, this is the blessing of the everlasting God upon the tribes of Israel, and the richer blessing upon the head of Ephraim and his fellows. (D&C 133:26–34.)

Thus, Joseph Smith knew that the lost ten tribes of Israel would return from their outcast state and receive the blessings of the restored gospel from their brethren of Ephraim.

Identity of the Ten Tribes

Who are these ten tribes? An answer to this question is found when one understands the identity of the twelve sons of the Old Testament patriarch Jacob. These sons were Reuben, Simeon, Levi, Judah, Issachar, Zebulun, Joseph, Benjamin, Gad, Asher, Dan, and Naphtali. (See Genesis 35:23–26.)

God changed Jacob's name to Israel (see Genesis 35:10), and from his twelve sons came the twelve tribes of Israel. However, a tribe is not named for each son. Levi was not numbered among the tribes (see Numbers 1:47–49) because his posterity was given the Levitical Priesthood and they ministered to all the tribes (see Numbers 3:12–13). Joseph was given a double portion through his sons Ephraim and Manasseh. Thus, the twelve tribes include ten of Jacob's sons and two of Joseph's. (See Joseph Fielding Smith, *Answers to Gospel Questions,* comp. Joseph Fielding Smith, Jr., 5 vols., Salt Lake City: Deseret Book Co., 1957–66, 1:115; see also JST, Genesis 48:5–6.)

The twelve tribes were united under King David and his son Solomon, but ten of the tribes rebelled against Solomon's son Rehoboam and set up their own kingdom, which became known as the Northern Kingdom of Israel. Judah and Benjamin remained in Jerusalem and became known as the Southern Kingdom, or Kingdom of Judah. There were remnants of all the tribes found among the people of Judah. (See 1 Kings 12; Smith, *Answers to Gospel Questions,* 1:115.)

The tribes of the Northern Kingdom were taken into captivity by the Assyrian king Shalmaneser about 721 B.C. (See 2 Kings 17.) These tribes have come to be known as the lost ten tribes. There appears to be a broader definition of these ten tribes than just limiting them to the ten who originally made up the Northern Kingdom of Israel. An entry in the *Encyclopedia of Mormonism* states: "For Latter-day Saints, the lost tribes are Israelites other than either the Jewish people or the Lamanites of the Book of Mormon (2 Ne. 29:13)." (2:709, s.v. "Israel: Lost Tribes of Israel.")

Where Are the Lost Tribes?

While it may seem silly to ask where the lost tribes are, there have been statements made by prophets and record keepers that help clarify this matter. Elder Parley P. Pratt, who was called as one of the first Apostles of these last days, observed, "The Jews are called dispersed because they are scattered among the nations: but the ten tribes are called outcasts, because they are cast out, from the knowledge of the nations, into a land by themselves." (*A Voice of Warning and Instruction to All People,* New York: W. Sandford, 1837, p. 57.)

While serving as a member of the Quorum of the Twelve Apostles, Elder Joseph Fielding Smith made several statements regarding the identity and whereabouts of the lost tribes:

> The Ten Tribes were taken by force out of the land the Lord gave to them. Many of them mixed with the peoples among whom they were scattered. A large portion, however, departed in one body into the north and disappeared from the rest of the world. Where they went and where they are, we do not know. *That they are intact we must believe,*

else how shall the scriptures be fulfilled? There are too many prophecies concerning them and their return in a body for us to ignore the fact. (WP, p. 130; italics added.)

You know, a lot of people have an idea that these tribes that are lost are not lost at all, they are just coming in among us all the time. They are not coming in among us all the time. *We are gathering scattered Israel, but those tribes have not come yet. They will come when the Lord gets ready. (ST, pp. 44–45; italics added.)*

Whether these tribes are in the north or not, I am not prepared to say. As I said before, they are "lost" and until the Lord wishes it, they will not be found. All that I know about it is what the Lord has revealed, and He declares that they will come from the North. He has also made it very clear and definite that *these lost people are separate and apart from the scattered Israelites now being gathered out. (ST, p. 186; italics added.)*

Visited by the Resurrected Savior

The resurrected Savior spoke of these "other tribes" when He visited the ancient inhabitants of the Americas (see 3 Nephi 15:20) and announced He had been commanded of His Father to visit these "other sheep" and bring them into his fold (see 3 Nephi 16:1–3). He then declared, "But now I go unto the Father, and also to show myself unto the lost tribes of Israel, for they are not lost unto the Father, for he knoweth whither he hath taken them." (3 Nephi 17:4.)

It is logical to believe that the Savior organized these separate and lost tribes under priesthood direction, just as He had done for the remnants of Lehi's colony as recorded in the Book of Mormon. (See 3 Nephi 12:1; 19:4–12.) Even though Christ had organized His church under the priesthood leadership of His Twelve Apostles in the land of His mortal ministry, He organized a second church in the Americas for His followers who were physically separated from, unknown by, and at that time not under the stewardship of the Twelve Apostles in the Holy Land. Would He not do the same for the other tribes who were located in an unknown and separate land?

President Joseph Fielding Smith wrote: "It is reasonable for us to conclude that among these others [the lost tribes], who were hidden from the rest of the world, he likewise chose *disciples*—perhaps *twelve*—to perform like functions and minister unto their people with the same fulness of divine authority." (*DS*, 3:159.)

In 1857 Elder Wilford Woodruff declared his belief that "there are Prophets among them." (*JD*, 4:231.) And in 1986 Elder Neal A. Maxwell spoke of a "third witness of Christ"—the records of the lost tribes of Israel—that will yet come forth to join with the Bible and the Book of Mormon to "complete a triad of truth." (*Ensign*, November 1986, p. 52.) This statement gives latter-day affirmation to the Lord's earlier declaration that he would "speak unto the other tribes of the house of Israel, which I have led away, and they shall write it." (2 Nephi 29:12–14.)

That prophets have been among the lost tribes is attested to in a statement made by the Prophet Joseph Smith in June 1831. Joseph said that "John the Revelator was then among the ten tribes of Israel . . . to prepare them for their return from their long dispersion." (*HC*, 1:176, footnote.)

The Keys Are with Ephraim

Because there is always order in the Lord's kingdom, it is reasonable to conclude that when the lost tribes return, they will not function as a body separate from the established priesthood authority. They will receive their blessings under the direction of the President and prophet of The Church of Jesus Christ of Latter-day Saints, he who holds the fulness of priesthood keys in this dispensation of time.

Based on the Savior's utterances in the Book of Mormon and Joseph Smith's declaration regarding John's ministry among the lost tribes, it can be assumed that there will be those among these tribes who have received the ordinance of baptism for the forgiveness of sins. However, they will need to be baptized anew in order to receive membership into the Lord's "only true and living church upon the face of the whole earth." (D&C 1:30.) This is consistent with what happened to the ancient Nephites, whose priesthood leaders had been baptizing them "unto repentance" with proper authority prior to the visit of the resurrected Redeemer among them. (See 3 Nephi 7:23–26.) However, when the Savior visited them, He gave His newly chosen disciples new authority to not only baptize "unto repentance" but also to baptize the people into His church and kingdom. (See 3 Nephi 12:1; 19:11–13.)

Certainly the worthy among the lost tribes will receive their saving ordinances, including the exalting ordinances of the temple, from the hands of Ephraim. As earlier noted, an 1831 revelation declared that upon their return, the lost tribes shall "fall down and be crowned with glory, even in Zion, by the hands of the servants of the Lord, even the children of Ephraim." (D&C 133:32.)

President Joseph Fielding Smith affirmed: "*The keys are with Ephraim.* It is Ephraim who is to be endowed with *power to bless* and *give to the other tribes, including the Lamanites, their blessings.* All the other tribes of Jacob, including the Lamanites, are to be crowned with glory in Zion *by the hands of Ephraim.*" (*DS,* 2:251.)

Other Theories on the Whereabouts of the Lost Tribes

Some have suggested that the Lost Tribes are not in a separate land but are scattered among the nations of the earth. Elder Bruce R. McConkie was a chief proponent of this school of thought. Regarding their location Elder McConkie wrote:

> There is something mysterious and fascinating about believing the Ten Tribes are behind an iceberg somewhere in the land of the north, or that they are on some distant planet that will one day join itself with the earth, or that the tribe of Dan is in Denmark, the tribe of Reuben in Russia, and so forth. A common cliché asserts: "If we knew where

the Lost Tribes were, they would not be lost." True it is that they are lost from the knowledge of the world; they are not seen and recognized as the kingdom they once were; but *in general terms, their whereabouts is known. They are scattered in all the nations of the earth, primarily in the nations north of the lands of their first inheritance.*" (*NWAF*, p. 520; italics added.)

Elder McConkie further noted that "these Ten Tribes, no matter where they are located, are in nations and places known in the days of Isaiah and Jeremiah and the ancient prophets as the north countries. Hence, their return to Palestine at least will be from the land of the north." (*MM*, p. 320.)

Regarding the identity of the "prophets" among the lost tribes, Elder McConkie commented:

> The President of the Church, who holds the keys to lead the Ten Tribes from the nations of the north wherein they now reside, holds also the keys of salvation for all men. There are not two true churches on earth, only one; there are not two gospels or two plans of salvation, only one; there are not two competing organizations, both having divine approval, only one. . . . Their prophets are members of The Church of Jesus Christ of Latter-day Saints. They are stake presidents and bishops and quorum presidents who are appointed to guide and direct the destinies of their stakes and wards and quorums.
>
> There is only one presiding prophet on earth at any one time, and he is the President of the Church. All other prophets are subject to him and his direction. There is not now on earth and there shall not be—as long as the earth shall stand or there is one man on the face thereof—a prophet who is not subject to and whose acts are not governed by the presiding prophet. Who, then, shall the prophets be among the Ten Tribes? They shall be the worthy and faithful members of the great latter-day kingdom who serve as all faithful elders now serve. (*MM*, pp. 325–26.)

Because of its widespread speculation, one more theory regarding the location of the lost tribes is included here. Elder Matthias F. Cowley reported the following having been said at a meeting in Logan, Utah, in 1867: "President [Brigham] Young is quoted as saying that the ten tribes of Israel are on a portion of the earth,—a portion separated from the main land. This view is also expressed in one of the . . . hymns written by Eliza R. Snow: 'And when the Lord saw fit to hide / The ten lost tribes away, / Thou, earth, was severed to provide / The orb on which they stay.'" (As quoted in *WW*, p. 448.)

However the prophecies are fulfilled, one fact remains: they will be fulfilled in the Lord's own way and in His own time. The restoration of the ten tribes as one of the signs of the last days is certain.

Chapter 15

THE GATHERING OF THE LAMANITES

"But before the great day of the Lord shall come, Jacob shall flourish in the wilderness, and the Lamanites shall blossom as the rose."

—D&C 49:24

Promises to Lehi's Posterity

Latter-day Saints believe firmly that one reason for the coming forth of the Book of Mormon is to assist in restoring the natives of the Americas to a knowledge of their forefathers and of the gospel of Jesus Christ. These natives, known anciently as Lamanites, are descendants of the prophet Lehi, whom the Lord led to the Americas from his home in Jerusalem around 600 B.C.

The Book of Mormon title page, which was written by the prophet-historian Moroni, states that the record was "written to the Lamanites, who are a remnant of the house of Israel. . . . and also to the convincing of the Jew and Gentile that Jesus is the Christ." Around five hundred years before Christ was born, an early record keeper of this people, Enos, stated that he "did cry unto God that he would preserve the records; and he covenanted with me that he would bring them forth unto the Lamanites in his own due time." (Enos 1:16.)

Over two millennia later, the Lord promised His latter-day prophet Joseph Smith that the testimony of the Savior, as preserved in the translation of that ancient record, would "come to the knowledge of the Lamanites." He then declared the purpose of the record: "And that the Lamanites might come to the knowledge of their fathers, and that they might know the promises of the Lord, and that they may believe the gospel and rely upon the merits of Jesus Christ, and be glorified through faith in his name, and that through their repentance they might be saved." (D&C 3:18, 20.)

Almost a century later, this purpose was reiterated by the sixth prophet of this last dispensation, President Heber J. Grant: "God gave us the Book of Mormon and the chief reason, as set forth in one of the revelations, is that it shall be the means of bringing to the descendants of Father Lehi the knowledge of the Redeemer of the world, and to establish them in the faith of their fathers." (CR, October 1926, p. 40.)

Around 545 B.C. the prophet Nephi prophesied that the Lamanites would be "restored unto the knowledge of their fathers, and also to the knowledge of Jesus Christ." (2 Nephi 30:4–5.) From the day that the first missionaries took copies of the Book of Mormon to the native Americans, that prophecy began to be fulfilled. It is still ongoing as the gospel continues to be taken to the natives of the Americas.

Gathered to Houses of Worship

The role of the Lamanites in latter-day theology is found in part in this declaration by the Prophet Joseph Smith: "One of the most important points in the faith of the Church of the Latter-day Saints, through the fullness of the everlasting Gospel, is the gathering of Israel (of whom the Lamanites constitute a part)—that happy time when Jacob shall go up to the house of the Lord, to worship Him in spirit and in truth, to live in holiness." (*HC*, 2:357.)

As noted in chapter 12, the Lamanites will ultimately *assist* in building the temple in the New Jerusalem. In the meantime these descendants of Lehi and Sariah assist in the other temples and houses of worship in their various locations. In 1947, as one of the newer members of the Quorum of the Twelve Apostles, Elder Spencer W. Kimball stated: "The Lamanites must rise in majesty and power. We must look forward to the day when they . . . shall be organized into wards and stakes of Zion, furnishing much of their own leadership; when they shall build and occupy and fill the temples, and serve in them." (CR, October 1947, p. 22.)

To Blossom as the Rose

An 1831 revelation addressing some of the false beliefs surrounding the Second Coming gave a great promise to the Lamanites: "But before the great day of the Lord shall come, Jacob shall flourish in the wilderness, and the Lamanites shall blossom as the rose." (D&C 49:24.)

Commenting on the progress being made by the descendants of Father Lehi's children, Elder Bruce R. McConkie stated: "Throughout the whole Book of Mormon account, the Lehite prophets looked forward to that glorious day when the Lamanites—then a dark and benighted and loathsome people—would again become pure and delightsome. The fulfillment of these promises is pre-Millennial, and it is now beginning to occur, particularly in South America, where Father Lehi's seed are coming into the Church in such great numbers." (*NWAF*, pp. 631–32.)

Consider the following examples of the fulfillment of these promises:

• While in Bolivia in the middle 1970s, President Marion G. Romney of the First Presidency stated that the descendants of Jacob in Bolivia would "live to see the day when millions of Indians will join The Church of Jesus Christ of Latter-day Saints." (As quoted in *DCE*, p. 273.) About the same time at a conference in Chile, Elder Bruce R. McConkie declared, "I foresee the day . . . when The Church of Jesus Christ of Latter-day Saints will be the most powerful influencing leaven in this entire nation." (Ibid., pp. 272–73.)

• At a special area conference held in Mexico City in 1977, President Spencer W. Kimball told of a dream he had experienced thirty years earlier. "Maybe it was a vision," he declared. In this dream he saw the flourishing and blossoming of the descendants of Lehi in Mexico as they rose to responsible positions in the Church and community in their native land. He also saw "stakes by the hundreds [and] a temple." (*Church News*, 19 February 1977, p. 3.)

• In remarks that clearly indicated a fulfillment of President Kimball's vision, President Gordon B. Hinckley stated the following during a general conference session of the Church:

> I have been to Mexico a number of times extending over a period of many years. Once our people there seemed so poor, their education so meager. They appeared to be seriously handicapped in many ways.
>
> Now, recently, when the Mexico City Temple was dedicated, they came by the thousands. They were clean, their faces bright and smiling, their clothes neat and attractive. They bore every mark of education and refinement. There was something of greatness apparent in them. Most of them have the blood of Lehi in their veins. The shackles of darkness have fallen from their eyes, as promised by the prophets of the Book of Mormon. They have become "a pure and delightsome people." (2 Ne. 30:6.) (*Ensign*, November 1985, p. 54.)

There is an interesting parallel between what is currently happening in the great countries of Latin America and South America and what occurred among the ancient inhabitants of the Americas just prior to their being visited by the resurrected Savior. Elder H. Verlan Andersen, while serving as a member of the First Quorum of Seventy, noted: "The history of the Lamanites just prior to the Lord's first appearance on this continent reveals an interesting parallel between what occurred then and what is happening today. Commencing about the year 92 B.C., the Lamanites began coming into the Lord's church by the tens of thousands. That *conversion miracle, which took place just shortly before the Lord's first advent, is being repeated now just prior to his second coming.*" (*Ensign*, November 1986, p. 23; italics added.)

To watch the miracle of Church growth among the Lamanite people is to see prophecy in process of fulfillment as we await the second coming of the Lord Jesus Christ.

Chapter 16

THE GATHERING AT ADAM-ONDI-AHMAN

*"Spring Hill is named by the Lord Adam-ondi-Ahman,
because, said he, it is the place where Adam shall come to visit
his people, or the Ancient of Days shall sit, as spoken of by
Daniel the prophet."*

—D&C 116:1

The Land Where Adam Dwelt

On May 19, 1838, Joseph Smith led several companions on a
surveying excursion to an area about seventy miles north of
present-day Kansas City known as Spring Hill, in Daviess
County, Missouri. The Prophet surprised his companions by
renaming the location "Adam-ondi-Ahman." Joseph explained
that the name was given "by the mouth of the Lord . . .
because, said He, it is the place where Adam shall come to visit
his people, or the Ancient of Days [Adam] shall sit, as spoken
of by Daniel the Prophet." (*HC,* 3:35; see also D&C 116; Daniel
7:9–14.)

We know that the name *Ahman,* or possibly *Ah Man,* is the
name of God the Father in the pure Adamic language. In
essence it means "Man of Holiness." Elder Orson Pratt of the
Quorum of the Twelve Apostles said that the "whole term
[Adam-ondi-Ahman] means *Valley of God, where Adam dwelt.* It
is in the original language spoken by Adam, as revealed to the
Prophet Joseph." (*JD,* 18:343; italics added.)

Early leaders of The Church of Jesus Christ of Latter-day
Saints taught that the Garden of Eden was located in what is
now Jackson County, Missouri. (See *JD,* 11:337.) When Adam

and Eve were driven from the Garden, they traveled north to Adam-ondi-Ahman, where they offered sacrifices to God. The Prophet Joseph Smith discovered in that area an ancient pile of stones that he identified as part of Adam's sacrificial altar.

The First Great Gathering

It was in the valley of Adam-ondi-Ahman that Adam gathered his righteous posterity three years before his death to bless them:

> Three years previous to the death of Adam, he called Seth, Enos, Cainan, Mahalaleel, Jared, Enoch, and Methuselah, who were all high priests, with the residue of his posterity who were righteous, into the valley of Adam-ondi-Ahman, and there bestowed upon them his last blessing.
>
> And the Lord appeared unto them, and they rose up and blessed Adam, and called him Michael, the prince, the archangel.
>
> And the Lord administered comfort unto Adam, and said unto him: I have set thee to be at the head; a multitude of nations shall come of thee, and thou art a prince over them forever.
>
> And Adam stood up in the midst of the congregation; and, notwithstanding he was bowed down with age, being full of the Holy Ghost, predicted whatsoever should befall his posterity unto the latest generation. (D&C 107:53–56.)

It is important to understand that this was a gathering of Adam's *righteous* posterity. Elder Orson Pratt noted that all of the eight generations who had been invited to attend "were righteous . . . , while millions of his children, descendants that were wicked," were not invited. (*JD*, 18:343.)

The Second Great Gathering

Before the ushering in of the Millennium, a second great gathering of Adam's righteous posterity will take place in the valley of Adam-ondi-Ahman. President Joseph Fielding Smith provides us with a description of this grand occasion:

Not many years hence there shall be another gathering of high priests and righteous souls in this same valley of Adam-ondi-Ahman. At this gathering Adam, the Ancient of Days, will again be present. At this time the vision which Daniel saw will be enacted. The Ancient of Days will sit. There will stand before him those who have held the keys of all dispensations, who shall render up their stewardships to the first Patriarch of the race, who holds the keys of salvation. This shall be a day of judgment and preparation. . . .

This council in the valley of Adam-ondi-Ahman is to be of the greatest importance to this world. At that time there will be a transfer of authority from the usurper and impostor, Lucifer, to the rightful King, Jesus Christ. Judgment will be set and all who have held keys will make their reports and deliver their stewardships, as they shall be required. Adam will direct this judgment, and then he will make his report, as the one holding the keys for this earth, to his Superior Officer, Jesus Christ. Our Lord will then assume the reins of government; directions will be given to the Priesthood; and He, whose right it is to rule, will be installed officially by the voice of the Priesthood there assembled. This grand council of Priesthood will be composed, not only of those who are faithful who now dwell on this earth, but also of the prophets and apostles of old, who have had directing authority. Others may also be there, but if so they will be there by appointment, for this is to be an official council called to attend to the most momentous matters concerning the destiny of this earth.

When this gathering is held, the world will not know of it; the members of the Church at large will not know of it, yet it shall be preparatory to the coming in the clouds of glory of our Savior Jesus Christ as the Prophet Joseph Smith has said. The world cannot know of it. The Saints cannot know of it—except those who officially shall be called into this council—for it shall precede the coming of Jesus Christ as a thief in the night, unbeknown to all the world. (*WP*, pp. 289–91; italics added; see also *TPJS*, pp. 157–58.)

In a revelation dealing with the sacrament, the Lord identified a number of individuals who would be present with him at some future occasion when he would "drink of the fruit of the vine with you on the earth." (D&C 27:5.) Could this be a grand sacrament meeting? Could it be the great gathering of the righteous in the valley of Adam-ondi-Ahman?

While we may not have all answers, this much we know: Before the great day of the Lord—the second coming of Son Ahman (Son of the Man of Holiness)—there will be a powerful meeting of prophets, apostles, and other righteous Saints in the valley of Adam-ondi-Ahman. Perhaps these inspired words of W. W. Phelps will be sung on that sacred occasion:

> *This earth was once a garden place,*
> *With all her glories common,*
> *And men did live a holy race,*
> *And worship Jesus face to face,*
> *In Adam-ondi-Ahman.*
> *We read that Enoch walked with God,*
> *Above the pow'r of mammon,*
> *While Zion spread herself abroad,*
> *And Saints and angels sang aloud,*
> *In Adam-ondi-Ahman.*
> *Her land was good and greatly blest,*
> *Beyond all Israel's Canaan;*
> *Her fame was known from east to west,*
> *Her peace was great, and pure the rest*
> *Of Adam-ondi-Ahman.*
> *Hosanna to such days to come,*
> *The Savior's second coming,*
> *When all the earth in glorious bloom*
> *Affords the Saints a holy home,*
> *Like Adam-ondi-Ahman.*

("Adam-ondi-Ahman," *Hymns,* 1985, no. 49.)

Chapter 17

THE NEW JERUSALEM OR CITY OF ZION

"And it shall come to pass that I will establish my people, O house of Israel. And behold, this people will I establish in this land, unto the fulfilling of the covenant which I made with your father Jacob; and it shall be a New Jerusalem. And the powers of heaven shall be in the midst of this people; yea, even I [Jesus Christ] will be in the midst of you."

—3 Nephi 20:21–22

Prophecies of an American Jerusalem

The terms *New Jerusalem* and *Zion* have been used interchangeably by the prophets throughout the ages. Old Testament prophets referred to the New Jerusalem as Zion. For instance, Isaiah spoke of millennial times when "out of Zion shall go forth the law, and the word of the Lord from [old] Jerusalem." (Isaiah 2:3; see also Micah 4:2.) The Apostle Paul wrote of a "Jerusalem which is above" (Galatians 4:26), and John the Revelator saw "the holy city, new Jerusalem, coming down from God out of heaven, prepared as a bride adorned for her husband" (Revelation 21:2; see also 3:12).

Ether, the last prophet of the Jaredite civilization, which flourished in ancient America from the time of the Tower of Babel to about 590 B.C., prophesied that "a new Jerusalem should be built upon this land [America], unto the remnant of the seed of Joseph." (Ether 13:6.) Then, speaking of millennial conditions, the prophet further proclaimed: "And there shall be a new heaven and a new earth; and they shall be like unto the old save the old have passed away, and all things have become new. And then cometh the New Jerusalem; and blessed are they who dwell therein, for it is they whose garments are white through the blood of the Lamb; and they are they who are numbered among the remnant of the seed of Joseph, who were of the house of Israel." (Ether 13:9–10.) The resurrected Savior also spoke of the New Jerusalem being established in the land of America and proclaimed that "the power of heaven shall be in the midst of this people; yea, even I will be in the midst of you." (3 Nephi 20:22.)

The Lord revealed the exact location of this future city in an 1831 revelation. It was to be in the "land of Missouri," which the Lord "appointed and consecrated for the gathering of the saints" and which "is the land of promise, and the place for the city of Zion." The Lord then identified the city of Independence as the "center place." (See D&C 57:1–5.) This city of Zion was to "be called the New Jerusalem, a land of peace, a city of refuge, a place of safety for the saints of the Most High God." (D&C 45:66.)

Based on the revelation he had received, Joseph Smith wrote the following as one of the basic beliefs of Latter-day Saints: "We believe . . . that Zion (the New Jerusalem) will be built upon the American continent." (Articles of Faith 1:10.) The Prophet's grandnephew, President Joseph Fielding Smith, added: "This western continent is known as the *land of Joseph* and is also designated as the *land of Zion*. . . . We should keep in mind that these terms (City of Zion, and New Jerusalem) have reference to the same sanctified place from whence shall go forth the law, with the word of the Lord from Jerusalem. Enoch's city was also called *Zion*, which means by interpretation, the *pure in heart*." (*DS*, 3:67.)

Relation of Zion to the Garden of Eden

As mentioned in the chapter on Adam-ondi-Ahman, early Church leaders taught that the Garden of Eden was just south of the present site of Independence, Missouri.

President Brigham Young instructed the Saints on this matter: "In the beginning . . . the Lord commenced his work upon what is now called the American continent, where the Garden of Eden was made. In the days of Noah, in the days of the floating of the ark, he took the people to another part of the earth." (*JD*, 8:195.) Apparently Brigham Young learned this from the Prophet Joseph Smith, for Brigham Young is quoted as having said: "Joseph, the Prophet, told me that the Garden of Eden was in Jackson County, Missouri. When Adam was driven out he went to the place we now call Adam-ondi-Ahman, Daviess County, Missouri. There he built an altar and offered sacrifices." (As quoted in *WW*, p. 481.)

This teaching has been repeated more recently by President Joseph Fielding Smith, who declared: "In accord with the revelations given to the Prophet Joseph Smith, we teach that *the Garden of Eden was on the American continent located where the City Zion, or the New Jerusalem, will be built. . . .*

"We are committed to the fact that Adam dwelt on this American continent. But when Adam dwelt here, it was not the American continent, nor was it the Western Hemisphere, for all the land was in *one* place, and all the water was in one place. There was no Atlantic Ocean separating the hemispheres." (*DS*, 3:74.)

The Gathering to Zion Deferred

The Saints in the days of Joseph Smith fully expected to build the glorious City of Zion but were prevented from doing so by the actions of their persecutors. Because of these difficulties, the Lord temporarily rescinded the requirement to build the New Jerusalem and its magnificent temple. On January 19, 1841, the voice of Deity declared: "Verily, verily, I say unto you, that when I give a commandment to any of the sons of men to do a work unto my name, and those sons of men go with all their might and with all they have to perform that work, and cease not their diligence, and their enemies come upon them and hinder them from performing that work, behold, it behooveth me to require that work no more at the hands of those sons of men, but to accept of their offering." (D&C 124:49.)

The Lord, who knows the end from the beginning, was aware that the establishment of the City of Zion was to be deferred. President Joseph Fielding Smith suggested that the Lord had hinted of this deferral in an 1831 revelation. (See D&C 58:3–4; *DS*, 3:77–78.) President Smith has noted that the city and temple will yet be built and that Latter-day Saints are still under a sacred obligation to work toward that divine purpose:

> Over one hundred years have passed since the site of Zion was dedicated and the spot for the temple was chosen, and some of the members of the Church seem to be fearful lest the word of the Lord should fail. Others have tried to convince themselves that the original plan has been changed, and that the Lord does not require at our hands this mighty work which has been predicted by the prophets of ancient times. We have not been released from this responsibility, nor shall we be. The word of the Lord will not fail. . . . It is true that the Lord commanded the saints to build to his name a temple in Zion. This they attempted to do, but were prevented by their enemies, so the Lord did not require the work at their hands at that time. The release from the building of the temple in 1833, did not, however, cancel the responsibility of building the city and the house of the Lord, at some future time. When the Lord is ready for it to be accomplished, he will command his people, and the work will be done." (*WP*, pp. 268–69.)

Return to Jackson County

There has been some speculation that civil disobedience or disasters may precede the future building of the City of Zion, or the New Jerusalem. Most, if not all, of this is based on two sources: first, a reported prophecy of Joseph Smith to General Alexander Doniphan, his friend and attorney in Missouri; and second, an alleged prophecy by President Heber C. Kimball, counselor in the First Presidency to Brigham Young.

The Joseph Smith prophecy was recorded by General Doniphan's brother-in-law some seventy years after it was reportedly spoken. According to the account, the Prophet warned Doniphan that "God's wrath hangs over Jackson County . . . and *you will live to see the day* when it will be visited by fire and sword. . . . The fields and farms and houses will be destroyed, and only the chimneys will be left to mark the desolation." (L. M. Lawson, as quoted in Junius F. Wells, "A Prophecy and Its Fulfillment," *Improvement Era*, November 1902, p. 9; italics added.)

General Doniphan is reported to have said that "the devastation of Jackson County [during the Civil War] forcibly reminded him of this remarkable prediction." (Ibid.) Elder B. H. Roberts used this account as well as vivid descriptions of the destruction in Jackson County during this terrible war to show the fulfillment of Joseph Smith's prophecy regarding this land of Zion. (See *Comprehensive History of the Church*, 1:537–59.)

The alleged prophecy of President Heber C. Kimball is often referred to as the "yellow dog" prophecy. This declaration focuses on some future destruction in Jackson County. Elder Graham W. Doxey, of the Seventy, has written the following regarding its origin:

> It seems to have originated in a conversation between Heber C. Kimball and Amanda H. Wilcox in Salt Lake City in May 1868. She reports him as saying, "The western boundaries of the State of Missouri will be swept so clean of its inhabitants that, as President Young tells us, when we return to that place, 'There will not be left so much as a yellow dog to wag his tail.'" (*Prophetic Sayings of Heber C. Kimball to Sister Amanda H. Wilcox*, n.p., n.d., p. 6.)
>
> There seem to be a number of questions about the authenticity of this account since Heber C. Kimball was apparently in Provo, not Salt Lake, during the month of May. Also, no other record exists of Brigham Young making a similar statement. However, it is sufficiently similar to Joseph Smith's statements, except for the "yellow dog," that someone may have remembered the original substance but in the retelling allowed embellishment to creep in. ("Missouri Myths," *Ensign*, April 1979, p. 65.)

One other statement should be considered regarding the return to Jackson County to build the City of Zion. As a counselor in the First Presidency, President Joseph F. Smith stated the following:

> When God leads the people back to Jackson County, how will he do it? Let me picture to you how *some* of us *may* be gathered and led to Jackson County. I think I see two or three hundred thousand people wending their way across the great plain enduring the nameless hardships of the journey, herding and guarding their cattle by day and by night, and defending themselves and little ones from foes on the right hand and on the left, as when they came here. They will find the journey back to Jackson County will be as real as when they came out here. Now, mark it. And though you may be led by the power of God "with a stretched out arm," it will not be more manifest than the leading the people out here to those that participate in it. They will think there are a great many hardships to endure in this manifestation of the power of God, and it will be left, perhaps to their children to see the glory of their deliverance, just as it is left for us to see the glory of our former deliverance from the hands of those that sought to destroy us. *This is one way to look at it.* It is certainly a practical view. Some might ask, what will become of the railroads? I fear that the sifting process would be insufficient were we to travel by railroads. We are apt to overlook the manifestations of the power of God to us because we are participators in them, and regard them as commonplace events. But when it is written in history—as it will be written—it will be shown forth to future generations as one of the most marvelous, unexampled and unprecedented accomplishments that has ever been known to history." (*JD,* 24:156–57; italics added.)

Elder Graham W. Doxey provided the following commentary on President Smith's statement: "This is a vivid mental picture, but people frequently remember the picture and forget he said '*some* of us' and '*may* be gathered.' We should also keep in mind that he said this is 'one way to look at it,' remembering also the perspective of 1882. From our perspective [today], it seems even less likely that we would sell our automobiles and herd cattle along our freeway systems. But we simply have no scriptural information about who—if any general Church members—will be called to go back and the means that they might use. The prophets of our day have not found it timely or necessary to speak on the matter." ("Missouri Myths," pp. 64–65.)

Zion Redeemed by Righteousness

In March 1831 the Lord admonished the Saints to "gather up your riches that ye may purchase an inheritance which shall hereafter be appointed unto you." (D&C 45:65.) That inheritance was shortly thereafter identified as the land of Zion, or Independence, Missouri; and again the Lord stressed the importance of purchasing the land. (D&C 57:1–5.)

In August 1831 the Saints were warned against obtaining the land of Zion through the shedding of blood: "Wherefore, the land of Zion shall not be obtained but by purchase or by blood, otherwise there is none inheritance for you. And if by purchase, behold you are blessed; And if by blood, as you are forbidden to shed blood, lo, your enemies are upon you, and ye shall be scourged from city to city, and from synagogue to synagogue, and but few shall stand to receive an inheritance." (D&C 63:29–31.)

The fifth prophet of this last dispensation, President Lorenzo Snow, emphasized that the lands upon which the New Jerusalem will be built shall not be obtained by force: "We will not take possession of the land of Zion by force. If we should do, it would turn out to us as it did with the people who were upon the land of Zion when this revelation [D&C 63] was given." (CR, October 1900, p. 62.) The Saints heeded the admonition and purchased many pieces of property in Jackson County, Missouri, in hopes of establishing their Zion. Persecution and mobocracy drove them from their lands, but they were instructed by revelation to "hold claim" to their properties even "though they should not be permitted to dwell thereon." (D&C 101:99.)

An interesting revelation was received near the conclusion of the march of Zion's Camp, a unit of about two hundred men who had gone to the relief of the beleaguered Latter-day Saints in Missouri. On June 22, 1834, while the relief group was encamped on the banks of Fishing River in Missouri, the Lord reaffirmed his desire to have the Saints purchase land in Jackson County and in the adjoining counties. He then declared:

> And after these lands are purchased, I will hold the armies of Israel guiltless in taking possession of their own lands, which they have previously purchased with their moneys, and of throwing down the towers of mine enemies that may be upon them, and scattering their watchmen, and avenging me of mine enemies unto the third and fourth generation of them that hate me.
>
> But first let my army become very great, and let it be sanctified before me, that it may become fair as the sun, and clear as the moon, and that her banners may be terrible unto all nations.
>
> That the kingdoms of this world may be constrained to acknowledge that the kingdom of Zion is in very deed the kingdom of our God and his Christ; therefore, let us become subject unto her laws. (D&C 105:28–32.)

Speaking of the people of Enoch's ancient Zion, Elder Orson Pratt asked, "What was it that made their banners terrible to the nations? It was not their numbers." Then, speaking of the future New Jerusalem, Elder Pratt continued: "If, then Zion must become great it will be because of her sanctification." (*JD*, 17:112.)

Thus, the great army that will redeem Zion will be one that is sanctified and holy before the Lord. This unified army of sanctified Saints will not be armed with weapons of war but with robes of righteousness and the power of the priesthood.

On another occasion, Elder Pratt spoke of the need for the Saints to be sanctified in order to redeem Zion: "When we go back to Jackson County, we are to go back with power. Do you suppose that God will reveal his power among an unsanctified people, who have no regard nor respect for his laws and institutions but who are filled with covetousness? No. When God shows forth his power among the Latter-day Saints, it will be because there is a union of feeling in regard to doctrine, and in regard to everything that God has placed in their hands; and not only a union, but a sanctification on their part, that there shall not be a spot or wrinkle as it were, but everything shall be as fair as the sun that shines in the heavens." (*JD*, 15:361.)

Not all of the millions of Latter-day Saints will be asked to return to the land where Adam and Eve once dwelt. President Brigham Young preached that "a portion of the Priesthood will go and redeem and build up the centre Stake of Zion." (*JD*, 11:16.)

In 1877 President Young further proclaimed: "Are we going back to Jackson County? Yes. When? As soon as the way opens up. Are we all going? O no! of course not. The country is not large enough to hold our present numbers. When we do return there, will there be any less remaining in these mountains than we number today? No, there may be a hundred then for every single one that there is now. It is folly in men to suppose that we are going to break up these our hard earned homes to make others in a new country. We intend to hold our own here, and also penetrate the north and the south, the east and the west, there to make others and to raise the ensign of truth." (*JD*, 18:355–56.)

Who will be invited to return and redeem Zion, to participate in the building of the Holy City and its attendant temple? A holy city can only be built by a holy people. Consider this observation by Elder Bruce R. McConkie:

> As to the building of the New Jerusalem, different criteria apply than those pertaining to the Second Coming. Zion could have been redeemed a century and a half ago. If the newly called saints of that day had kept the commandments and seen eye to eye as did the saints of Enoch's day, they too could have built a City of Holiness, called Zion, and the glory of God would have rested upon it. That day of opportunity passed, however, and the Lord's

people began the arduous process of establishing stakes of Zion in all nations as part of a schooling process to prepare them for the day when they would build Zion itself.

The stakes of Zion that now are must be strengthened and perfected before they can uphold and sustain that Zion which is destined to be. When Zion is fully established, it will be by obedience to the law of the celestial kingdom, which law is operative in the stakes of Zion only in part. As of now, we are living under a preparatory law, as it were; as the Mosaic law was a schoolmaster to prepare Israel for the fulness of the gospel, so the church and kingdom, as now constituted, is a schoolmaster to prepare the saints for an inheritance in that perfect society of souls of which Zion will be composed. The most obvious illustration of this concept is that we today have the law of tithing, which we do not live perfectly, but when Zion is built we will have the law of consecration in its fulness. It follows that the righteousness of the saints can hasten the redemption of Zion. And, viewing the present state of the Church, good as it is when compared with the world, the day of the building of Zion seems to be some years away. (*NWAF*, pp. 591–92.)

While serving as a counselor in the First Presidency, President Joseph F. Smith taught that those who are called upon to return and build the New Jerusalem must be able to live the law of consecration and sacrifice: "When shall I be prepared to go there? Not while I have in my heart the love of this world more than the love of God. Not while I am possessed of that selfishness and greed that would induce me to cling to the world or my possessions in it, at the sacrifice of principle or truth. But when I am ready to say, 'Father, all that I have, myself included, is Thine; my time, my substance, everything that I possess is on the altar, to be used freely, agreeable to Thy holy will, and not my will, but Thine, be done,' then perhaps I will be prepared to go and help to redeem Zion. For Zion can only be built up by the law that God revealed for that purpose, which is the law of consecration—not the law of tithing." (*Millennial Star*, 56:385–86.)

Led by a Man like Moses

The Lord revealed that "the redemption of Zion must needs come by power." He then declared, "Therefore, I will raise up unto my people a man, who shall lead them like as Moses led the children of Israel." (D&C 103:15–16.)

There has been some confusion and speculation regarding the identity of the "man . . . like as Moses." Elder John Taylor, while serving as the editor of the *Times and Seasons*, the official Church publication in Nauvoo, declared, "The president [of the Church] stands in the same relationship to the Church as Moses did the Children of Israel." (6:922.) Elder John A. Widtsoe of the Quorum of the Twelve Apostles stated emphatically, "The man like unto Moses in the Church is the President of the Church." (*Evidences and Reconciliations*, arr. G. Homer Durham, Salt Lake City: Bookcraft, 1960, p. 248.)

When the land of Zion is redeemed, it will be under the direction of the Lord's prophet on earth—the President of The Church of Jesus Christ of Latter-day Saints. Whether he physically stands at the head of those who are directed to return to build the New Jerusalem, or whether he simply stands as the spiritual leader under whose direction the move takes place, is of little consequence. In either case, he will be acting as a modern-day Moses, with full authority to do whatever needs to be done.

A World Capital

The Old Testament prophets Isaiah and Micah foresaw that the New Jerusalem would be a world capital out of which the law of the Lord would go forth. (See Isaiah 2:2–3; Micah 4:1–2.) In this last dispensation, the Council of the Twelve Apostles issued a proclamation to the world in 1845:

> He [God] will assemble the Natives, the remnants of Joseph in America; and make them a great, and strong, and powerful nation: and he will civilize and enlighten them, and will establish a holy city, and temple, and seat of government among them, which shall be called Zion.

And there shall be his tabernacle, his sanctuary, his throne, and seat of government for the whole continent of North and South America forever.

In short, it will be to the western hemisphere what Jerusalem will be to the eastern. . . .

The city of Zion, with its sanctuary and priesthood, and the glorious fulness of the gospel, will constitute a *standard* which will put an end to jarring creeds and political wranglings, by uniting the republics, states, provinces, territories, nations, tribes, kindred, tongues, people, and sects of North and South America in one great and common bond of brotherhood.

While truth and knowledge shall make them free, and love cement their union. The Lord also shall be their king and their lawgiver; while wars shall cease and peace prevail for a thousand years." (As quoted in James R. Clark, comp., *Messages of the First Presidency of The Church of Jesus Christ of Latter-day Saints,* 6 vols., Salt Lake City: Bookcraft, 1965–75, 1:259–60.)

Two Other Holy Cities Yet to Come

Yet to come are two other holy cities that should not be confused with the millennial New Jerusalem: the city of Enoch and the celestial Jerusalem of the postmillennial period. "John the Revelator saw in vision the holy city come down from God in heaven twice. First he saw the City of Enoch, a Holy City called the New Jerusalem, come down after the Second Coming to remain with men on earth a thousand years. Then with seeric eyes he beheld the celestial Jerusalem, the Holy City where God and angels dwell, come down from heaven to be with men forever in that day when this earth becomes a celestial sphere." (*NWAF,* p. 588; see also Revelation 21.)

Prepare to Abide the Day

While we anxiously await that glorious day when the New Jerusalem shall be established, one might be inclined to say, "What does the concept of a future New Jerusalem have to do with me personally today?"

The answer to that question is at least partially found in a statement by Elder G. Homer Durham of the Seventy: "The vision of the New Jerusalem has moved generations of mankind. It has moved our people. We look to the day when 'Christ will reign personally upon the earth.' (A of F 1:10.) But, as the prophet Malachi asked, 'Who may abide the day of his coming? and who shall stand when he appeareth?' (Mal. 3:2.) Let us prepare to abide the day of his coming by building Zion in our hearts, in our families." (*Ensign*, May 1982, p. 68.)

Our task is to strive to live worthy of being among those who will be called upon to build the Holy City and the magnificent temple. And if we are among the many who, though worthy, are not called to assist in this glorious undertaking, our task is to so live as to make the places where we do dwell similar to the center stake of Zion, "for this is Zion—THE PURE IN HEART." (D&C 97:21.)

Chapter 18

THE RETURN OF THE CITY OF ENOCH

"And the Lord said unto Enoch: Then shalt thou and all thy city meet them there, and we will receive them into our bosom, and they shall see us; and we will fall upon their necks, and they shall fall upon our necks, and we will kiss each other."

—MOSES 7:63

Faith and Power of the Prophet Enoch

Few names evoke more feelings of awe than that of the prophet Enoch. His own personal history gives hope to those who struggle with feelings of inadequacy, especially when matters of faith are concerned. When the Lord first called Enoch to His work, the young prophet cried, "Why is it that I have found favor in thy sight, and am but a lad, and all the people hate me; for I am slow of speech; wherefore am I thy servant?" (Moses 6:31.)

Although feeling unqualified for the call he received, Enoch was humble and responded in faith. And though "all men were offended because of him" (Moses 6:37), he taught and testified, leading the people to new heights of spirituality. The scriptures tell us:

> And so great was the faith of Enoch that he led the people of God, and their enemies came to battle against them; and he spake the word of the Lord, and the earth trembled, and the mountains fled, even according to his command; and the rivers of water were turned out of their course; and the roar of the lions was heard out of the wilderness; and all nations feared greatly, so powerful was

the word of Enoch, and so great was the power of the language which God had given him. . . .

And the Lord called his people ZION, because they were of one heart and one mind, and dwelt in righteousness; and there was no poor among them.

And Enoch continued his preaching in righteousness unto the people of God. And it came to pass in his days, that he built a city that was called the City of Holiness, even ZION. . . .

And lo, Zion, in process of time, was taken up into heaven. (Moses 7:13, 18–19, 21.)

Status of the City of Enoch

Elder Joseph Young, the second man in seniority among those called to preside over the Seventy in this last dispensation, provided some interesting insights into the taking up of the City of Enoch: "The people, and the city, and the foundations of the earth on which it stood, had partaken of so much of the immortal elements, bestowed upon them by God through the teachings of Enoch, that it became philosophically impossible for them to remain any longer upon the earth; consequently, Enoch and his people, with the city which they occupied, and the foundations on which it stood, with a large piece of earth immediately connected with the foundations and the city, had assumed an aerial position within the limits of our solar system; and this in consequence of their faith." (*History of the Organization of the Seventies*, Salt Lake City: Deseret News, 1878, p. 11.)

Elder Young's comments about the actual ground also being taken up appear to be based on a statement Joseph Smith was alleged to have made that "the City of Enoch would again take its place in the identical spot from which it had been detached, now forming that chasm of the earth, filled with water, called the Gulf of Mexico." (Ibid., p. 12n.)

While some may debate the issue of the transplanting of ground and structures, there should be no question about the fact that the people of the City of Enoch were taken from this earth. These people had raised themselves to a higher order of living that was incompatible with the other residents of this world. In the words of President Joseph Fielding Smith, they "were as pilgrims and strangers on the earth . . . due to the fact that they were living the celestial law in a telestial world." (*CHMR*, 1:195.)

What does it mean to say that the people of the City of Enoch were "taken up"? Not only were they separated physically from this earth without experiencing death, but they also underwent a physical change in which their bodies were raised to a terrestrial order. They were no longer subject to death or disease and were then in the same status later granted to John the Beloved and the Three Nephites. (See John 21:20–23; D&C 7; 3 Nephi 28:1–10.)

According to Elder Bruce R. McConkie, Enoch and his people are no longer in a state of translation but went through the change of instantaneous death and resurrection when Jesus Christ rose from the tomb. They were evidently among the righteous who had lived from the time of Adam and Eve to the time of Christ's resurrection and who were raised to a resurrected status, as mentioned in both the Bible and the Book of Mormon. (See Matthew 27:52–53; 3 Nephi 23:9.) Elder McConkie stated, "[Among] those who were with [Christ] in his resurrection [were] those of Enoch's city, a righteous people who first were translated and who then gained full immortality when Christ rose from his tomb." (*MM*, p. 636.)

Ministers to Other Worlds

The Prophet Joseph Smith provided some insights regarding translated beings: "Many have supposed that the doctrine of translation was a doctrine whereby men were taken immediately into the presence of God, and into an eternal fullness, but this is a mistaken idea. Their place of habitation is that of the terrestrial order, and a place prepared for such characters He held in reserve to be *ministering angels unto many planets*, and who as yet have not entered into so great a fullness as those who are resurrected from the dead." (*TPJS*, p. 170; italics added.)

President John Taylor wrote that the people of the City of Enoch may be serving as "ministering angels unto many planets":

> It would appear that the translated residents of Enoch's city are under the direction of Jesus, who is the Creator of worlds; and that He, holding the keys of the government of other worlds, could, in His administrations to them, select the translated people of Enoch's Zion, if He thought proper, to perform a mission to these various planets, and as death had not passed upon them, they could be prepared by Him and made use of through the medium of the Holy Priesthood to act as ambassadors, teachers, or messengers to these worlds over which Jesus holds the authority. . . .
>
> It is recorded that to Jesus has been given all power in heaven and in earth, and . . . he evidently had power which he used to commission the citizens of the Zion of Enoch to go to other worlds on missions. (*The Mediation and Atonement,* reprint of 1882 edition, Salt Lake City: Deseret News Press, 1964, pp. 76–77.)

City of Enoch to Return

The Lord declared that the people of Enoch "were separated from the earth, and were received unto myself—a city reserved until a day of righteousness shall come." (D&C 45:12.)

A description of this "day of righteousness" is found in the Joseph Smith Translation of Old Testament writings:

> And the bow shall be in the cloud; and I will look upon it, that I may remember the everlasting covenant, which I made unto thy father Enoch; that, when men should keep all my commandments, Zion should again come on the earth, the city of Enoch which I have caught up unto myself. And this is mine everlasting covenant, that *when thy posterity shall embrace the truth, and look upward, then shall Zion look downward,* and all the heavens shall shake with gladness, and the earth shall tremble with joy; And the general assembly of the church of the first-born shall come down out of heaven, and possess the earth, and shall have place until the end come. And this is mine everlasting covenant,

which I made with thy father Enoch. (JST, Genesis 9:21–23; italics added.)

A hymn to be sung when the Savior returns to earth includes these words: "The Lord hath brought down Zion from above. The Lord hath brought up Zion from beneath." (D&C 84:100; see verses 98–102.) The third prophet of this last dispensation, President John Taylor, said the following regarding the Zion which should be "brought up . . . from beneath": "And Zion that is on the earth will rise, and the Zion above will descend, as we are told, and we will meet and fall on each other's necks and embrace and kiss each other." (*JD*, 21:253.)

Elder Orson Pratt suggested that this city of holiness will return to the earth "at the commencement of the Millennium to meet the Zion [New Jerusalem] here." (*JD*, 2:103.) In a revelation given anciently to Enoch, the Lord declared that these righteous inhabitants of "Zion, a New Jerusalem," would meet with Enoch and his city in a glorious reunion accompanying the Second Coming. (Moses 7:62–65.)

People's Righteousness to Unite the Two Zions

The thing that will make it possible for these two cities of holiness to intermingle in fellowship will be their common ground of celestial living. Those who will inhabit the New Jerusalem will be of the same character as those of the ancient City of Zion. Elder Orson Pratt provided the following commentary on this subject: "The Latter-Day Zion will resemble, in most particulars, the Zion of Enoch: it will be established upon the same celestial laws—be built upon the same gospel, and be guided by continued revelation. Its inhabitants, like those of the antediluvian Zion, will be the righteous gathered out from all nations: the glory of God will be seen upon it; and His power will be manifested there, even as in Zion of old. All the blessings and grand characteristics which were exhibited in ancient Zion will be shown forth in the Latter-Day Zion." (*Seer*, May 1854, p. 265.)

The commencement of the Millennium will not be hastened by the righteousness or the wickedness of the people of this world, for the time is set and is unalterable. However, the building of the City of Holiness, the New Jerusalem, can be hastened by the development of a Zion-like people. To become a people "pure in heart," a prerequisite for Zion (D&C 97:21), should be a goal towards which we all strive. "Enoch and his city of Zion are powerful symbols among the Latter-day Saints, affirming that supreme righteousness can be attained on earth as it is in heaven." (*EM*, s.v. "Enoch.")

SECTION 4

THE SECOND COMING

Chapter 19

Preparedness and the Second Coming

"Ye hear of wars in far countries, and you say that there will soon be great wars in far countries, but ye know not the hearts of men in your own land . . . ; wherefore, treasure up wisdom in your bosoms, lest the wickedness of men reveal these things unto you by their wickedness, in a manner which shall speak in your ears with a voice louder than that which shall shake the earth; but if ye are prepared ye shall not fear."

—D&C 38:29–30

Panic and Complacency

The commotion and tribulations of the last days surely lead to much fear, anxiety, and panic. Adverse economic conditions cause people to fear losing their jobs and consequently their ability to provide food and shelter for themselves and those who depend upon them. Raging violence causes many to fear for their personal safety. Dim prospects for the future create discouragement and despair.

Indeed, one of the signs of the last days will be "men's hearts failing them for fear." (Luke 21:26; see also D&C 45:26.) As a result of fear, many people panic, forgetting their faith in the Lord and his words, "If ye are prepared ye shall not fear." (D&C 38:30.)

At the other extreme are those who do not fear because of their complacency. Consequently, they do not prepare for the prophesied calamities of the future or even for the unforeseen disasters or setbacks that can occur without warning. There is great danger in complacency. President Ezra Taft Benson warned "Too often we bask in our comfortable complacency and rationalize that the ravages of war, economic disaster, famine, and earthquake cannot happen here. Those who believe this are either not acquainted with the revelations of the Lord, or they do not believe them. Those who smugly think these calamities will not happen, that they somehow will be set aside because of the righteousness of the Saints, are deceived and will rue the day they harbored such a delusion." (*Ensign*, November 1980, p. 34.)

Prophecies of the last days have been given so that we might properly prepare to meet the predicted challenges. Whether or not we will ultimately experience a calamity or challenge to our safety and security makes no difference. Our task is to be prepared—to keep both our temporal and spiritual lamps trimmed and ready and to follow the Savior's admonition to "watch" and be prepared. (See Matthew 25:1–13.)

A Personal Responsibility

From the time it was organized in 1830, The Church of Jesus Christ of Latter-day Saints has stressed personal preparedness, taking care of oneself and one's family, and seeking to alleviate the condition of the poor. The primary responsibility for taking care of oneself rests first with the individual and second with the family. Resources of the Church and community are to be used only after relying upon oneself and one's family.

Bishop Victor L. Brown expressed concern that "because the Church program includes production projects, canneries, bishops' storehouses, Deseret Industries, and other visible activities, our people are mistakenly led to believe these things replace the need for them to provide for themselves." He then declared, "This simply is not so." (*Ensign*, November 1980, p. 81.) Elder L. Tom Perry of the Quorum of the Twelve Apostles added: "We must remind ourselves that the Church welfare system was never designed or intended to care for the healthy member who, as a result of his poor management or lack of preparation, has found himself in difficulty." (*Ensign,* May 1981, p. 87.) "No true Latter-day Saint," President Spencer W. Kimball admonished, "while physically or emotionally able will voluntarily shift the burden of his own or his family's well-being to someone else." (*Ensign,* November 1977, p. 77.)

Latter-day Saints are taught to take seriously the Apostle Paul's pointed counsel that "if any provide not for his own, and specially for those of his own house, he hath denied the faith, and is worse than an infidel." (1 Timothy 5:8.) An 1832 revelation stressed the fact that women have "claim" upon their husbands and that children have claim upon their parents "for their maintenance." (D&C 83.)

While serving as a counselor in the First Presidency, President Marion G. Romney emphasized that preparedness and welfare services are "not a doomsday program, but a program for today." (*Ensign,* November 1982, p. 93.) Taking care of oneself and one's family is an ongoing responsibility. President Spencer W. Kimball taught that "we could refer to all the components of personal and family preparedness, not in relation to holocaust or disaster, but in cultivating a life-style that is on a day-to-day basis its own reward." (*Ensign,* November 1977, p. 78.)

The present welfare services program of the Church is designed to assist members to live providently now and to be prepared for future emergencies. This was emphasized by Bishop Victor L. Brown: "I fear that many think the welfare services program was designed primarily for doomsday. This is not true. The principles of the welfare services program are designed to help us live providently each day and to cope successfully with serious problems as they come into our lives." (*Ensign,* November 1982, p. 79.)

Admonitions from Church Leaders

What have Latter-day Saints, and for that matter all people, been admonished by Church leaders—the Lord's servants—to do in terms of personal preparedness? While serving as a counselor in the Presiding Bishopric of the Church, Bishop J. Richard Clarke said: "The greatest test for any generation is how it responds to the voice of the prophets. Our prophets have admonished us to—

1. Increase our personal righteousness.

2. Live within our means and get out of debt.

3. Produce, can, and store enough food, clothing, and, where possible, fuel for one year." (*Ensign*, November 1980, p. 82.)

Let's look at each of these items.

Counsel on Food Storage and Debt

Initially, the welfare program of the Church was called the "security" program. In an address at the April 1937 general conference of the Church, President J. Reuben Clark, Jr., first counselor in the First Presidency, admonished "every head of every household . . . [to have] on hand enough food and clothing, and, where possible, fuel also, for at least a year ahead." (CR, April 1937, p. 26.)

Regarding the type of food one should store, Elder Harold B. Lee, then an apostle, counseled: "Perhaps if we think not in terms of a year's supply of what we ordinarily would use, and think more in terms of what it would take to keep us alive in case we didn't have anything else to eat, that last would be very easy to put in storage for a year . . . just enough to keep us alive if we didn't have anything else to eat." (Welfare conference, 1 October 1966.)

President Ezra Taft Benson emphasized that "the Church has not told you what foods should be stored. This decision is left up to individual members." However, he did indicate that wheat and water should have high priority and that the "other basics could include honey or sugar, legumes, milk products or substitutes, and salt or its equivalent." (*Ensign*, November 1980, p. 33.)

President Benson cautioned people about going into debt for their food storage and added this counsel:

> You do not need to go into debt . . . to obtain a year's supply. Plan to build up your food supply just as you would a savings account. Save a little for storage each pay-check. Can or bottle fruit and vegetables from your gardens and orchards. Learn how to preserve food through drying and possibly freezing. Make your storage a part of your budget. Store seeds and have sufficient tools on hand to do the job. If you are saving and planning for a second car or a TV set or some item which merely add to your comfort or pleasure, you may need to change your priorities. We urge you to do this prayerfully and *do it now.*
>
> I speak with a feeling of great urgency. I have seen what the days of tribulation can do to people. (Ibid.)

Perhaps the most urgent statement made by President Benson on the subject was this: "The revelation to produce and store food may be as essential to our temporal welfare today as boarding the ark was to the people in the days of Noah." (Ibid.)

"Let us avoid debt as we would avoid a plague," words spoken by President J. Reuben Clark, Jr., well over half a century ago, are even more appropriate in today's world of credit cards—the buy-now-and-pay-later philosophy—and rising consumer debt.

A basic part of preparedness is financial planning. Wise management of our income precludes impulse spending and the consequent loss of personal peace through debt. President Heber J. Grant, who was a master at handling financial matters, observed: "If there is any one thing that will bring peace and contentment into the human heart, and into the family, it is to live within our means. And if there is any one thing that is grinding and discouraging and disheartening, it is to have debts and obligations that one cannot meet." (*Gospel Standards,* Salt Lake City: Improvement Era, 1941, p. 111.)

Another master in financial matters, President N. Eldon Tanner, who served as a counselor in the First Presidency to three presidents of the Church, provided this sage commentary: "*Live on less than you earn.* I have discovered that there is no way that you can ever earn *more* than you can spend. I am

177

convinced that it is not the amount of money an individual earns that brings peace of mind as much as it is having *control* of his money. . . . Those who structure their standard of living to allow a little surplus, control their circumstances. Those who spend a little more than they earn are controlled by their circumstances." (*Ensign*, November 1979, p. 81.)

Specific counsel regarding how to avoid debt was given by Elder M. Russell Ballard, who had spent years in the business world before his call to serve as a General Authority in 1976:

> 1. Avoid debt-pooling where exorbitant fees are charged. We may want to consolidate debts using a bank or credit union loan that can be repaid at a sensible interest rate over a reasonable length of time. We may need to stop using our credit cards.
>
> 2. Exercise self-discipline by telling ourselves 'We can't afford it' and refusing to take on further credit obligations. . . .
>
> 3. Make a budget and stick to it.
>
> 4. Cut expenses by distinguishing between wants and needs. Economize by controlling the use of goods, services, and energy.
>
> 5. Increase homemaking skills and have family members complete home and car repairs, when feasible.
>
> 6. Invest wisely. Avoid speculations and get-rich-quick schemes. (*Ensign*, May 1981, p. 87.)

Obviously, there are some legitimate areas where debt must be incurred. These would include a home mortgage and possibly the need to borrow for legitimate, sound business investments and "reasonable debt for education." (See "The Dangerous Threat of Increasing Indebtedness," *Church News*, 17 March 1962, p. 13; and "Stay Free from Debt," ibid., 12 April 1975, p. 18.)

Insurance and Retirement Planning

I once had a friend who should have known better than not to plan for his retirement. He said to me that he was not saving anything for retirement because the Second Coming would be here before then. How foolish! We need to plan for retirement as if the Second Coming would not come in our lifetime yet live our lives in such a way that we would be worthy of greeting the Savior if he did come during our lifetime.

On one occasion, President Lorenzo Snow spoke of those who refused to put down their roots and live in the present because of their singular focus on anticipated events of the future: "The time is speedily coming—we do not want to talk very much, though, about going to Jackson County, Missouri, because through our foolishness and weakness we would not care anything about building houses and making ourselves comfortable here. I know when we first started a colony in Brigham City, the people generally thought it was nonsense, perfectly useless, to plant peach trees, apple trees, currant bushes and the like, because we were going to Jackson County so speedily; and it was with the utmost effort that we were enabled to disabuse them of this idea." (CR, April 1898, p. 64.)

We need to "plant" not only for ourselves, but also for those who will follow after us. I believe the Lord taught this principle to the Saints in Ohio in an 1831 revelation when he said the land would be consecrated unto them "for a little season" and then admonished them to "act upon this land as for years." (D&C 51:16–17.)

Because "no man knoweth" the exact time of the Second Coming, all should "act upon this land as for years," preparing for the future. Too many are not adequately providing for the future or falsely believe they can depend upon what in fact has become an endangered social security system. A recent report on retirees is frightening: "Financial prospects for many Americans on the eve of retirement are grim: Forty percent have no pension income other than Social Security. One in five households has no assets. One in seven individuals has no health insurance. And 20 percent are disabled.

"Those are the principal findings of the largest federal study of Americans approaching retirement ever undertaken."

("Older Americans Face Uncertain Future," *Salt Lake Tribune,* 18 June 1993, p. A1.)

Planning for the future includes providing adequate insurance protection for oneself and any dependents. President N. Eldon Tanner counseled: "Nothing seems so certain as the unexpected in our lives. With rising medical costs, health insurance is the only way most families can meet serious accident, illness, or maternity costs, particularly those for premature births. Life insurance provides income continuation when the provider prematurely dies. Every family should make provision for proper health and life insurance." (*Ensign,* November 1979, p. 82.)

With regard to the amount of insurance one should obtain, perhaps the words of Jacob would suffice: "O be wise; what can I say more?" (Jacob 6:12.)

The Most Important Preparation

So far in this chapter we have focused on temporal preparedness. This is appropriate, for there is an interrelationship between temporal and spiritual matters, expressed in the Lord's declaration that "all things unto me are spiritual." (D&C 29:34.) "It has always been a cardinal teaching with the Latter-day Saints," said President Joseph F. Smith, "that a religion which has not the power to save the people temporally and make them prosperous and happy here cannot be depended upon to save them spiritually, and exalt them in the life to come." (As quoted in *EM,* s.v. "Welfare Services.")

While serving in the Presiding Bishopric of the Church, Bishop J. Richard Clarke stated, "Most important of all, brothers and sisters, with all our storing, let us store righteousness that we may stand approved of the Lord." (*Ensign,* November 1980, p. 84.) Elder John Longden, who served as a General Authority from 1951 until his death in 1969, wisely observed, "We may survive physically and materially but unless we survive spiritually these things avail nothing." (CR, October 1960, p. 112.)

The storage of food, clothing, and fuel and the avoidance of debt will ultimately mean little if we have not stored up sufficient spiritual oil to keep our lamps lit and shining brightly. In commenting on the parable of the ten virgins, half of whom were wise enough to have sufficient oil in their lamps and half of whom were foolishly unprepared, President Spencer W. Kimball said: "I believe that the Ten Virgins represent the people of the Church of Jesus Christ. . . . They had the saving, exalting gospel, but it had not been made the center of their lives." (*Faith Precedes the Miracle*, Salt Lake City: Deseret Book Co., 1972, pp. 253–54; see also Matthew 25:1–13.)

While serving as a member of the Quorum of the Twelve Apostles, Elder Harold B. Lee spoke of some requisites for preparing ourselves to meet and associate with the Savior and the Saints who are worthy of His presence:

> Now, I have asked myself, this being the time to prepare for the millennial reign, how shall we set about to prepare a people to receive the coming of the Lord? . . . This preparation demands first that a people, to receive the coming of the Lord, must be taught the personality and the nature of God and his Son, Jesus Christ. . . .
>
> Another requisite . . . demands that the people be taught to accept the divinity of the mission of Jesus as the Savior of the world. . . .
>
> We must be cleansed and purified and sanctified to be made worthy to receive and abide that holy presence. . . .
>
> We must accept the divine mission of the Prophet Joseph Smith as the instrumentality through which the restoration of the gospel and the organization of the Church of Jesus Christ was accomplished. (*Improvement Era*, December 1956, pp. 941–42.)

In other words, strengthening one's testimony is one of the best ways to prepare for Christ's coming. President Harold B. Lee stated, "There is nothing better that we can do to prepare ourselves spiritually than to read the Book of Mormon." (*Improvement Era*, January 1969, p. 13.) "In the Book of Mormon we find a pattern for preparing for the Second Coming" said President Ezra Taft Benson, who then gave these

181

insights: "A major portion of the book centers on the few decades just prior to Christ's coming to America. By careful study of that time period, we can determine why some were destroyed in the terrible judgments that preceded His coming and what brought others to stand at the temple in the land of Bountiful and thrust their hands into the wounds of His hands and feet." (*Ensign*, November 1986, pp. 6–7.)

It is of interest to note that Sister Virginia Lee Perry, deceased wife of Elder L. Tom Perry of the Quorum of the Twelve Apostles, made the Book of Mormon a "fundamental part of her storage program." In addition to the cans of wheat and other food supplies, Sister Perry maintained "a supply of a dozen copies of the Book of Mormon," true spiritual food that she replenished as regularly as she gave them out. (*Ensign*, May 1975, p. 33.)

Perhaps an appropriate conclusion to this chapter on preparing for the Second Coming is the following sure witness by Elder Neal A. Maxwell: "An economic depression would be grim, but it would not change the reality of immortality. The inevitability of the second coming is not affected by the unpredictability of the stock market. . . . A case of cancer does not cancel the promises of the temple endowment." Elder Maxwell adds this assurance: "All that matters is gloriously intact. The promises are in place. It is up to us to perform." (*Notwithstanding My Weakness*, Salt Lake City: Deseret Book Co., 1981, p. 57.)

Chapter 20

THE SIGN OF THE SON OF MAN

"There will be wars and rumors of wars, signs in the heavens above and on the earth beneath, the sun turned into darkness and the moon to blood, earthquakes in divers places, the seas heaving beyond their bounds; then will appear one grand sign of the Son of Man in Heaven. But what will the world do? They will say it is a planet, a comet. . . . But the Son of Man will come as the sign of the coming of the Son of Man, which will be as the light of the morning cometh out of the east."
—*HC*, 5:337

Signs in the Sun, Moon, and Stars

In taking to task the scurrilous writings of one newspaper of his day, the Prophet Joseph Smith commented on the newspaper's report of a claim that a Mr. Hyrum Redding of Ogle County, Illinois, had already "seen the sign of the Son of Man." The Prophet noted that the Lord would reveal such an event to His earthly prophet and that no man had yet seen such a sign, "nor will any man, until after the sun shall have been darkened and the moon bathed in blood." (*HC*, 5:290–91.)

There are Biblical and latter-day references to a forthcoming time preceding the Second Coming when great signs shall be shown that will affect the sun, moon, and stars. For example, during his nocturnal visit to Joseph Smith on September 21, 1823, the angel Moroni quoted from the Old Testament prophet Joel: "And I will shew wonders in the heavens and in the earth, blood, and fire, and pillars of smoke. The sun shall be turned into darkness, and the moon into blood, before the great and the terrible day of the Lord come." (Joel 2:30–31; see also JS–H 1:41.)

The prophet Isaiah proclaimed: "Behold the day of the Lord cometh, cruel both with wrath and fierce anger, to lay the land desolate: and he shall destroy the sinners thereof out of it. For the stars of heaven and the constellations thereof shall not give their light: the sun shall be darkened in his going forth, and the moon shall not cause her light to shine." (Isaiah 13:9–10.) John the Revelator spoke of these signs in the heavens occurring at the time the "sixth seal" was to be opened: "And I beheld when he had opened the sixth seal, and, lo, there was a great earthquake; and the sun became black as sackcloth of hair, and the moon became as blood; and the stars of heaven fell unto the earth, even as a fig tree casteth her untimely figs, when she is shaken of a mighty wind." (Revelation 6:12–13.)

The Savior warned of the terrible days of trial prior to his coming and declared, "Immediately after the tribulation of those days shall the sun be darkened, and the moon shall not give her light, and the stars shall fall from heaven, and the powers of the heavens shall be shaken." (Matthew 24:29; see also Joseph Smith–Matthew 1:33.) The Lord affirmed these signs in several latter-day revelations given to the Prophet Joseph Smith: "But, behold, I say unto you that before this great day [the Second Coming] shall come the sun shall be darkened, and the moon shall be turned into blood, and the stars shall fall from heaven, and there shall be greater signs in heaven above and in the earth beneath." (D&C 29:14; see also 34:9; 45:42; 88:87; 133:49.)

One of the means whereby these signs could occur is suggested by a statement of President Brigham Young, who declared, "When man fell, the earth fell into space, and took up its abode in this planetary system, and the sun became our light." (JD, 17:143.) At some future point this earth will be rolled back into its former paradisiacal planetary orbit. At that time its source of light will be from God's presence rather than from the sun. (This is similar to the source of light in the New Jerusalem Temple; see chapter 12.) In this sense, then, the face of the sun will be hidden or darkened. (See *DCE*, pp. 364, 435, 570.)

Another possible means whereby the sun might be darkened is by being obscured by heavy clouds of volcanic ash, such as what might have occurred in ancient America at the time of the Crucifixion (see 3 Nephi 8:20–23) or because of smoke from great fires caused by warfare. Recall the scenes of the blackened skies and consequent obliterated sun when the invading Iraqis set fire to the oil fields of Kuwait during the Persian Gulf War.

How shall the moon be turned into blood? This is yet to be revealed. However, its blood-red color might be a result of volcanic ash or nuclear dust and clouds in the atmosphere. The moon might also undergo a real or perceived change of color as a result of its changed condition when the earth is rolled back into its terrestrial or paradisiacal orbit.

What about the stars falling from heaven? Once again, the starry spectacle could occur when the earth is rolled back to its former orbit near the abode of God. In the process of such a move, as the earth hurtles through space, it could well appear that the stars are falling from the heavens.

Other explanations for the falling stars could be meteor showers or missiles and bombs streaking through the skies. Dr. Sidney B. Sperry suggested that the falling stars spoken of "are probably not the distant suns we see in space, but the falling of bodies that will create tremendous light when they pass through the layers of our earthly atmosphere." (*Doctrine and Covenants Compendium*, Salt Lake City: Bookcraft, 1960, p. 434.)

Whatever the final cause of these heavenly wonders may be, it seems apparent that these signs will be visible and will precede the great sign of the Son of Man.

The Great Sign Seen by All

Isaiah, who pronounced so many messianic prophesies, declared, "And the glory of the Lord shall be revealed, and all flesh shall see it together: for the mouth of the Lord hath spoken it." (Isaiah 40:5.)

The Savior Himself prophesied that after the above-mentioned heavenly wonders occur, "then shall appear the sign of the Son of man in heaven: and then shall all the tribes of the earth mourn, and they shall see the Son of man coming in the clouds of heaven with power and great glory." (Matthew 24:30.) In latter-day revelation, He reaffirmed that "all people shall see [the great sign in heaven] together." (D&C 88:93; see also 101:23.)

What is this great sign that all people shall see? That it will be accompanied by a very brilliant and visible light is evidenced by the words of Jesus, who said, "As the light of the morning cometh out of the east, and shineth even unto the west, and covereth the whole earth, so shall also the coming of the Son of Man be." (JS–M 1:26.)

There is at least one tradition suggesting that this great sign will be "the return of the City of Enoch to the earth." (Wandle Mace, in "Sayings of Joseph Smith as reported by those who claimed to hear him make the statements," JSP.) We do know that the Savior will be accompanied by the righteous hosts of heaven, including the apostles from His earthly ministry: "For I will reveal myself from heaven with power and great glory, with all the hosts thereof, and dwell in righteousness with men on earth a thousand years, and the wicked shall not stand. And again, verily, verily, I say unto you, and it hath gone forth in a firm decree, by the will of the Father, that mine apostles, the Twelve which were with me in my ministry at Jerusalem, shall stand at my right hand at the day of my coming in a pillar of fire, being clothed with robes of righteousness, with crowns upon their heads, in glory even as I am, to judge the whole house of Israel, even as many as have loved me and kept my commandments, and none else." (D&C 29:11–12.)

Although the entire population of this planet will see the sign, whatever it may be, the Prophet Joseph indicated that the world "will say it is a planet, a comet." (*HC*, 5:337.) As with other signs, spiritually discerning people will recognize the great sign's true meaning and prepare themselves to worship the Son of God. They understand the significance of the following words of the Lord: "And it shall come to pass that he that feareth me shall be looking forth for the great day of the Lord to come, even for the signs of the coming of the Son of Man. And they shall see signs and wonders, for they shall be shown forth in the heavens above, and in the earth beneath. . . . And then they shall look for me, and, behold, I will come; and they shall see me in the clouds of heaven, clothed with power and great glory; with all the holy angels; and he that watches not for me shall be cut off." (D&C 45:39–40, 44.)

And so we watch . . . and wait to see the grand sign of the coming of the Son of Man.

Chapter 21

THE SAVIOR COMES AGAIN

"And his feet shall stand in that day upon the mount of Olives, which is before Jerusalem on the east, and the mount of Olives shall cleave in the midst thereof toward the east and toward the west, and there shall be a very great valley; and half of the mountain shall remove toward the north, and half of it toward the south."

—(ZECHARIAH 14:4.)

The Savior's Coming in Relation to Armageddon

The terrible nature of Armageddon has already been discussed in chapter 10. Its relationship to the Second Coming has been described by Elder Bruce R. McConkie:

> When the Lord Jesus comes again, it will be not as the Prince of Peace, not as the Suffering Servant, not as one who descends below all things, but as the Man of War and the God of Battles who will wage war and overthrow kingdoms and spread destruction as he did when Joshua and Gideon and David led his people anciently. *The Millennial era will not be ushered in by the righteousness of the people. Christ will come in the midst of war such as has never been known before in the whole history of the world.* All the nations of the earth will be engaged. Those who oppose freedom and liberty and Christianity and the Jews will attack Jerusalem. The focal point will be the ancient battlegrounds of Megiddo and Armageddon. In the midst of this war, "this same Jesus" who ascended from Olivet "shall so come in like manner" as he went up into heaven. (Acts 1:11.) His feet shall once again stand upon the Mount of Olives. And in the Valley of Jehoshaphat, which is between

188

Jerusalem and Olivet, he shall sit to judge the heathen nations. (*NWAF,* p. 637; italics added.)

Jerusalem will be under a terrible siege when the Savior appears. The prophet Zechariah described the plight of the city's inhabitants: "For I will gather all nations against Jerusalem to battle; and the city shall be taken, and the houses rifled, and the women ravished; and half of the city shall go forth into captivity, and the residue of the people shall not be cut off from the city." (Zechariah 14:2.) Isaiah also described the cruelty to be inflicted upon Jerusalem's citizens and "every one that is joined unto them": "Their children also shall be dashed to pieces before their eyes; their houses shall be spoiled, and their wives ravished." (Isaiah 13:15–16.)

Only the coming of Jesus Christ will save the people from utter destruction. The valley created by the splitting of the Mount of Olives will offer an escape route for the beleaguered people, and then they will see and recognize their true Messiah, even Jesus Christ: "And then shall the Jews look upon me and say: What are these wounds in thine hands and in thy feet? Then shall they know that I am the Lord; for I will say unto them: These wounds are the wounds with which I was wounded in the house of my friends. I am he who was lifted up. I am Jesus that was crucified. I am the Son of God. And then shall they weep because of their iniquities; then shall they lament because they persecuted their king." (D&C 45:51–53; see also Zechariah 12:10; 13:6.)

Not only the Jews, but those in all nations shall weep and mourn because of their unbelief and wickedness. The more righteous of the people will repent and be baptized, cleansing them of their "sin and uncleanness." (See Zechariah 13:1.)

The Great Earthquake

Latter-day revelation informs us that the Savior's voice "shall be heard among all people," and it shall "break down the mountains, and the valleys shall not be found." (D&C 133:21–22.) Indeed, His very presence "shall be as the melting fire that burneth, and as the fire which causeth the waters to boil." When He comes "the mountains [shall] flow down." (D&C 133:41, 44.)

As noted in chapter 3, the occurrence of a great earthquake at the time of the Second Coming will split the Mount of Olives and shake the entire earth. John the Revelator tells us that "cities of the nations" of the world will fall as a result of this great quake and that islands will flee and mountains would disappear. (Revelation 16:18, 20.)

The prophet Micah described the effect of the Lord's coming: "For, behold, the Lord cometh forth out of his place, and will come down, and tread upon the high places of the earth. And the mountains shall be molten under him, and the valleys shall be cleft, as wax before the fire, and as the waters that are poured down a steep place." (Micah 1:3–4.) Another Old Testament prophet, Ezekiel, added this description of the shaking of the earth at Christ's appearance: "And it shall come to pass at the same time when Gog shall come against the land of Israel, saith the Lord God, that my fury shall come up in my face. For in my jealousy and in the fire of my wrath have I spoken, Surely in that day there shall be a great shaking in the land of Israel; So that the fishes of the sea, and the fowls of the heaven, and the beasts of the field, and all creeping things that creep upon the earth, and all the men that are upon the face of the earth, shall shake at my presence, and the mountains shall be thrown down, and the steep places shall fall, and every wall shall fall to the ground." (Ezekiel 38:18–20.)

John the Revelator gave specific numbers to the destruction and death that would take place in Jerusalem during this great earthquake: "And the same hour was there a great earthquake, and the tenth part of the city fell, and in the earthquake were slain of men seven thousand: and the remnant were affrighted, and gave glory to the God of heaven." (Revelation 11:13.)

Dr. Richard D. Draper suggests that the tenth represents "the Lord's portion—his tithe that he will demand of the wicked." He further suggests that "the figure seven thousand. . . . is probably not to be taken literally. Rather, it signifies . . . fullness and completeness." (*OSS*, p. 124.)

The Savior's Red Apparel

In contrast to the clothing "of most exquisite whiteness" (Joseph Smith–History 1:31) normally attributed to heavenly beings, when the Savior appears He "shall be red in his apparel, and his garments like him that treadeth the wine-vat." (D&C 133:48; see also Isaiah 63:1–3.) This could be symbolic of the blood of the wicked who are slain at His coming, for the Lord declared, "And I have trampled them in my fury, and I did tread upon them in mine anger, and their blood have I sprinkled upon my garments, and stained all my raiment; for this was the day of vengeance which was in my heart." (D&C 133:51.)

His red apparel could also be representative of the blood He shed during His atoning sacrifice, having "trodden the wine-press alone." (D&C 76:107; 88:106; 133:50.) Elder Neal A. Maxwell observed: "Having bled at every pore, how red His raiment must have been in Gethsemane, how crimson that cloak!

"No wonder, when Christ comes in power and glory, that He will come in reminding red attire (see D&C 133:48), signifying not only the winepress of wrath, but also to bring to our remembrance how He suffered for each of us in Gethsemane and on Calvary!" (*Ensign*, May 1987, p. 72; see also Luke 22:44; D&C 19:18.)

144,000 to Stand with the Savior

One of the intriguing aspects of the Savior's second coming and the ushering in of the Millennium is the appearance of the 144,000 with Him. John the Revelator spoke of these being "sealed in their foreheads" (Revelation 7:2–8) and then said, "And I looked, and, lo, a Lamb stood on the mount Sion, and with him an hundred forty and four thousand, having his

Father's name written in their foreheads." (Revelation 14:1; see also D&C 133:17–18.)

Latter-day revelation gives understanding to the mission of this body of 144,000:

"Q. What are we to understand by sealing the one hundred and forty-four thousand, out of all the tribes of Israel—twelve thousand out of every tribe?

"A. We are to understand that those who are sealed are high priests, ordained unto the holy order of God, to administer the everlasting gospel; for they are they who are ordained out of every nation, kindred, tongue, and people, by the angels *to whom is given power over the nations of the earth, to bring as many as will come to the church of the Firstborn.*" (D&C 77:11; italics added.)

Thus, it appears that this 144,000 will have a special missionary assignment. President Joseph Fielding Smith wrote: "This certainly is a great honor to be one of the 144 thousand who are specially called by the power of 'the angels to whom is given power over the nations of the earth,' to bring souls unto Christ. John the Apostle had the great desire to bring souls to Christ. Three of the Nephite disciples likewise sought this great honor and it was granted to them. It is one of the noblest desires that a man can have. It will be a wonderful blessing to those who are called in this great group." (*CHMR*, 1:302.)

The Prophet Joseph Smith referred to the 144,000 as "saviors on Mount Zion" and added they would be accompanied by "an innumerable host that no man can number." (*HC*, 6:365.)

Regarding the location of the "Mount Zion" where they will appear, Elder Bruce R. McConkie has written:

> All of the references to Mount Zion which talk of the Second Coming and related latter-day events appear to have in mind the new Mount Zion in Jackson County, Missouri. Thus we read [in D&C 133:17–18]: "Prepare ye the way of the Lord, and make his paths straight, for the hour of his coming is nigh—When the Lamb shall stand upon Mount Zion, and with him a hundred and forty-four

thousand, having his Father's name written on their fore-heads."

Then comes this explanatory comment [in verse 20] which shows the Lord will appear many places at his coming: "For behold, he shall stand upon the mount of Olivet, and upon the mighty ocean, even the great deep, and upon the islands of the sea, and upon the land of Zion." And then, [in verses 21–22,] using some language borrowed from Rev[elation] 14:2, the revelation continues: "And he shall utter his voice out of Zion, and he shall speak from Jerusalem, and his voice shall be heard among all people; And it shall be a voice as the voice of many waters, and as the voice of a great thunder, which shall break down the mountains, and the valleys shall not be found." (D&C 133:17–22.)

It seems clear that the Lord and his exalted associates shall stand in glory upon the American Mount Zion, although it may well be that in his numerous other appearances, including that on the Mount of Olivet, which is itself but a few stones' throw from old Mount Zion, he shall also be accompanied by the 144,000 high priests, "for they follow the Lamb whithersoever he goeth." [Revelation 14:4.] (*DNTC*, 3:525–26.)

Just how the Savior will deploy this force of 144,000 special emissaries remains to be revealed. It seems obvious that because of the "innumerable host" that will accompany them, missionary work will move forward with great zeal among those who escape the wrath of God when the world as we now know it comes to an end.

Chapter 22

THE END OF THE WORLD

"For, behold the day cometh, that shall burn as an oven; and all the proud, yea, and all that do wickedly, shall be stubble: and the day that cometh shall burn them up, saith the Lord of hosts, that it shall leave them neither root nor branch."

—MALACHI 4:1

The Great and Dreadful Day

An Old Testament prophecy refers to the second coming of Jesus Christ as "the great and dreadful day of the Lord." (Malachi 4:5.) It is significant that the resurrected Savior recited this prophecy to the ancient people of the Americas during His visit with them. (See 3 Nephi 24:1; 25:5.) It is also of interest to note that the angel Moroni quoted this statement three times on the night he first visited young Joseph Smith in 1823. (See Joseph Smith–History 1:36–38, 44–46.) The scripture is also repeated twice in the Doctrine and Covenants. (See D&C 2:1; 110:14.) Thus, reference to "the great and dreadful day of the Lord" appears in all four standard works of The Church of Jesus Christ of Latter-day Saints.

This "great and dreadful day" is also referred to by other descriptive terms such as the "day of visitation, and of judgment, and of indignation" (D&C 56:16), the "day of wrath" (D&C 63:6), the "day of vengeance" (D&C 133:51), and the "day . . . that shall burn as an oven" (Malachi 4:1; D&C 133:64).

Such a day will truly be a *great* day to those who are righteous, but to the wicked it shall be a *dreadful* day of exquisite sorrow. Elder Orson Pratt defined this momentous day as follows: "The day in which wickedness should be entirely swept from the earth, and no remnants of the wicked left, when every branch of them and every root of them should become as stubble, and be consumed from the face of the earth." (*JD*, 7:77.)

The Wicked Shall Be Burned

The great and dreadful day of the Lord is the promised day in which the wheat and tares will no longer be allowed to grow together (see Matthew 13:24–30; D&C 86:1–11), for the tares, or the wicked, will be "bound in bundles to be burned" (JST, Matthew 13:29), while the wheat, or the righteous, shall be "secured in the garners to possess eternal life, and be crowned with celestial glory" (D&C 101:65).

The Prophet Joseph's inspired rendering of the parable of the wheat and the tares declares: "The harvest is the end of the world, or the destruction of the wicked. The reapers are the angels or the messengers sent of heaven. As, therefore, the tares are gathered and burned in the fire, so shall it be in the end of this world, or the destruction of the wicked. . . . For the world shall be burned with fire." (JST, Matthew 13:39–42, 44.)

The Book of Mormon similarly records the burning of the wicked: "For behold, saith the prophet, the time cometh speedily that Satan shall have no more power over the hearts of the children of men; for the day soon cometh that all the proud and they who do wickedly shall be as stubble; and the day cometh that they must be burned." (1 Nephi 22:15.)

As the earth was cleansed of wickedness in the days of Noah through the great flood, at the Second Coming the earth will be cleansed by fire so that "wickedness shall not be upon the earth." (D&C 29:9.) While serving as an editor of the official Church publication in Nauvoo, Elder John Taylor wrote: "The earth, a part of the creation of God, has [fulfilled] and will fulfil the measure of its creation. It has been baptized by water, it will be baptized by fire." (*Times and Seasons*, 15 January 1844, p. 408.) The baptism of fire will be preparatory to the final change that will occur at the end of the Millennium when the earth will be transformed into a celestial sphere and take up its abode in the presence of God.

The Fall of Babylon

The burning of the wicked is the destruction of the kingdom of Babylon—the symbol of all that is wicked and evil. While Babylon anciently was an actual city of wickedness, in modern times the Lord referred to the name as a representation of those in all nations whose wicked actions would qualify them for citizenship in ancient Babylon. His plea has been, "Go ye out from among the nations, even from Babylon, from the midst of wickedness, which is spiritual Babylon." (D&C 133:14.)

Spiritual Babylon is also referred to as "the great whore, which did corrupt the earth" (Revelation 19:2), the "church of the devil [and the] mother of abominations" (1 Nephi 14:10), and "the great and abominable church" (D&C 29:21). The Lord gave further clarification regarding those who would be classified among Babylon: "Wherefore, he that fighteth against Zion, both Jew and Gentile, both bond and free, both male and female, shall perish; for they are they who are the whore of all the earth; for they who are not for me are against me, saith our God." (2 Nephi 10:16.)

The Apostle John from the New Testament and Nephi from the Book of Mormon both refer to Babylon as "the great whore that sitteth upon many waters." (Revelation 17:1; see also verse 15; 1 Nephi 14:11.) The description of "many waters" is symbolic of the power Babylon has to enslave many nations and people with her wicked ways.

Elder Bruce R. McConkie provided the following definition of Babylon and her forthcoming destruction:

> The destruction of Gog and Magog constitutes the fall of Babylon, the overthrow of the great and abominable church, and the destruction of the wicked. Babylon is the world; it is carnality, sensuality, and devilishness; it is the

church of the devil; it is every religious and political kingdom and power that is not of God. Within its folds are
found Catholics, Protestants, and Latter-day Saints; com-
munists, worldly peoples, and godless nations; the Islamics,
the Buddhists, and all who worship any God but the Lord;
atheists, humanists, and evolutionists—yes, within its folds
are all those who live after the manner of the world. And
they all "shall be cast down by devouring fire" (D&C
29:21), as Ezekiel said with reference to Gog and Magog.
(*NWAF*, pp. 638–39.)

The Destruction of the Wicked

When the Prophet Joseph Smith declared that "the destruction
of the wicked . . . is the end of the world" (Joseph Smith–
Matthew 1:4), he was referring to the end of wickedness in the
world and not to the end of the earth, for that time will come
at the end of the Millennium when the earth as we now know it
will be changed and become a celestial sphere. (See chapter
26.)

When the wicked are destroyed, those of a telestial nature
will be swept from the face of the earth, and only those capable of living celestial and terrestrial lives will remain. While
this is not the final judgment, which will come at the end of the
Millennium, it is a judgment that illustrates the efficacy of
these principles: "For he who is not able to abide the law of a
celestial kingdom cannot abide a celestial glory. And he who
cannot abide the law of a terrestrial kingdom cannot abide a
terrestrial glory." (D&C 88:22–23.)

The millennial earth will be a terrestrial sphere, and those
who cannot live at this level will not be permitted to live
there, at least until the "little season" at the end of the one-
thousand-year period. President Joseph Fielding Smith
explained: "When the reign of Jesus Christ comes during the
millennium, *only those who have lived the telestial law will be
removed.* The earth will be cleansed of all its corruption and
wickedness. Those who have lived *virtuous lives,* who have been
honest in their dealings with their fellow men and have *endeav-*

ored to do good to the best of their understanding, shall remain." (*DS,* 3:62.)

The Lord revealed that "every corruptible thing, both of man, or of the beasts of the field, or of the fowls of the heavens, or of the fish of the sea, that dwells upon all the face of the earth, shall be consumed." (D&C 101:24.)

Satan to Be Bound

Along with the destruction of the wicked will come the binding of Satan. The Lord revealed that at the beginning of the Millennium, "Satan shall be bound, that old serpent, who is called the devil, and shall not be loosed for the space of a thousand years." (D&C 88:110.) During that period of time, "Satan shall not have power to tempt any man" (D&C 101:28), and he "shall have no place in the hearts of the children of men" (D&C 45:55).

The Revelator described the binding of Satan: "And I saw an angel come down from heaven, having the key of the bottomless pit and a great chain in his hand. And he laid hold on the dragon, that old serpent, which is the Devil, and Satan, and bound him a thousand years." (Revelation 20:1–2.)

The limitation of the adversary's power was also described by Nephi: "For behold, saith the prophet, the time cometh speedily that Satan shall have no more power over the hearts of the children of men; for the day soon cometh that all the proud and they who do wickedly shall be as stubble; and the day cometh that they must be burned. . . . And because of the righteousness of his [God's] people, Satan has no power; wherefore, he cannot be loosed for the space of many years; for he hath no power over the hearts of the people, for they dwell in righteousness, and the Holy One of Israel reigneth." (1 Nephi 22:15, 26.)

There are several points of view regarding the binding of Satan. President Joseph Fielding Smith explained the limitation of Satan's power this way: "There are many among us who teach that the binding of Satan will be merely the binding which those dwelling on the earth will place upon him by their refusal to hear his enticings. This is not so. He will not have the privilege during that period of time to tempt any man." (*CHMR*, 1:192.)

President Daniel H. Wells, counselor to Brigham Young, held a different view, believing that the righteousness of the people would bind Lucifer: "How is [the binding of Satan] to be accomplished? By our becoming so impregnated with the principles of the Gospel—with the Holy Ghost—that the enemy will have no place in us or in our families. . . . He will be chained to all intents and purposes when he can have no influence—no power—no tabernacles into which he can enter." (*JD*, 5:43.) This same position was taken by Elder Bruce R. McConkie, who stated:

> What does it mean to bind Satan? How is he bound? Our revelation says: "And in that day Satan shall not have power to tempt any man." (D&C 101:28.) Does this mean that power is withdrawn from Satan so that he can no longer entice men to do evil? Or does it mean that men no longer succumb to his enticements because their hearts are so set on righteousness that they refuse to forsake that which is good to follow him who is evil? Clearly it means the latter. Satan was not bound in heaven, in the very presence of God, in the sense that he was denied the right and power to preach false doctrine and to invite men to walk away from that God whose children they were; nay, in this sense, he could not have been bound in heaven, for even he must have his agency.
>
> How, then, will Satan be bound during the Millennium? It will be by the righteousness of the people. . . . The destruction of the wicked sets the stage for millennial righteousness. (*MM*, p. 668.)

However he is bound, the fact is that his reign of blood and terror on this earth will be terminated for a millennium. Peace will prevail and enmity will cease for a thousand years. The work of the kingdom will move forward under the direction of Him whose kingdom it is, for "Christ will reign personally upon the earth." (Articles of Faith 1:10.)

SECTION 5

THE MILLENNIUM

Chapter 23

THE MILLENNIUM: RIGHTEOUSNESS PREVAILS

"For I will reveal myself from heaven with power and great glory, with all the hosts thereof, and dwell in righteousness with men on earth a thousand years, and the wicked shall not stand."

—D&C 29:11

The First Resurrection: A Look Back

On the Sunday morning following His crucifixion, Jesus Christ became the "first fruits" of the Resurrection as He rose from the grave and defeated death. But He was not alone, for following His resurrection, "the graves were opened; and many bodies of the saints which slept arose." (Matthew 27:52; see also 3 Nephi 23:6–13.)

Elder Parley P. Pratt, one of the original apostles of this last dispensation, described this "first resurrection": "The first general resurrection took place in connection with the resurrection of Jesus Christ. This included the Saints and Prophets of both hemispheres, from Adam down to John the Baptist; or, in other words, all those who died in Christ before His resurrection." (*Key To Theology,* Liverpool: Albert Carrington, 1883, p. 138.)

Among those resurrected at the time of Christ's resurrection were those who had been temporarily spared from death through the process of translation. These translated beings, who included Moses and Elijah, went through an instantaneous death and resurrection at the time. President Joseph Fielding Smith explained the reason for their translation:

> Elijah and Moses were preserved from death: because *they had a mission to perform,* and it had to be performed *before* the crucifixion of the Son of God, and *it could not be done in the spirit. They had to have tangible bodies.* Christ is the first fruits of the resurrection; therefore if any former prophets had a work to perform preparatory to the mission of the Son of God, or to the dispensation of the meridian of times, it was essential that they be preserved to fulfill that mission *in the flesh.* . . . The Lord preserved [Moses], so that he could come at the proper time and *restore his keys,* on the heads of Peter, James, and John, who stood at the head of the dispensation of the meridian of time. He reserved Elijah from death that he might also come and bestow his keys upon the heads of Peter, James, and John and prepare them for their ministry. (*DS,* 2:110–11.)

Because there was no necessity for Moses and Elijah to remain as translated beings following the resurrection of Christ, they went through death and resurrection in the twinkling of an eye. Thus, when they restored priesthood keys to the Prophet Joseph Smith and Oliver Cowdery in 1836 (see D&C 110), they did so as resurrected beings.

Since the time of the first resurrection, there have been others who have been granted translated bodies in order to continue their ministry upon this earth, notably the Apostle John (see D&C 7) and the Three Nephite Disciples (see 3 Nephi 28.) There have also been individuals resurrected since the time of Christ who had special missions to perform in the flesh, namely Peter, James, and Moroni. The former two joined with the Apostle John in restoring the keys of the Melchizedek Priesthood to Joseph Smith and Oliver Cowdery in 1829. (See D&C 27:12.) Moroni appeared to the Prophet as a resurrected angel to instruct him regarding the translation of the Book of Mormon. (See JS–H 1:27–54.)

As to where resurrected beings now reside, we turn again to the writings of Elder Parley P. Pratt: "Those raised left the earth and ascended, or were transplanted far on high, with the risen Jesus, to the glorified mansions of His Father, or to some planetary system already redeemed and glorified. The reasons for thus leaving the earth are obvious. Our planet was still in its rudimental state, and therefore subject to the rule of sin and death. It was necessary that it should continue thus, until the full time of redemption should arrive; it was, therefore, entirely unfitted for the residence of immortal man." (Pratt, *Key to Theology,* p. 139.)

It is noteworthy to consider the present status of three ancient prophets who were resurrected at the time of Christ. The Lord revealed that "Abraham, . . . Isaac, . . . and Jacob . . . have entered into their exaltation, according to the promises, and sit upon thrones, and are not angels but are gods." (D&C 132:37.)

Millennial Resurrection of the Righteous

With few exceptions, all who have died from the time of Christ to the present await the day when their spirits shall be reunited with the flesh. To the righteous, this resurrection—the resurrection of the just—will come at the beginning of the Millennium. "While there was a general resurrection of the righteous at the time Christ arose from the dead," declared President Joseph Fielding Smith, "it is customary for us to speak of the resurrection of the righteous at the Second Coming of Christ as the *first resurrection.* It is the first *to us,* for we have little thought or concern over that which is past. The Lord has promised that at the time of his Second Advent the graves will be opened, and the just shall come forth to reign with him on the earth for a thousand years." (*DS,* 2:295.)

Elder Bruce R. McConkie gave further understanding to the meaning of the "first resurrection": "No matter when they lived, the righteous dead, those destined to gain eternal life in our Father's kingdom, always come forth in the next available resurrection. That resurrection to them is the first resurrection." (*MM,* p. 634.)

Those who receive patriarchal promises that they shall be

raised in the "*morning* of the first resurrection" are those who are worthy to be "first caught up to meet him" in the heavens prior to His earthly descent. (D&C 88:97–98.)

As discussed in chapter 21, when Christ returns at His second coming, He will be accompanied by a specially designated group of 144,000 (see Revelation 14:1; D&C 133:18), as well as an innumerable company of resurrected Saints who have qualified for celestial glory (see D&C 76:50–70). In addition, "the saints that are upon the earth, who are alive shall be quickened and be caught up to meet him." (D&C 88:96; see also 1 Thessalonians 4:16–17.)

While the worthy Saints among the living are "quickened and . . . caught up to meet him," it seems reasonable to believe that not all will pass through death and resurrection at this time. In order for mortal children to be born during the Millennium, they must be begotten by mortal parents. Much is yet to be revealed regarding these matters.

Those who are resurrected after the morning of the first resurrection are "those who are Christ's at his coming." (D&C 88:99.) President Joseph Fielding Smith explained their status: "In this resurrection will come forth those of the *terrestrial order,* who were not worthy to be caught up to meet him, but who are worthy to come forth to enjoy the millennial reign." (*DS,* 2:296–97.)

Only those worthy of celestial or terrestrial glory will inhabit the earth during the Millennium. All others must wait for the resurrection of the unjust when the thousand years of peace will be disrupted for a little season prior to the final judgment. Until then, the wicked and unrepentant remain unresurrected. President Joseph Fielding Smith noted: "It is decreed that the unrighteous shall have to spend their time during this thousand years in the prison house prepared for them where they can repent and cleanse themselves through the things which they shall suffer." (*DS,* 3:60.) Such, for example, will be the status of King David, whose adulterous relationship with

Bathsheba led him to take the life of the faithful Uriah. (See *TPJS*, pp. 188–89.)

Human Lifespan

This earth will be a paradisiacal planet during the Millennium, and death—at least as it now exists in our present telestial world—will cease. The Lord revealed: "And there shall be no sorrow because there is no death. In that day an infant shall not die until he is old; and his life shall be as the age of a tree. And when he dies he shall not sleep, that is to say in the earth, but shall be changed in the twinkling of an eye, and shall be caught up, and his rest shall be glorious." (D&C 101:29–31.)

The "age of a tree" has been identified as "one hundred years old." (Joseph Fielding Smith; as quoted in *DCE*, p. 9.) The prophet Isaiah foretold that "the child shall die an hundred years old." (Isaiah 65:20.)

Membership in Christ's Church

It is of interest to note that the Prophet Joseph Smith said: "There will be wicked men on the earth during the thousand years." (*TPJS*, pp. 268–69.) Commenting on this statement, President Joseph Fielding Smith explained: "The saying that there will be *wicked* men on the earth during the millennium has been misunderstood by many, because the Lord declared that the wicked shall not stand, but shall be consumed. In using this term *wicked* it should be interpreted in the language of the Lord as recorded in the Doctrine and Covenants, section 84, verses 49–53. Here the Lord speaks of those who have not received the gospel as being *wicked* as they are still under the bondage of sin, having not been baptized. *The inhabitants of the terrestrial order will remain on the earth during the millennium, and this class is without the gospel ordinances.*" (*DS*, 3:63–64.)

While every knee shall bow and every tongue confess that Jesus is the Christ (see Philippians 2:10–11), according to Brigham Young not all who remain on the millennial earth will be members of His true church: "In the millennium men will have the privilege of being Presbyterians, Methodists or Infidels, but they will not have the privilege of treating the name and character of Deity as they have done heretofore. No, but every knee shall bow and every tongue confess to the glory of God the Father that Jesus is the Christ." (*JD*, 12:274.)

On another occasion, President Young said: "When all nations are so subdued to Jesus that every knee shall bow and every tongue shall confess, there will still be millions on the earth who will not believe in him; but they will be obliged to acknowledge his kingly government. You may call that government ecclesiastical, or by whatever term you please; yet there is no true government on earth but the government of God, or the holy Priesthood." (*JD*, 7:142; see also 2:316–17.)

President Joseph Fielding Smith also expressed his belief that not all inhabitants of the millennial earth would be members of Christ's church: "From the words of the prophets it is quite evident that there will be on the earth some who will not belong to the Church, but they will have to pay homage to the government of God. If, in that day, a man shall die unrepentant he shall be accursed. (Isa. 65:20.) We cannot help thinking, however, that under such conditions of righteousness and influence of the teachings of heavenly beings, the time will not be very long before all people will forsake the ways of the world, and even the heathens will come unto the brightness of the Gospel light." (*WP*, p. 312.)

Elder Bruce R. McConkie, however, took a different view regarding the existence of other churches than "the only true and living church" of Jesus Christ (D&C 1:30) during the Millennium:

> How and in what manner will men worship their God during the Millennium? In answer, we can only call attention to the pure and perfect worship ordained to be in that blessed age. . . . This we know: the Millennium is designed to save souls; Satan will be bound, and sin as we know it will cease; all false religions and every rite and practice that is not of God will go the way of all the earth; and true wor-

ship, untainted, unalloyed, unabridged, will fill the hearts of all men. The gospel in its fulness and perfection will fill every heart; all people will be baptized; all shall glory in the gift of the Holy Ghost; all men will hold the priesthood and magnify their callings; and there will be no marriage but eternal marriage. (*NWAF*, p. 643.)

Millennial Government

Two Old Testament prophets foresaw two world capitals during the Millennium: "for out of Zion [the New Jerusalem] shall go forth the law, and the word of the Lord from [old] Jerusalem." (Isaiah 2:3; Micah 4:2.)

Thus, there will be two world capitals during the millennial era, one in the western hemisphere and one in the eastern hemisphere. "There will be no conflict," declared President Joseph Fielding Smith, "for *each city shall be headquarters for the Redeemer of the world,* and *from each he shall send forth his proclamations as occasion may require.*" (*DS,* 3:70.)

Regarding the nature of government during the Millennium, President Smith stated:

> When our Savior comes to rule in the millennium, all governments will become subject unto his government, and this has been referred to as the kingdom of God, which it is; but this is the *political kingdom* which will *embrace all people whether they are in the Church or not. . . . But the kingdom of God is the Church of Jesus Christ, and it is the kingdom that shall endure forever.* When the Savior prayed, "Thy kingdom come," he had reference to the kingdom in heaven which is to come when the millennial reign starts.
>
> *When Christ comes, the political kingdom will be given to the Church.* The Lord is going to make an *end* to all nations; that means this nation as well as any other. The kingdom of God is the Church, but during the millennium, the multitudes upon the face of the earth who are not in the Church will have to be governed, and many of *their officers,* who will be elected, may not be members of the Church. (*DS,* 1:229–30.)

The separate nature of the church of God and the kingdom of God was described by President George Q. Cannon:

> We are asked, Is the Church of God and the Kingdom of God the same organization? and we are informed that some of the brethren hold that they are separate.
>
> This is the correct view to take. *The Kingdom of God is a separate organization from the Church of God.* There may be men acting as officers in the Kingdom of God who will not be members of the Church of Jesus Christ of Latter-day Saints. On this point the Prophet Joseph gave particular instructions before his death, and gave an example, which he asked the younger Elders who were present to always remember. It was to the effect that men might be chosen to officiate as members of the Kingdom of God who had no standing in the Church of Jesus Christ of Latter-day Saints. The Kingdom of God when established will not be for the protection of the Church of Jesus Christ of Latter-day Saints alone, but for the protection of all men, whatever their religious views or opinions may be. Under its rule, no one will be permitted to overstep the proper bounds or to interfere with the rights of others." (*Juvenile Instructor,* 1 March 1896, p. 140; italics added; see also *HC,* 7:382.)

President Brigham Young further clarified the difference between the Church and the political kingdom of God. Speaking of the kingdom of God, he said: "That kingdom grows out of the Church of Jesus Christ of Latter-day Saints, but it is not the church; for a man may be a legislator in that body which will issue laws to sustain the inhabitants of the earth in their individual rights and still not belong to the Church of Jesus Christ at all. And further though a man may not even believe in any religion it would be perfectly right, when necessary, to give him the privilege of holding a seat among that body which will make laws to govern all the nations of the earth and control those who make no profession of religion at all; for that body would be governed, controlled and dictated to acknowledge others in those rights which they wish to enjoy themselves." (*HC,* 7:382.)

Temple Work

A major effort during the thousand-year period of Christ's reign on earth will be the focus on temple work. This will be *"the great work of the millennium,"* said President Joseph Fielding Smith, who then explained: "The work of the millennium will be largely work for the dead who did not have an opportunity when living to obtain the blessings, but who would have accepted the blessings if they had lived. Justice demands this. We need not worry, therefore, because young men or young women die without being married. All who are worthy will be blessed just the same as if they had lived and obtained the blessings." (*DS,* 2:167, 177.)

President Wilford Woodruff added this testimony regarding the extent of temple work during the Millennium: "This work of administering the ordinances of the house of God to the dead, I may say, will require the whole of the Millennium, with Jesus at the head of the resurrected dead to attend to it. The ordinances of salvation will have to be attended to for the dead who have not heard the Gospel, from the days of Adam down, before Christ can present this world to the Father, and say, 'It is finished.'" (*JD,* 13:327.)

In September 1877, at a time when there was only one operating temple on the earth, President Woodruff said: "When the Savior comes, a thousand years will be devoted to this work of redemption; and Temples will appear all over this land of Joseph,—North and South America—and also in Europe and elsewhere." (*JD,* 19:230.)

As discussed in chapter 12, we are presently in the greatest era of temple building the world has ever experienced as we prepare for this millennial work. But there will yet be "thousands" of temples built, said President Brigham Young, and "tens of thousands of men and women will go into those temples and officiate for people who have lived as far back as the Lord shall reveal." (*JD,* 3:372.)

In order to accomplish this mighty work of redemption, temples will need to have extended operating hours. In 1899

211

President Lorenzo Snow foresaw such a day: "The time will come when there will be Temples established over every portion of the land, and we will go into these Temples and work for our kindred dead night and day." (*Millennial Star,* 31 August 1899, p. 546.) More recently, at the rededication of the Arizona Temple in 1975, President Spencer W. Kimball saw a time when "temples will be used around the clock and throughout the year. We have been promised hundreds of temples and hundreds of thousands of people who want to go to the temples." (*Church News,* 19 April 1975, p. 3.)

John the Revelator saw this around-the-clock labor of redemption in vision: "And one of the elders answered, saying unto me, What are these which are arrayed in white robes? and whence came they? . . . Therefore are they before the throne of God, and *serve him day and night in his temple,* and he that sitteth on the throne shall dwell among them." (Revelation 7:13, 15; italics added.) President Spencer W. Kimball commented on the Revelator's vision, saying, "John saw that sometime in the future (and it is still in the future to us), those who [are] faithful and have cleansed their lives will work night and day in the holy temples. Evidently there will be then a constant succession of groups going through the temple." (*Ensign,* January 1977, p. 7.)

Interaction of Mortals and Resurrected Beings

Regarding the question of who will actually perform or participate in the ordinances of the temple, President Joseph Fielding Smith stated: "Will resurrected beings during the millennium actually take part in the endowment work of the temple along with mortal beings?

"The answer to this question is no! That is, they will not assist in performing the ordinances. Resurrected beings will assist in furnishing information which is not otherwise available, but mortals will have to do the ordinance work in the temples." (*DS,* 2:178.)

Much divine assistance will be provided to those who perform temple work during the Millennium. President John Taylor observed that "communications from the heavens will be received in regard to our labors, how we may perform them, and for whom." (*JD*, 25:185.) President Joseph Fielding Smith added this testimony: "Those who will be living here then will be in *daily* communication with those who have passed through the resurrection, and they will come with this information, this knowledge that we do not have and will give it to those who are in mortality saying, 'Now go into the temples and do this work; when you get this done, we will bring you other names.' And in that way every soul who is entitled to a place in the celestial kingdom of God will be ferreted out, and not one soul shall be overlooked." (*DS*, 2:167.)

Two statements by President Brigham Young add insight in how interaction with immortals will facilitate temple work during the Millennium:

> Before this work is finished, a great many of the Elders of Israel in Mount Zion will become pillars in the Temple of God, to go no more out: they will eat and drink and sleep there; and they will often have occasion to say—"Somebody came into the Temple last night; we did not know who he was, but he was no doubt a brother, and told us a great many things we did not before understand. He gave us the names of a great many of our forefathers that are not on record, and he gave me my true lineage and the names of my forefathers for hundreds of years back. He said to me, You and I are connected in one family: there are the names of your ancestors; take them and write them down, and be baptised and confirmed, and save such and such ones, and receive of the blessings of the eternal Priesthood for such and such an individual, as you do for yourselves." (*JD*, 6:295.)

> Some of those who are not in mortality will come along and say, "Here are a thousand names I wish you to attend to in this temple, and when you have got through with them I will give you another thousand." (*JD*, 3:372.)

Those who work in the temples will have direct knowledge that the work they are doing is acceptable to those for whom it is being done. President Anthon H. Lund, counselor in the First Presidency to President Joseph F. Smith, said: "The veil, I believe, will be much thinner between the spirit world and this; and we will work for the dead, not only in faith that those for whom we labor will accept the Gospel, but with an actual knowledge that they are longing for the work to be done." (CR, October 1903, p. 82.)

The Abode of Resurrected Beings

Regarding the abode of resurrected beings, President John Taylor said, "There will be a peculiar habitation for the resurrected bodies. This habitation may be compared to paradise, whence man, in the beginning was driven." (*The Gospel Kingdom,* Salt Lake City: Bookcraft, 1964, p. 218.)

President Joseph Fielding Smith added this statement: "During all these years men dwelling in mortality will have the privilege of associating with those who have received their resurrection. Our Lord and Savior will be a familiar figure among the righteous saints. Instruction will be given by resurrected prophets. How could wickedness remain under such conditions? Those who have passed through resurrection will not, however, dwell with those in mortality. They will not stay in earthly, or human homes nor sleep in the beds of mortals. Such a thing would be inconsistent." (*WP,* pp. 312–13.)

While much remains to be made known regarding this final chapter in the earth's history, we rejoice in that which has been revealed and look forward to the further light and knowledge that shall be forthcoming.

Chapter 24

THE MILLENNIUM:
A PARADISIACAL GLORY

"We believe . . . that the earth will be renewed and receive its paradisiacal glory."

—ARTICLES OF FAITH 1:10

Enmity to Cease

The Millennium will be a period of peace not only to mankind—"violence shall no more be heard in thy land" (Isaiah 60:18)—but also to the brute creation and every living thing. The Lord declared: "And in that day the enmity of man, and the enmity of beasts, yea, the enmity of all flesh, shall cease from before my face." (D&C 101:26.) The writings of the prophet Isaiah are very descriptive of this period of peace: "The wolf and the lamb shall feed together, and the lion shall eat straw like the bullock; and dust shall be the serpent's meat. They shall not hurt nor destroy in all my holy mountain, saith the Lord." (Isaiah 65:25; see also 11:6–9; 2 Nephi 21:6–9; 30:12–15.)

During the march of Zion's Camp, the Prophet Joseph Smith preached a mini-sermon on eliminating enmity. He recorded these words in his journal:

> In pitching my tent we found three massasaugas or prairie rattlesnakes, which the brethren were about to kill, but I said, "Let them alone—don't hurt them! How will the serpent ever lose its venom, while the servants of God possess the same disposition, and continue to make war upon it? Men must become harmless before the brute creation, and when men lose their viscious dispositions and

cease to destroy the animal race, the lion and the lamb can dwell together, and the sucking child can play with the serpent in safety." The brethren took the serpents carefully on sticks and carried them across the creek. I exhorted the brethren not to kill a serpent, bird, or an animal of any kind during our journey unless it became necessary in order to preserve ourselves from hunger. (*TPJS,* p. 71.)

While the millennial earth may not be a paradise for hunters, surely it will be a place of peace for all God's creatures.

Paradisiacal Glory Returns to Earth

The lack of enmity between animals and humans is indicative of the terrestrial, or paradisiacal, state of the earth during the Millennium. As noted at the beginning of the chapter, "We believe . . . the earth will be renewed and receive its paradisiacal glory." (Articles of Faith 1:10.) The footnote to this scripture identifies paradisiacal glory as "a condition like the Garden of Eden." President Joseph Fielding Smith provided further insight into the meaning of this "paradisiacal glory":

> Too many have the idea that this has reference to the celestialized earth, but this *is not* the case. It refers to the *restored earth* as it will be when Christ comes to reign. This is taught in Isaiah 65:17–25, and in the Doctrine and Covenants, section 101:23–31. . . .
>
> Now in time past this earth had a paradisiacal glory, and then came the fall, bringing a change, and that change has been upon the earth in the neighborhood of 6,000 years. . . .
>
> *This earth is to be renewed and brought back to the condition in which it was before it was cursed through the fall of Adam.* When Adam passed out of the Garden of Eden, then the earth became a telestial world, and it is of that order today. I do not mean a telestial glory such as will be found in telestial worlds after the resurrection, but a telestial condition which has been from the days of Adam until now and will continue until Christ comes. . . .

It will become a terrestrial world then and will so remain for 1,000 years. . . .

At the end of the world *the earth will die; it will be dissolved, pass away, and then it will be renewed, or raised with a resurrection*. It will receive its resurrection to become a celestial body. (*DS*, 1:84–88; see also *DCE*, p. 411.)

The Earth Transfigured

The change the earth will undergo is called a "day of transfiguration." (D&C 63:20.) Part of this change is bringing the mass of the earth back to the condition it was in before the continents and islands were separated, when the earth was "divided." This occurred in the days of Peleg, who was a great-great-great-grandson of Noah. (See Genesis 9:18; 10:21–25.)

Isaiah described this as a time when the "land shall be married." (Isaiah 62:4.) In a revelation received in 1831, the Lord declared: "He shall command the great deep, and it shall be driven back into the north countries, and the islands shall become one land; And the land of Jerusalem and the land of Zion shall be turned back into their own place, and the earth shall be like as it was in the days before it was divided." (D&C 133:23–24.)

President Joseph Fielding Smith provided this insightful information:

> We are committed to the fact that Adam dwelt on this American continent. But when Adam dwelt here, it was not the American continent, nor was it the Western Hemisphere, for all the land was in *one place,* and all the water was in one place. There was no Atlantic Ocean separating the hemispheres. . . .
>
> Then we read in Genesis that there came a time when the earth was divided. There are some people who believe that this simply means that the land surface was divided among the various tribes, but this is not the meaning; *it was an actual dividing of the surface of the earth,* and it was broken up as we find it now. (*DS*, 3:74–75; see also *DCE*, pp. 144–45.)

Elder Bruce R. McConkie suggested it is possible that "the very axis of the earth will shift so that the seasons cease and the whole earth enjoys both seedtime and harvest at all times." (*NWAF*, pp. 649–50.) The marrying of the land mass and the combining of the oceans may be, in part, the result of land changes at the time of the Second Coming.

John the Revelator prophesied of the time when "every mountain and island were moved out of their places." (Revelation 6:14; see also 16:20.) Isaiah foresaw the mountains flowing at the presence of the Lord: "Oh that thou wouldest rend the heavens, that thou wouldest come down, that the mountains might flow down at thy presence, as when the melting fire burneth, the fire causeth the waters to boil, to make thy name known to thine adversaries, that the nations may tremble at thy presence! When thou didst terrible things which we looked not for, thou camest down, the mountains flowed down at thy presence." (Isaiah 64:1–3.)

Micah spoke of the mountains being "molten under him" (Micah 1:4), and the Doctrine and Covenants includes three references to this great event (see 49:23; 109:74; 133:22). Elder Bruce R. McConkie added this commentary:

> Not only will the Lord come in flaming fire, but that fire will produce fervent, glowing, intense heat, heat that has not been known in the entire history of the earth, heat that will cause the very elements to melt, the mountains to flow down at his presence, and the very earth itself, as now constituted, to dissolve. Nowhere is this better expounded than by Peter. "The day of the Lord will come as a thief in the night," he says, "in the which the heavens shall pass away with a great noise, and the elements shall melt with fervent heat, the earth also and the works that are therein shall be burned up." In this dread day when "the heavens being on fire shall be dissolved, and the elements shall melt with fervent heat," there will come into being "new heavens and a new earth, wherein dwelleth righteousness." (2 Peter 3:10–13.) (*NWAF*, p. 645.)

The Millennial and Postmillennial
New Heaven and New Earth

The concept of a new heaven and new earth includes both a *millennial* and a *postmillennial* aspect.

Isaiah prophesied of "new heavens and a new earth" and then proceeded to describe millennial conditions. (See Isaiah 65:17–25.) In commenting on Isaiah's writings, President Joseph Fielding Smith said: "[Isaiah's writings have] reference to the change which shall come to the earth and all upon it, at the beginning of the Millennial reign, as we declare in the tenth article of the Articles of Faith. This is the renewed earth when it shall receive its paradisiacal glory, or be restored as it was before the fall of man." (*CHMR*, 1:143.)

The Lord setting his foot upon the Mount of Olives and the occurrence of the great earthquake may be what triggers the reuniting of the land masses, for "the earth shall tremble, and reel to and fro, and the heavens also shall shake." (D&C 45:48; see also 49:23; 88:87.)

The postmillennial new heaven and earth is described in latter-day revelation: "And again, verily, verily, I say unto you that when the thousand years are ended, and men again begin to deny their God, then will I spare the earth but for a little season; and the end shall come, and the heaven and the earth shall be consumed and pass away, and there shall be a new heaven and a new earth. For all old things shall pass away, and all things shall become new, even the heaven and the earth, and all the fulness thereof, both men and beasts, the fowls of the air, and the fishes of the sea." (D&C 29:22–24.)

This postmillennial change "is the final change, or resurrection, of the earth, after the 'little season' which shall follow the Millennium," stated President Joseph Fielding Smith. (*CHMR*, 1:143.)

Isaiah spoke of the earth reeling to and fro like a drunkard and being "utterly broken down, . . . dissolved, . . . [and] moved exceedingly." (Isaiah 24:19–20.) President Smith wrote: "The interpretation is that [the earth] should not be restored to the same mortal or temporal condition. When the earth passes away and is dissolved, it will pass through a similar condition which the human body does in death, but, like the human body, so shall the earth itself be restored in the resurrection and become a celestial body, through the mercy and mission of Jesus Christ." (*CHMR*, 1:143.)

John the Revelator spoke of this changed earth as a "sea of glass" (Revelation 4:6), which the Lord identified as "the earth, in its sanctified, immortal, and eternal state" (D&C 77:1). "After [the earth] hath filled the measure of its creation, it shall be crowned with glory, even with the presence of God the Father." (D&C 88:19.) Before the earth fills the "measure of its creation," however, the forces of evil will once again assemble their hellish hosts for one last battle before they are everlastingly banished.

Chapter 25

THE MILLENNIUM: A LITTLE SEASON

"And again, verily, verily, I say unto you that when the thousand years are ended, and men again begin to deny their God, then will I spare the earth but for a little season."

—D&C 29:22

An Ancient Zion Society Destroyed

The Book of Mormon provides a classic example of what creates a Zion and how that celestial society can be destroyed.

Following the visit of the resurrected Redeemer, the ancient inhabitants of the Americas enjoyed almost two hundred years of happiness. This celestial society was one in which "there were no contentions and disputations among them, and every man did deal justly one with another." (4 Nephi 1:2.) Furthermore, "they did walk after the commandments which they had received from their Lord and their God, continuing in fasting and prayer, and in meeting together oft both to pray and to hear the word of the Lord." (Verse 12.)

The happiness of this people was described by Mormon, their prophet-scribe: "And it came to pass that there was no contention in the land, because of the love of God which did dwell in the hearts of the people. And there were no envyings, nor strifes, nor tumults, nor whoredoms, nor lyings, nor murders, nor any manner of lasciviousness; and *surely there could not be a happier people among all the people who had been created by the hand of God. . . .* They were in one, the children of Christ, and heirs to the kingdom of God." (Verses 15–17; italics added.)

Only eighty-four years later, the first signs of a breakdown began to appear as a "small part of the people . . . revolted from the church." (Verse 20.) The majority of the people continued to live their lives "after the manner of happiness" (2 Nephi 5:27) and to enjoy the Spirit of the Lord in their lives for about another one hundred years. Ultimately, however, their peace was destroyed. They "were lifted up in pride, such as the wearing of costly apparel." (4 Nephi 1:24.) They "began to be divided into classes . . . and began to deny the true church of Christ." (Verse 26.) Wickedness spread, and Satan "did get hold upon their hearts." (Verses 24–26, 28.) Secret oaths and combinations spread, and hatred filled the hearts of the people. Eventually, because of their exceeding anger towards one another, they not only lost their love of others, but began to "thirst after blood and revenge continually." (Moroni 9:3–5.) Their society was completely destroyed.

The Great Last Struggle

Unfortunately, the celestial society of the Millennium will face some similar challenges near the end of the thousand-year period of peace and reign of righteousness. The Lord warned that the time would come when "men [would] again begin to deny their God." (D&C 29:22.) It seems likely that many of the main factors in the destruction of the ancient society in the Americas will once again be present: pride, loss of love, creation of social classes, selfishness, fault-finding, hatred, and the pursuit of pleasure through wickedness.

Satan will be "loosed a little season" to work his wickedness in one last effort to gather souls to his evil cause. (See Revelation 20:1–3; D&C 43:30–31; 88:110–111.) One must remember that Satan has no hope of winning! His war is the destruction of souls, for "the devil will not support his children at the last day, but doth speedily drag them down to hell." (Alma 30:60.) Nephi reminded us that Lucifer "seeketh that all men might be miserable like unto himself." (2 Nephi 2:27; see verse 18.)

What is "a little season"? President Joseph Fielding Smith suggested it may be close to one thousand years: "Our Lord came about 4,000 years from the time of the fall. The millennium is to come some time following the 2,000 years after his coming. Then there is to be the millennium for 1,000 years, and following that a '*little season,*' the length of which is not revealed, but which may *bring 'time' to its end* about 8,000 years from the beginning." (*DS,* 1:81.)

If the Fall of Adam and Eve took their paradisiacal world to a telestial state, what will happen to the paradisiacal earth of the Millennium when many people turn to wickedness and Satan once again rages in their hearts? President Joseph Fielding Smith provided an answer: "Will the earth go back to the telestial order after the millennium? No, but the people on the face of the earth, many of them, will be like the Nephites who lived 200 years after the coming of Christ. They will rebel against the Lord knowingly, and the great last struggle will come, and the devil and his forces will be defeated; then the earth will die and receive its resurrection and become a celestial body. The resurrection of the wicked will take place as one of the last events before the earth dies." (*DS,* 1:87.)

Resurrection of the Unjust

The first resurrection, which commenced with Christ and will continue through the Millennium, includes all who are worthy of a celestial or a terrestrial glory. The second resurrection, or the resurrection of the unjust (see D&C 76:17), will first include telestial beings, those who have been "thrust down to hell" and "who shall not be redeemed from the devil until the last resurrection." (D&C 76:84–85.) Finally, rising from the grave with a resurrected body of no glory will be the sons of perdition.

Elder Bruce R. McConkie provided this commentary: "At the end of the millennium, and in the morning of this second resurrection, those shall come forth who merit telestial bodies, and they shall be rewarded accordingly. Finally, in the afternoon of the second resurrection, those who 'remain filthy still,' those who having been raised in immortality are judged and found wholly wanting, those whom we call sons of perdition, shall be cast out with Lucifer and his angels." (*DNTC,* 1:196–97.)

Those who come forth in the morning of the second resurrection will be redeemed to inherit a telestial glory. However, the sons of perdition—"vessels of wrath" (D&C 76:33)—"shall not be redeemed" (verse 38) and are "doomed to suffer the wrath of God, with the devil and his angels in eternity" (verse 33).

Some of these vessels of wrath will come from among those who live near the end of the Millennium. President Joseph Fielding Smith explained: "After the thousand years Satan will be loosed again and will go forth again to deceive the nations. Because men are still mortal, Satan will go out to deceive them. Men will again deny the Lord, but in doing so they will act with their eyes open and because they love darkness rather than light, and so *they become sons of perdition.* Satan will gather his hosts, both those on the earth and the wicked dead who will eventually also be brought forth in the resurrection. Michael, the Prince, will gather his forces and the last great battle will be fought. Satan will be defeated with his hosts. Then will come the end. Satan and those who follow him will be banished into outer darkness." (*DS,* 1:87.)

Second Battle of Gog and Magog

As noted in chapter 10, there will be two future battles of Gog and Magog: one at the time of Armageddon, preceding the Second Coming; and, as taught by the Prophet Joseph Smith, one "will be after the millennium." (*TPJS,* p. 280.)

Elder Bruce R. McConkie taught: "The great war involving Gog and Magog is both premillennial . . . and also postmillennial in the sense that there will be another great conflict with wicked nations just before this globe becomes a celestial sphere. . . .

"Postmillennial events will be revealed in full to those who live during the Millennium. The knowledge then given will stand as a warning for those of future generations, even as the words of Ezekiel [39:1–16] warn us to live as becometh saints. We speculate that much the same thing that happens in the first war with Gog and Magog will be repeated in the second." (*MM*, p. 488.)

The apocalyptic writings of the Apostle John include this description of this final battle between good and evil: "And when the thousand years are expired, Satan shall be loosed out of his prison, and shall go out to deceive the nations which are in the four quarters of the earth, Gog and Magog, to gather them together to battle: the number of whom is as the sand of the sea. And they went up on the breadth of the earth, and compassed the camp of the saints about, and the beloved city: and fire came down from God out of heaven and devoured them." (Revelation 20:7–9.) The "fire" mentioned by John could be symbolic of the glory of Michael the archangel, who is Adam, as he descends with his heavenly hosts in the power of God to battle Lucifer.

What will this final conflict consist of, and who will be involved? According to Elder McConkie, it will consist mainly of a war of ideologies: "The war in heaven was a war of ideologies; it was a war to determine how men would be saved; and so it is in the warfare of the world today. Lucifer's forces advocate a plan of salvation that is contrary to the Lord's true plan. And in the process, armies assemble and wars are fought, for the devil delights in destruction. And so shall it be after the Millennium." (*MM*, pp. 696–97.)

Truth and righteousness will prevail in this final conflict, just as it did when Michael led the hosts of heaven to victory over the devil and his followers in the premortal war in heaven. (See Revelation 12:7–9.) Latter-day revelation describes this coming conflict: "And Michael, the seventh angel, even the archangel, shall gather together his armies, even the hosts of heaven. And the devil shall gather together his armies; even the hosts of hell, and shall come up to battle against Michael and his armies. And then cometh the battle of the great God;

and the devil and his armies shall be cast away into their own place, that they shall not have power over the saints any more at all. For Michael shall fight their battles, and shall overcome him who seeketh the throne of him who sitteth upon the throne, even the Lamb." (D&C 88:112–15.)

What a glorious day that shall be! The adversary and his wicked ways and followers "shall not have power over the saints any more at all." Surely one will want to be found in the Lord's army on this occasion.

IMMORTALITY FOR ALL, ETERNAL LIFE FOR SOME

Chapter 26

ALL WILL BE JUDGED

"We shall all stand before the judgment seat of Christ. For it is written, As I live, saith the Lord, every knee shall bow to me, and every tongue shall confess to God. So then every one of us shall give account of himself to God."

—ROMANS 14:10–12

Judgment: A Process

At least from the time when the great plan of salvation was presented in the premortal world—and perhaps before—the children of God have been in a constant process of being judged.

Those who chose to reject God as their Father and Christ as their Savior were judged not worthy of "advancing" to mortality. All who have been or will be born on this earth were supportive of their premortal Mentors and qualified to come to earth to continue their progression. Here Deity declared, "We will prove them herewith, to see if they will do all things whatsoever the Lord their God shall command them." (Abraham 3:25.)

The process of judgment continues throughout mortality. Those who accept the gospel of Jesus Christ in this life and who are judged worthy of receiving the ordinance and covenant of baptism are brought into God's kingdom and church on earth. Throughout their mortal lives, these Saints of God receive regular checkups by ecclesiastical judges. Worthiness interviews are conducted in order for Church members to hold office or participate in sacred ordinances.

Furthermore, all are encouraged to constantly evaluate and judge their own progress through this mortal schooling. Each is urged to evaluate his or her thoughts, words, and deeds and to repent where necessary. (See Mosiah 4:30.) Perhaps the quintessential questions we need to ask ourselves are those postured by the prophet Alma: "And now behold, I ask of you, my brethren of the church, have ye spiritually been born of God? Have ye received his image in your countenances? Have ye experienced this mighty change in your hearts? . . . I say unto you, can ye look up to God at that day [of judgment] with a pure heart and clean hands? I say unto you, can you look up, having the image of God engraven upon your countenances?" (Alma 5:14, 19.)

At the time of death, as the spirit separates from the body, there is a judgment passed regarding the abode of the newly disembodied spirit. Those who are judged righteous will enter into a state of happiness and peace in the paradise of God, while others are consigned to a spirit prison. (See Alma 40:6–14.) But there is still hope for those in the latter part of the spirit world. During the three days in which the Savior's spirit was separated from the body following His death on Calvary, the Savior organized those in paradise to take the gospel to those in the spirit prison. (See 1 Peter 3:18–20; 4:6; D&C 138.)

As noted elsewhere in this volume, a judgment is passed at the time of resurrection. Those judged worthy of a celestial or terrestrial resurrection will be brought forth in the first resurrection, while others are required to await the second resurrection.

Ultimately, He to whom all judgment has been committed, even Jesus Christ, will pass a final and "just" judgment upon all. (See John 5:22–30.) This judgment will evidently include a review of the records kept in heaven and on earth (see Revelation 20:12; D&C 128:6–7), as well as input from prophets and apostles whose writings, teachings, and stewardships will impinge on that final judgment (see 1 Nephi 12:9–10; Jacob 6:8–9, 13; Mormon 3:19; Moroni 10:34.)

It is of interest to note that the Greek New Testament word for judgment (*krinō*) means to separate or to decide. Thus, the final judgment will be an act of separating people not only into kingdoms of glory, but also into degrees of glory within each of those kingdoms.

Many Mansions in Heaven

When all things are complete and the Lord Jesus Christ turns to His Father and utters the irrevocable words "It is finished!" each individual will receive his or her just reward.

Alma taught that all people would "be judged according to their works, according to the law and justice. . . . And thus, none but the truly penitent are saved." (Alma 42:23–24.) According to the Prophet Joseph Smith, "Salvation consists in the glory, authority, majesty, power and dominion which Jehovah possesses and in nothing else; and no being can possess it but himself or one like him." (As quoted in *MM*, p. 705.) Therefore, in the ultimate sense, salvation, or exaltation, consists of partaking of eternal life, being co-heirs with the Father and Son, and living the kind of life that God does: possessing all things and enjoying all the blessings of a celestial glory.

Yet, all who have not committed the unpardonable sin will partake of a degree of salvation and glory in some kingdom. (See *TPJS*, pp. 356–57.) The Gospel of John records the Savior as saying, "In my Father's house are many mansions. . . . I go to prepare a place for you." (14:2.) The Prophet Joseph Smith gave further understanding to John's words, suggesting they should be rendered, "In my Father's kingdom are many kingdoms." (*TPJS*, p. 366.) Furthermore, the Prophet indicated that the Savior's next words were "I go to prepare a kingdom for you, that the exaltation that I receive you may receive also." (As quoted in Andrew E. Ehat and Lyndon W. Cook, *The Words of Joseph Smith*, Salt Lake City: Publisher's Press, 1988, p. 371.)

The Final Judgment

As revealed in the great vision to Joseph Smith and Sidney Rigdon (see D&C 76), the hereafter does not consist of merely a heaven and a hell. There are three kingdoms of glory—celestial, terrestrial, and telestial—and each of these kingdoms has subdivisions. In addition, there is a space known as "outer darkness," which has absolutely no glory. Here the devil, his unembodied so-called angels, and the sons of perdition are sent to remain throughout eternity.

Within the *celestial kingdom*, which reflects the glory of the sun, are three degrees of glory, with the highest being reserved for those who qualify for eternal lives. (See D&C 76:50–70; 131:1–4; 132:15–17.) These persons will be resurrected with gloriously renewed and sanctified bodies of a celestial nature. And none but those possessing such bodies will enter this kingdom, "for he who is not able to abide the law of a celestial kingdom cannot abide a celestial glory." (D&C 88:22.) Celestial beings "shall dwell in the presence of God and his Christ forever and ever." (D&C 76:62.)

The glory of those who inherit the *terrestrial kingdom* will differ from those of the celestial kingdom as the moon differs from the sun. Heirs of this kingdom will "receive of the presence of the Son, but not of the fulness of the Father." (D&C 76:77; see verses 71–80.) Only those who qualify for this kingdom will enter, for "he who cannot abide the law of a terrestrial kingdom cannot abide a terrestrial glory." (D&C 88:23.)

The glory of the *telestial kingdom* will differ from that of the terrestrial kingdom as the stars differ from the moon. Into this kingdom will pass those individuals who will continue to pay the price of penitence throughout the Millennium and who will have to await the second resurrection before being redeemed. Yet the Lord in His mercy will grant them a glory that "surpasses all understanding." (D&C 76:89.) President Brigham Young taught: "The glory of those who are *not* permitted to enter into the presence of the Father and the Son will be greater than mortals can imagine, in glory, excellency, exquisite pleasure, and intense bliss." (*JD*, 9:315; italics added.)

Regarding the numerous gradations of glory within the kingdoms of glory, Elder James E. Talmage has written:

> The three kingdoms of widely differing glories [sun, moon, and stars] are severally organized on a plan of gradation. The Telestial kingdom comprises subdivisions; this also is the case, we are told, with the Celestial; and, by analogy, we conclude that a similar condition prevails in the Terrestrial. Thus the innumerable degrees of merit amongst mankind are provided for in an infinity of graded glories. The Celestial kingdom is supremely honored by the personal ministrations of the Father and the Son. The Terrestrial kingdom will be administered through the higher, without a fulness of glory. The Telestial is governed through the ministrations of the Terrestrial, by "angels who are appointed to minister for them." (*Articles of Faith*, Salt Lake City: Deseret Book Co., 1984, pp. 370–371.)

The *sons of perdition*, those who commit the unpardonable sin and knowingly and openly rebel against and deny Christ, are "doomed to suffer the wrath of God, with the devil and his angels in eternity." (D&C 76:33.) They are consigned to "a kingdom which is not a kingdom of glory." (D&C 88:24.)

Perhaps there will be a great degree of self-judgment involved in the process of determining to what kingdom or glory one is assigned, for the scriptures teach that "your glory shall be that glory by which your bodies are quickened." (D&C 88:28.) We will naturally be assigned to places where beings of a glory similar to our own will reside.

This may give added meaning to Isaiah's declaration that "the shew of their countenance doth witness against them." (Isaiah 3:9; 2 Nephi 13:9.) To the wicked, who are filled with darkness, one may ask, "Where is thy glory?" (Moses 1:12–14.) Yet the righteous "shall shine forth in the kingdom of God" (Alma 40:25), and of them it will be said they are "glorious beyond description [with a] countenance truly like lightning" (JS–H 1:32).

Chapter 27

THE MEASURE OF CREATION

"For after [the earth] hath filled the measure of its creation, it shall be crowned with glory, even with the presence of God the Father."

—D&C 88:19

The Gifts of Immortality and Eternal Life

The essence and purpose of earth life could be summed up in this declaration of Deity: "For behold, this is my work and my glory—to bring to pass the immortality and eternal life of man." (Moses 1:39.)

The infinite atonement of Jesus Christ makes this divine purpose possible. By willingly allowing His life to be taken on Calvary, then rising in the Resurrection, the Redeemer overcame death and hell. His act of mercy and love freed us from eternal servitude to Satan. (See 2 Nephi 9:6–12.) Truly we sing: "Let the whole wide earth rejoice. Death is conquered, man is free. Christ has won the victory." ("He Is Risen!" *Hymns,* 1985, no. 199.)

The free gift of *immortality,* given through the grace of Christ, will be granted to every living thing. (See D&C 29:24–25.) All will be raised from the grave, and the spirit and the body will be inseparably reunited for eternity. *Eternal life,* however, or that life which God lives, will only be granted to those who qualify. Eternal life is the reward of the righteous— not only they who have lived valiantly, but also they who have accepted the saving covenants and ordinances of the gospel of Jesus Christ, including baptism and temple sealings.

Those who are granted eternal life have fully accepted that holy and sinless blood shed for them in Gethsemane and on Calvary. (See D&C 19:15–20; 2 Nephi 2:7.) These are they who in spite of their good works "know that it is by grace that we are saved, after all we can do." (2 Nephi 25:23.) These are they who have truly come to "know . . . the only true God, and Jesus Christ." (John 17:3; see also D&C 132:24.) Only these will be exalted and dwell in the presence of the Father and Son throughout eternity.

Truly, these are they who will have filled the measure of their creation.

Celestialization of the Earth

In preparation for its final destiny, filling "the measure of its creation," the earth will go through one final refiner's fire. Elder Bruce R. McConkie taught that the earth would go through a second burning in preparation for its final destiny: "After the Millennium, plus a little season, which we assume will be a thousand years, the earth will again be burned; it will again be changed; there will again be new heavens and a new earth, but this time it will be a celestial earth. This is also spoken of as the resurrection of our planet." (*MM*, p. 536.)

President Joseph Fielding Smith spoke of the earth dying and being resurrected: "At the end of the world *the earth will die; it will be dissolved, pass away, and then it will be renewed, or raised with a resurrection.* It will receive its resurrection to become a celestial body, so that they of the celestial order may possess it forever and ever. Then *it will shine forth as the sun and take its place among the worlds that are redeemed.* When this time comes the terrestrial inhabitants will also be taken away and be consigned to another sphere suited to their condition. Then the words of the Savior will be fulfilled, for the meek shall inherit the earth." (*DS*, 1:87–88.)

The physical change the earth will undergo in preparation for its celestialization was taught by President Brigham Young: "When it becomes celestialized, [this world] will be like the sun, and be prepared for the habitation of the Saints, and be brought back into the presence of the Father and the Son. It will not then be an opaque body as it now is, but it will be like the stars of the firmament, full of light and glory: it will be a body of light. John compared it, in its celestialized state, to a sea of glass [Rev. 4:6; 15:2]." (*JD*, 7:163.)

In 1843 the Prophet Joseph Smith gave some inspired items of instruction, including the following description of the new earth: "[Angels] reside in the presence of God, on a globe like a sea of glass and fire, where all things for their glory are manifest, past, present, and future, and are continually before the Lord. The place where God resides is a great Urim and Thummim. This earth, in its sanctified and immortal state, will be made like unto crystal and will be a Urim and Thummim to the inhabitants who dwell thereon, whereby all things pertaining to an inferior kingdom, or all kingdoms of a lower order, will be manifest to those who dwell on it; and this earth will be Christ's." (D&C 130:7–9.)

The ancient revelator John described the surface of this celestial sphere as "a sea of glass like unto crystal." (Revelation 4:6.) The modern-day revelator Joseph Smith said that the "sea of glass spoken of by John . . . is the earth, in its sanctified, immortal, and eternal state." (D&C 77:1.) All inhabitants of this celestial sphere will be given their own personal Urim and Thummim "whereby, things pertaining to a higher order of kingdoms will be made known." (D&C 130:10.) John described this Urim and Thummim as "a white stone" that has written on it a "new name . . . which no man knoweth saving he that receiveth it." (Revelation 2:17; see also D&C 130:11.)

The Celestial City of Zion

In the twenty-first chapter of Revelation, John describes two holy cities: the "new Jerusalem" that will reign during the Millennium (see Revelation 21:2–3) and the "holy Jerusalem" that will descend from heaven to take up its abode on the newly celestialized earth (see Revelation 21:9–11).

John then proceeded to describe the "holy Jerusalem": "[It] had a wall great and high, and had twelve gates, and at the gates twelve angels, and names written thereon, which are the names of the twelve tribes of the children of Israel: On the east three gates; on the north three gates; on the south three gates; and on the west three gates. And the wall of the city had twelve foundations, and in them the names of the twelve apostles of the Lamb." (Revelation 21:12–14.) Richard D. Draper provided the following informative commentary:

> The city resembles the temple of Ezekiel (see 48:31–35.) But there are differences. First, at each of John's gates stands an angel as sentinel. The prophet Brigham Young provided insight into the duty of these angels. Defining the endowment, he stated: "Your *endowment* is, to receive all those ordinances in the House of the Lord, which are necessary for you, after you have departed this life, to enable you to walk back to the presence of the Father, passing the angels who stand as sentinels, being enabled to give them the key words, the signs and tokens, pertaining to the Holy Priesthood, and gain your eternal exaltation in spite of earth and hell." [*JD*, 2:31.] Appropriately, these angels are placed at the gates of the celestial city, symbolizing that only those who have made and kept their covenants in God's holy house will enter his kingdom. . . .
>
> The repetition of number twelve in the stones and gates stands as a constant reminder of the priestly power that guards and envelops all aspects and operations of the holy city. This is seen especially in the measurement of the walls. John notes they are 144 cubits [see Revelation 21:17], after the measure of an angel. The size of an angelic cubit is unknown. What is important is the number—twelve squared—signifying the fullness of priesthood authority. This is what surrounds and stands as a great bulwark to the city." (*OSS*, pp. 235–36.)

John saw that the city had no temple, for the whole face of this celestial sphere will be a temple: "And I saw no temple therein: for the Lord God Almighty and the Lamb are the temple of it. [The whole earth is the Lord's temple or Holy of Holies.] And the city had no need of the sun, neither of the moon to shine in it: for the glory of God did lighten it, and the Lamb is the light thereof. (Revelation 21:22–23.)

In light of the magnificence to be bestowed both upon this planet and the people who inherit it, the words of Elder Orson Pratt are well worth pondering: "O man, remember the future destiny and glory of the earth, and secure thine everlasting inheritance upon the same, that when it shall be glorious, thou shalt be glorious also." (*Millennial Star,* 1 March 1850, p. 72.)

"Then Shall They Be Gods"

The Lord's promise to those who qualify for the highest degree within the celestial kingdom is "Then shall they be gods." (D&C 132:20.) These gods are eternally sealed husbands and wives who are given the promise of a "continuation of the seeds" (procreative power) throughout the eternities. (D&C 132:19.) In 1916 the First Presidency and the Twelve Apostles declared: "Only resurrected and glorified beings can become parents of spirit offspring. Only such exalted souls have reached maturity in the appointed course of eternal life; and the spirits born to them in the eternal worlds will pass in due sequence through the several stages or estates by which the glorified parents have attained exaltation." (James R. Clark, comp., *Messages of the First Presidency of The Church of Jesus Christ of Latter-day Saints,* 6 vols. Salt Lake City: Bookcraft, 1965–75, 5:34.)

These gods will have traveled the same path trodden by their Father in Heaven eons before. The Prophet Joseph Smith declared, "God himself was once as we are now, and is an exalted man, and sits enthroned in yonder heavens!" (*TPJS,* p. 345; see also *DCE,* pp. 214–16.)

The truth of the divine destiny of worthy husbands and wives was revealed originally to Elder Lorenzo Snow, who stated it in poetic form: "As man now is, God once was; as God now is, man may be." Elder Snow, who lived to become the fifth prophet of this last dispensation, said of that revelation:

"Nothing was ever revealed more distinctly than that was to me." (*Improvement Era,* June 1919, p. 661.)

Men and women who qualify for godhood will have been true to the purpose of their creation. While they will still have much to learn and experience before truly becoming as God is, they will have filled in large part the measure of their creation.

It should be remembered that a man who holds the priesthood does not have an advantage over a woman who can bear children, nor she over him. Exaltation is a joint process. It requires a worthy man and a worthy woman—husband and wife joined by the sealing powers of the priesthood and sealed by the Holy Spirit of Promise—to qualify for this exalted status. The Apostle Paul said it well: "Neither is the man without the woman, neither the woman without the man, in the Lord." (1 Corinthians 11:11.)

Elder Bruce R. McConkie provided an appropriate summary statement on the destiny of those who receive a fulness of the Father's blessings and dominions: "Thus those who gain eternal life, which is exaltation, become like God. They believe what he believes, know what he knows, and exercise the same powers he possesses. Like him they become omnipotent, omniscient, and omnipresent. They have advanced and progressed and become like him. They are the ones who receive an inheritance in the Celestial City." (*MM,* p. 706.)

And so the possibilities of eternity begin to unfold, and the wonders of the universe become manifest. The blessed will forever associate with their God and Father in Heaven. This will be but the beginning of an eternity of association with Him who is known as the "Beginning and the End." Joy and peace will reign supreme as righteous husbands and wives live together in love in a family unit where time no longer exists.

Index

Fasting, 35
Fathers, 55–56
Fear: of Second Coming, 19–20;
  causing panic, 173
Financial planning, 177 78
Floods, 30
Food storage, 176–77

Gadianton robbers, 66
Garden of Eden, 147–48,
  152–53
Gathering: of seed of Abraham,
  108–14; of Judah, 123–34; of
  Ten Tribes, 135–42; of
  Lamanites, 143–46
Godhood, qualifications for,
  238–39
Gog, 33, 96–97, 103–4, 190,
  196–97, 224–25
Gospel preached to all nations,
  109–12
Government, Millennial, 209–10

Hailstorms, 33–34
Heavenly messengers, 8–9
Homicide, 47–48
Homosexuality, 39–44, 47, 58
Hosts of heavens, 186
House of Israel, 103, 189. See
  also Israel; Judah
Hyde, Orson, 127–28

Illegitimacy, 47, 54
Immorality, 39–45, 58
Immortality. See Eternal life
Independence, Missouri:
  temple to be built at, 117–20;
  near Garden of Eden,
  152–53; property in, 157. See

also Jackson County,
  Missouri; New Jerusalem
Insurance protection, 180
Israel: nations to fight against,
  96–97; gathering of House
  of, 97, 126, 131; dedication
  of, 127–29; as independent
  country, 132; scriptural
  gathering of, not yet
  accomplished, 98–99, 133

Jackson County, Missouri:
  disaster to occur in, 154–55;
  Saints to return to, 156–60.
  See also Independence,
  Missouri; New Jerusalem
Jaredites, 84
Jerusalem: and the great
  earthquake, 28; overrun,
  101–2; temple to be built at,
  118, 121–24; as gathering
  place of tribe of Judah,
  135–36; celestial, of the
  postmillennial period, 162; at
  time of Second Coming,
  188–89; Holy, 236–37. See also
  New Jerusalem
Jesus Christ: knew time of His
  second coming, 17–21; work
  of, to go forth, 70–71, 93–94;
  to return during earthquake,
  93, 103, 186–89; clothed in
  red at Second Coming, 191;
  government of, 209;
  atonement of, 234
Judah: tribe of, 125–26;
  gathering of, 126–30. See also
  Israel
Judgments, 229–33